Children's Theatre and Creative Dramatics: An Annotated Bibliography of Critical Works

Rachel Fordyce

G. K. HALL & CO., 70 LINCOLN STREET, BOSTON, MASS.

Copyright © 1975 by Rachel Fordyce

Library of Congress Cataloging in Publication Data

Fordyce, Rachel.
    Children's theatre and creative dramatics.

    Includes index.
    1.   Children's plays--Presentation, etc.--Bibliog-
raphy.   2.   Drama in education--Bibliography.   I.   Title.
Z5784.C5F67   [PN3157]   016.792'0226   75-11868
ISBN 0-8161-1161-8

FOR

BARBARA M. McINTYRE

Preface

Children's Theatre and Creative Dramatics: An Annotated
Bibliography of Critical Works is a comprehensive and
verified enumeration of 2269 source materials related to
drama with and for children, and available in the United
States. Only works of a critical, instructional, or evalua-
tive nature are included. Book reviews that do not go beyond
the strict limitations of the review article are not included,
nor are anthologies of children's plays unless they are
prefaced by or include some type of critical material.

There has been an attempt, for historical reasons, to
maintain separate categories for Children's Theatre and
Creative Dramatics. However, because discussion of these
two disciplines so frequently overlaps, several categories
in the bibliography contain citations pertinent to each. The
cross-indexing, at the conclusion of each category, shows
further the interdisciplinary nature of the entire study and
should be used in conjunction with the major entry list for
all reference work.

The first major category, "Children's Theatre and
Creative Dramatics", contains those types of entries most
frequently including information and criticism that cover
both fields. Works available in this country but pertinent
to child drama outside the USA are also included here because
the American distinction between Children's Theatre and
Creative Dramatics is not nearly so clear cut outside the
United States. Although the distinction in this country in
recent years has been none too obvious, historically a division has been made between Children's Theatre and Children's
Drama, hence the breakdown in subsequent major categories.

The second major category, "Children's Theatre", contains
those works related to the general history and development of
Children's Theatre, to specific theatres and directors, and
to technical considerations in Children's Theatre, as well as
its practice in the schools. Within this category are also

PREFACE

some works that pertain, secondarily, to creative dramatics.
However, if the major portion of the work is concerned with
Children's Theatre, the work is listed here and cross-indexed
after the relevant second, third or fourth category.

The third major category, "Creative Dramatics", encom-
passes works on the general history and development of the
discipline, as well as a major sub-category, "Creative
Dramatics in Education and the Schools." Once again there
is considerable overlapping of materials. The indices should
be consulted.

Approximately ninety per cent of the bibliography is
annotated; however, entries for which the title is an
adequate descriptor are not annotated.

The bibliographical work of Drs. William Kingsley,
Wesley Van Tassel and Mary Klock in Children's Theatre and
Creative Dramatics deserves recognition. It has strengthened
scholarship in the fields, as I hope this book will.

Contents

CONTENTS

BIBLIOGRAPHIES, DIRECTORIES AND REFERENCE WORKS

1   ADAMS, RICHARD C. "Appendix B: Composite Course Outlines for
    Children's Theatre and Creative Dramatics at the College
    Level." Children's Theatre and Creative Dramatics.
    Geraldine Brain Siks and Hazel Brain Dunnington, eds.
    Seattle: University of Washington Press, 1961.

2   ADLER, RICHARD R. AND LAWANA TROUT. Comps. Creative Drama-
    tics: A Selected Bibliography. Champaign, Illinois:
    National Council of Teachers of English, 1971.
        An annotated bibliography of forty-seven entries for
    the "uninitiated teacher."

3   ANDERSON, VERNA D. Comp. Readings in the Language Arts.
    New York: Macmillan Company, 1964.

4   BAKER, BLANCH. Theatre and the Allied Arts: A Guide to
    Books Dealing with the History, Criticism and Technic
    of the Drama and Theatre and Related Arts and Crafts.
    New York: H. W. Wilson Company, 1952.

5   BLOCK, DOROTHY. Ed. Guide to Lists of Masters Thesis.
    Chicago: American Library Association, 1965.

6   BOYER, MARTHA MAY. "An Annotated Bibliography of Assembly
    and Auditorium Practice in Elementary and Secondary
    Schools." Master's thesis, University of Wisconsin,
    1936.

7   BRIGGS, ELIZABETH D. Comp. Subject Index to Children's
    Plays. Chicago: American Library Association, 1940.

8   BRITISH CHILDREN'S THEATRE ASSOCIATION. Selected Bibliogra-
    phy of Plays Recommended for Performance to Child
    Audiences. 2nd ed. London: British Children's Theatre
    Association, 1962.

1

Children's Theatre and Creative Dramatics

CHILDREN'S THEATRE AND CREATIVE DRAMATICS

9   BROCKETT, OSCAR G. Ed. A Bibliographical Guide to Research
    in Speech and Dramatics Art. Chicago: Scott, Foresman
    and Company, 1963.

10 BURKART, ANN KAMMERLING. "A Preliminary Bibliography for
    Creative Dramatics." Master's thesis, Ohio State
    University, 1958.

11 CHICOREL, MARIETTA. Chicorel Index to Children's Plays.
    Vol. 9. New York: Chicorel Library Publishing Company,
    1973.

12 COLLINS, JOAN M. Books and Materials for School and Youth
    Drama. New York: Dennis Dobson, n. d.

13 CROTHERS, J. FRANCES. Puppeteer's Library Guide: A Biblio-
    graphical Index to the Literature of the World of
    Puppet Theatre. Metuchen, New Jersey: Scarecrow Press,
    1971.

14 DALZELL, CLOYDE DUVAL. "Sections from a Bibliography of the
    Arts for Children." Theatre and School, March 1932, n. p.

15 DAVIS, IRENE POOLE. "Short Reference Lists for the Elemen-
    tary Teacher's Bookshelf." Quarterly Journal of Speech.
    21 (November 1935), 549-53.

16 DAVIS, JED H. "Prospectus for Research in Children's
    Theatre." Educational Theatre Journal, 13 (December
    1961), 274-77.

17 _____. Ed. A Directory of Children's Theatre in the United
    States. Washington, D.C.: American Educational Theatre
    Association, 1968.

18 Directory of American Colleges and Universities Offering
    Training in Children's Theatre and Creative Dramatics.
    Washington, D.C.: American National Theatre Association,
    1966.

19 "Directory: Children's Theatre in the Southeast." Southern
    Speech, 16 (Winter 1972-1973), 25-30.
        Gives a list of the major theatres preparing work for
    children in the ten states belonging to the Southeast
    Conference.

20 Dissertation Abstracts. Ann Arbor, Michigan: University
    Microfilms, Inc., 1938-   .

Children's Theatre and Creative Dramatics

BIBLIOGRAPHIES, DIRECTORIES AND REFERENCE WORKS

21   Doctorial Dissertations Accepted by American Universities
       [1933-1955]. New York: H. W. Wilson Company, 1934-1955.

22   DZIURA, WALTER T. Ed. A Bibliography of Theatre Arts
       Publications in English, 1963. Washington, D.C.:
       American Educational Theatre Association, 1965.

23   ECKELMAN, DOROTHY A. AND MARGARET PARRET. "Source Materials
       for Speech in the Elementary Schools." Quarterly Journal
       of Speech, 36 (April 1950), 251-59.

24   ERVIN, JEAN. "Bibliography of Dramatics in the Elementary
       School." Speech Teacher, 3 (December 1954), 259-63.

25   FINLEY, ROBERT AND IAN HERBERT. Who's Who in the Theatre.
       15th ed. New York: Pitman Publishing Corporation, 1972.

26   FITCH, JOE. Ed. "Creative Dramatics in the Elementary
       School." Bozeman, Montana: Montana State University,
       1963. [typescript]

27   FRANCIS W. PARKER SCHOOL. Studies in Education: Experience
       in English Composition and Literature, Grades I-VIII.
       Chicago: Francis W. Parker School, 1932.

28   GARRISON, GERALDINE. "Bibliography of Puppetry for the
       Elementary School." Speech Teacher, 3 (September 1954),
       202-10.

29   GIBSON, JAMES W. AND ROBERT J. KIBLER. "Creative Thinking
       in the Speech Classroom: A Bibliography of Related
       Research." Speech Teacher, 14 (January 1965), 30-34.

30   GOHDES, CLARENCE. Literature and Theatre of the States and
       Regions of the U.S.A.: An Historical Bibliography.
       Durham, North Carolina: Duke University Press, 1967.

31   GUIMAUD, JEAN. International Bibliography: Theatre and Youth.
       Paris: International Theatre Institute, 1956.

32   HAAGA, AGNES. Ed. "A Directory of American Colleges and
       Universities Offering Training in Children's Theatre and
       Creative Dramatics." Educational Theatre Journal, 10
       (May 1958), 150-63.

33   HARMS, THELMA. "Evaluating Settings for Learning." Young
       Children, 25 (May 1970), 304-08.

CHILDREN'S THEATRE AND CREATIVE DRAMATICS

(HARMS, THELMA)
This work is a checklist of films, books and pamphlets for a teacher to use in evaluating the calibre of environment for learning in the classroom.

34   HARTMAN, GERTRUDE AND ANN SHUMAKER, Eds. Creative Expression The Development of Children in Art, Music, Literature and Dramatics. New York: The John Day Company, 1932.
Contains fourteen articles directly related to Children's Theatre and Creative Dramatics.

35   HAZELTINE, ALICE I. "Plays for Children." Public Library Monthly Bulletin, vol. 16. St. Louis: St. Louis Public Library, 1913. [typescript]

36   HENRY, MABLE WRIGHT. Ed. Creative Experiences in Oral Language. Champaign, Illinois: National Council of Teachers of English, 1967.
Contains twelve articles related to the language arts and creative dramatics.

37   HERRICK, VIRGIL E. AND LELAND B. JACOBS. Eds. Children and The Language Arts. Englewood Cliffs, New Jersey: Prentice-Hall, 1955.
Contains two articles related to drama and the language arts.

38   HUNTER, FREDERICK J. Ed. Drama Bibliography: A Short-Title Guide to Extended Reading in Dramatic Art for the English-Speaking Audience and Students in Theatre. Boston: G. K. Hall, 1971.

39   HYATT, AEOLA L. Comp. Index to Children's Plays. 3rd ed. Chicago: American Library Association, 1931.

40   Index to American Doctoral Dissertation. [1957-58-   ]. Ann Arbor, Michigan: University Microfilms, 1959- .

41   INTERNATIONAL THEATRE INSTITUTE. Theatre for Youth: An International Report on Activities For and By Children in 27 Countries. London: British Center of the International Theatre Institute, 1956.

42   JACOBS, LELAND B. Ed. Using Literature with Young Children. New York: Bureau of Publications, Columbia University Teachers College, 1965.
Of the twelve articles in this volume, two are directly related to drama and the language arts.

BIBLIOGRAPHIES, DIRECTORIES AND REFERENCE WORKS

43   JOHN, MALCOLM. Ed. Music Drama in Schools. Cambridge:
         Cambridge University Press, 1971.
         A valuable anthology including seven articles
         particularly concerned with music and drama, plus a
         list of thirty-four reference sources.

44   JOHNSON, ALBERT. Best Church Plays: A Bibliography of
         Religious Drama. Philadelphia: Pilgrim Press, 1968.

45   KIBLER, ROBERT J. AND JAMES W. GIBSON. "Creative Thinking
         in the Speech Classroom: A Bibliography of Related
         Research." Speech Teacher, 14 (January 1965), 30-34.

46   KLOCK, MARY EILEEN. "Writings in Creative Dramatics Concerned
         with Children of Elementary School Age (Pre-School
         Through Sixth Grade): An Annotated Bibliography from
         1890 Through 1970." Ph.D. dissertation, University of
         Denver, 1971.
         The bibliography contains 1129 entries, plus conclu-
         sions based on the research and recommendations for
         further research.

47   KNOWER, FRANKLIN H. Comp. "Graduate Theses - A Combined
         Index of Reports of Graduate Work in the Field of
         Speech and Dramatic Art, 1902-1944." Speech Monographs,
         12 (Research Annual 1945), 9-29.

48   KOZELKA, PAUL. "Bibliography." Children's Theatre and
         Creative Dramatics. Geraldine B. Siks and Hazel B.
         Dunnington, eds. Seattle: University of Washington
         Press, 1961.

49   _____. "Bibliography." Creative Dramatics. Margaret
         Rasmussen, ed. Washington, D.C.: Association of
         Childhood Education International, 1961.

50   KREIDER, BARBARA. Index to Children's Plays in Collections.
         Metuchen, New Jersey: Scarecrow Press, 1972.
         An index of over 500 short plays for children in
         collections from 1965-1969, plus a brief cast analysis.

51   LAW, MAUZON. Ed. "A Directory of American Colleges and
         Universities Offering Curricular Programs in Children's
         Theatre." Educational Theatre Journal, 6 (March 1954),
         40-46.

CHILDREN'S THEATRE AND CREATIVE DRAMATICS

52   LETTVIN, LORELEI JOY. "Stories to Dramatize." Elementary
      English, 39 (December 1962), 766-69.

53   LEWIS, GEORGE L. "Children's Theatre and Creative Dramatics:
      A Bibliography." Educational Theatre Journal, 7 (May
      1955), 139-46.

54   _____. AND ANN KAMMERLING BURKART. "Creative Dramatics: A
      Selective Bibliography." Elementary English, 39
      (February 1962), 91-100.

55   LITTO, FREDRIC M. American Dissertations on the Drama and
      Theatre: A Bibliography. Kent, Ohio: Kent State
      University Press, 1969.

56   LOOMIS, AMY GOODHUE. Guide for Drama Workshops in the
      Church: Prepared for Leaders and Instructors. New York:
      National Council of Churches, 1964.
          Two articles pertain directly to child-related drama.

57   MacCAMPBELL, JAMES C. Ed. Readings in the Language Arts in
      the Elementary School. Boston: D. C. Heath and Company,
      1964.
          Of the sixty-six articles in this volume, three
      concern creative dramatics and the language arts.

58   MACKAY, CONSTANCE D'ARCY. Children's Theatre and Plays.
      New York: D. Appleton-Century Company, 1927.

59   _____. "Fifty Plays for Children." Woman's Home Companion,
      58 (August 1931), 22, 113.

60   _____. "Patriotic Plays for Children and Young People."
      Horn Book, 17 (September-October 1941), 374-79.

61   Masters Abstracts: Abstracts of Selected Masters Theses on
      Microfilm, 1962-1968. Ann Arbor, Michigan: University
      Microfilms, 1962-1968.

62   McCASLIN, NELLIE. "A History of Children's Theatre in the
      United States." Ph.D. dissertation, New York University,
      1957.

63   McDOWELL, JOHN H. AND CHARLES J. McGRAW. Eds. "A Bibliogra-
      phy on Theatre and Drama in American Colleges and
      Universities, 1937-47." Speech Monographs, 16
      (November 1949), 1-124.

BIBLIOGRAPHIES, DIRECTORIES AND REFERENCE WORKS

64   McGraw-Hill Encyclopedia of World Drama, 4 vols. New York:
      McGraw-Hill, 1972.

65   McPHARLIN, PAUL. Guide to Puppet Plays. By the author,
      1932.

66   MELNITZ, WILLIAM W. Ed. Theatre Arts Publications in the
      United States, 1947-52. East Lansing, Michigan:
      American Educational Theatre Association, 1959.

67   MENDELSON, MARILYN. "Eighteen Body Plays for Primaries."
      Instructor, 78 (March 1969), 72.
         Lists various children's dramatic and recreational
      activities, and shows their value as teaching tools.

68   MICHAELIS, JOHN U. AND PAUL R. GRIM. Eds. The Student
      Teacher in the Elementary School. New York: Prentice-
      Hall, 1953.
         Of the thirteen articles, two are related to informal
      dramatics.

69   MICHAELOFF, GONI. "Resource Materials: Check List of
      Articles on Educational Theatre, September 1967 - May
      1969." Speech Teacher, 18 (November 1969), 318-22.
         Gives only references to non-standard theatre journals.

70   OGILVIE, MARDEL. "Assemblies in the Elementary School: A
      Bibliography." Speech Teacher, 5 (March 1956), 134-36.

71   OGLEBAY, KATE AND MARJORIE SELIGMAN. Eds. Plays for
      Children: A Selected List. 3rd ed. New York: H. W.
      Wilson Company, 1928.

72   OTTEMILLER, JOHN HENRY. Index to Plays in Collections.
      4th ed. Washington, D.C.: The Scarecrow Press, 1964.

73   PALFREY, THOMAS R. AND HENRY E. COLEMAN, JR. Guide to
      Bibliographies of Theses: United States and Canada.
      2nd ed. Chicago: American Library Association, 1940.

74   PATTEN, CORA MEL. "Children's Outdoor Plays." Drama, 10
      (May 1920), 284.

75   _____. "Christmas Plays for Children." Drama, 11 (November
      1920), 65.

CHILDREN'S THEATRE AND CREATIVE DRAMATICS

76 PATTEN, CORA MEL. Comp. Plays for Children. Chicago: Drama
    League of America, 1923.

77 _____. Comp. "Plays for Children." Drama, 16 (March 1926),
    233-35.

78 _____. Comp. "Plays for Juniors." Drama, 20 (January 1930),
    20, 123-24.

79 PAULMIER, HILAH. Comp. An Index to Holiday Plays for
    Schools. New York: H. W. Wilson Company, 1936.

80 POOLE, IRENE. "Reference Bibliography for Teachers of
    Speech in the Elementary Schools." Speech Bulletin,
    3 (May 1932), 29-39.

81 POPOVICH, JAMES E. "A Bibliography of Research in Child
    Drama (1926-1964)," University of South Florida: By the
    author, 1964. [typescript]

82 Portfolio for Kindergarten Teachers. Washington, D.C.:
    Association for Childhood Education International, n. d.
        Of the twelve pamphlets contained in the portfolio,
    two are related to dramatic play and rhythmic movement
    for children.

83 POSSEMIERS, JEAN. Comp. International Bibliography:
    Theatre and Youth. Paris: Olivier Perrin, 1955.

84 PRINTER, CALVIN L. AND STEPHEN ARCHER. Eds. Secondary
    School Theatre Bibliography. Washington, D.C.: American
    Theatre Association, 1970.
        Contains numerous entries that are also relevant to
    drama in early education.

85 PUGH, MICHAEL. "The International Bibliography of Children's
    Theatre Plays." Children's Theatre Review, 16
    (February 1966), 10-11.

86 _____. Ed. "International Bibliography of Children's
    Theatre Plays in Translation." 3rd ed. Somerset,
    England: By the author for the British Children's
    Theatre Association, 1966.

87 RANSOME, GRACE GREENLEAF. Ed. Puppets and Shadows: A
    Bibliography. Boston: F. W. Faxon Company, 1931.

BIBLIOGRAPHIES, DIRECTORIES AND REFERENCE WORKS

88 RASMUSSEN, CARRIE. Ed. Guides to Speech Training in the
    Elementary School: A Report on the Elementary Committee
    of the National Association of Teachers of Speech.
    Boston: Expression Company, 1943.

89 ____. Ed. The Role of Speech in the Elementary School:
    Vitalizing the Elementary Curriculum Through Speech.
    Bulletin of the Department of Elementary School
    Principals. Washington, D.C.: National Education
    Association, 1945-46.
      Of the thirty-one articles contained in this volume,
    eight are specifically related to dramatic activities.

90 RASMUSSEN, MARGARET. Ed. Creative Dramatics. Washington,
    D.C.: Association for Childhood Education International,
    1961.
      This brief bulletin contains seven articles, all of
    which are related to some aspect of creative drama.

91 REARDON, WILLIAM R. AND THOMAS D. PAWLEY. Black Teacher and
    the Dramatic Arts: A Dialogue, Bibliography and
    Anthology. Westport, Connecticut: Negro University
    Press, 1970.

92 REED, FRIEDA. "Theatre for Children." Dramatics, 30
    (December 1958), 18-19.
      A checklist of books for the director of children's
    theatre in high schools.

93 ROACH, HELEN. Spoken Records. 3rd ed. Metuchen, New
    Jersey: Scarecrow Press, 1970.
      This reference work includes, among other categories,
    one related to children's records, and is therefore a
    source for children's theatre and creative dramatics
    materials.

94 ROGERS, MARY BROWN AND LUCIANO L'ABATE. Bibliography of
    Play Therapy and Children's Play. Atlanta: Georgia
    State College Child Development Lab, 1969.
      A check list of materials, 1928-68.

95 ROSENBERG, RALPH P. "Bibliographies of Theses in America."
    Bulletin of Bibliography, 19 (1945-46), 181-82, 201-03.

CHILDREN'S THEATRE AND CREATIVE DRAMATICS

96   SALISBURY, BARBARA. Ed. "Directory of American Colleges
     and Universities Offering Training in Children's Theatre
     and Creative Dramatics: Revised - 1963." Children's
     Theatre Conference Newsletter, 12 (August 1963), 3-22.

97   _____. Ed. "Fourth Addendum to the Directory of American
     Colleges and Universities Offering Training in Children's
     Theatre and Creative Dramatics." Children's Theatre
     Review, 16 (August 1967), n. p.

98   _____. AND GERALDINE B. SIKS. Ed. "Directory of American
     Colleges and Universities Offering Training in Children's
     Theatre and Creative Dramatics: Revised." Children's
     Theatre Conference Newsletter, 14 (May 1965), 4-10.

99   Select List of References on Children's Drama and Theatre.
     Washington, D.C.: Library of Congress, 1913.

100 SELIGMAN, MARJORIE. "A Selected List for the School
     Theatre." Progressive -Education, 8 (January 1931), 95-98.

101 SHANE, HAROLD G. Research Helps in Teaching the Language
     Arts. Bulletin of the Association for Supervision and
     Curriculum Development. Washington, D.C.: National
     Education Association, 1955.

102 SMITH, PATRICIA HART. Ed. "December Program Ideas."
     Instructor, 79 (December 1969), 72-73.
          A check list of plays, pantomimes and songs to be
     used for Christmas.

103 SNOW, KATHLEEN M. Ed. Canadian Books for Schools: A
     Centennial Listing. Champaign, Illinois: National
     Council of Teachers of English, 1968.
          This is an annotated bibliography of works by
     Canadian authors about Canada; one sub-section is
     devoted to plays.

104 SUTORIUS-LANGLEY, PAULINE. "List of Plays for Thanksgiving,
     and Some Recent Volumes of Plays for Children." Drama,
     16 (October 1925), 30.

105 TAUBER, ABRAHAM. "A Guide to the Literature on Speech
     Education." Quarterly Journal of Speech, 20
     (November 1934), 507-24.

106 THIESS, CAROLYN; DONNA L. BUTLER; ROBERT V. DENBY. Comps.
     ERIC Documents on the Teaching of English. 4 vols.

BIBLIOGRAPHIES, DIRECTORIES AND REFERENCE WORKS

(THIESS, CAROLYN)
Champaign, Illinois: National Council of Teachers of
English, 1956-70.
    These four volumes contain 3751 bibliographic entries,
many of which are concerned with the use of creative
dramatics, pantomime, play acting and play therapy in
the English classroom.

107   VAN TASSEL, WESLEY HARVEY. "Theory and Practice in Theatre
       for Children: An Annotated Bibliography of Comment in
       English Circulated in the United States from 1900 Through
       1968." Ph.D. dissertation, University of Denver, 1969.
          A bibliography of 1033 entries specifically related
       to children's theatre.

See also the following entries. 251, 277, 312, 343, 362, 370,
442, 538, 540, 575, 610, 640, 821, 1005, 1054-55, 1175, 1338,
1522, 1555, 1599, 1620, 1631-33, 1638, 1670, 1683, 1701,
1718, 1731, 1736, 1757, 1766, 1809, 1833, 1840, 1853, 1870,
1874, 2005, 2016, 2040, 2048, 2072, 2109, 2200, 2220, 2234.

THEORY AND EVALUATION OF THE FIELDS

108   ABERNATHY, ROSE LORETTA. "A Study of Existing Practices of
       Storytelling for Children in the United States." Ph.D.
       dissertation, Northwestern University, 1964.

109   AD HOC COMMITTEE OF THE SPEECH ASSOCIATION OF AMERICA.
       "Speech Education in the Public Schools." Speech
       Teacher, 16 (January 1967), 79-82.
          The official statement of the Speech Association of
       America on policy and procedure for speech and drama
       related subjects.

110   ADCOCK, VIRGINIA. "The 'Big' Play." Instructor, 70
       (November 1960), 31.
          States that formal and informal drama are of equal
       value in the school situation, and both should be used
       to their utmost.

111   ALDRICH, DOROTHY. "A Study of Child Audience Reaction to a
       Controversial Character in a Children's Play." Master's
       thesis, University of Pittsburgh, 1965.
          Thesis is concerned with moral implications in
       children's plays and focuses on Arthur Fauquez'
       Reynard the Fox.

CHILDREN'S THEATRE AND CREATIVE DRAMATICS

112   ALEXANDER, ROBERT. Comp. Development of a Theatre Arts
       Curriculum for Young Children. Washington, D.C.: CAREL,
       1969.
           A project of CAREL (Central Atlantic Regional
       Educational Lab) which discusses the atmosphere necessary
       for a workshop curriculum, its objectives and limitations,
       as well as the range of theory involved in such a project.

113   ANDERSON, JOHN E. "Psychological Aspects of the Child
       Audience." Educational Theatre Journal, 2 (December
       1950), 285-92.

114   AUSTIN, MARY. "Reasons for Failure of Children's Theatre in
       This Country - Lesson of Two Popular Productions."
       New York Drama Magazine, 76 (December 1916), 7.

115   AYLLON, MAURIE AND SUSAN SNYDER. "Behavioral Objectives in
       Creative Dramatics." Journal of Educational Research,
       62 (April 1969), 255-59.
           The authors discuss the results of testing first
       graders in a creative dramatics situation and the effect
       verbal prompting and child demonstrations had on producing
       overt action.

116   BEDNERIK, MARYA. "A Critical Analysis of Problems in
       Adapting Folklore to Children's Theatre Plays."
       Master's thesis, Bowling Green State University, 1962.

117   BELL, CAMPTON. "The Psychology of the Child Audience."
       World Theatre, 2:3 (1952), 23-29.

118   BOGEN, MELVIN. "Values Transmitted to Children's Theatre
       Audiences by Children's Theatre." Master's thesis,
       Wayne State University, 1966.

119   BONAR, HUGH S. "Drama in the Kindergarten." American
       Childhood, 21 (June 1936), 45-46, 54.
           Research in Manitowoc, Wisconsin, shows that dramatic
       activities are the best for stimulating creative
       thinking in the kindergarten.

120   BORGERS, EDWARD W. "Children's Plays." Educational
       Theatre Journal, 13 (May 1961), 131-35.
           Sets up criteria for evaluating children's plays;
       stresses the value of Nicholas Gray's work.

THEORY AND EVALUATION OF THE FIELDS

121 BOURNE, JOHN. "Children's Theatre." Theatre and Stage.
Harold Downs, ed. London: Pitman, 1951.
Analyzes the role of child actors performing plays
for children.

122 BRAUCHER, MRS. HOWARD S. "Making Children's Dramatics Worth
While." Playground, 9 (July 1915), 116-20.
The author asks for purification of dramatic modes
for children; she advocates only informal drama up to
age twelve.

123 _____. "Problems of Dramatic Play." Playground, 6 (December
1912), 319-24.
An address given at the Sixth Annual Convention of the
Playground and Recreation Association, calling for an
assessment of the values and applications of formal and
informal dramatics.

124 BRUSH, MARTHA. "The Seventh Annual Children's Theatre
Conference." Educational Theatre Journal, 3 (October
1951), 192-97.
Concerned with mass media and its effect on a child
audience.

125 CARMER, CARL. "Children's Theatres." Theatre Arts
Monthly, 15 (May 1931), 410-25.
Carmer surveys major work in children's theatre in
1931; specific groups and attitudes are analyzed.

126 CARPENTER, REGAN. "Creativity: Its Nature and Nurture."
Education, 82 (March 1962), 391-95.
Defines creativity as it applies to an educational
situation; advocates much more involvement on the
teacher's part.

127 CHAMBERS, ROBERT E. "Creative Dramatics: Learning or
Playing? A Study of Three Informal Educational Situations." Master's thesis, Ohio State University, 1956.

128 CHANDLER, EDWARD H. "How Much Children Attend the Theatre,
the Quality of the Entertainment They Choose and Its
Effect Upon Them." Pedagogical Survey, 16 (September
1909), 367-71.

129 CHANDLER, M. CORRINE. "An Analysis of and Suggested Methods
of Organization and Conduct for Drama for Children."
Master's thesis, University of Oklahoma, 1932.

CHILDREN'S THEATRE AND CREATIVE DRAMATICS

CHILDREN'S THEATRE AND CREATIVE DRAMATICS

(CHANDLER, M. CORRINE)
Concerned primarily with formal dramatics, with child actors as well as professionals.

130 CHORPENNING, CHARLOTTE B. "Adults in Plays for Children." Educational Theatre Journal, 3 (May 1951), 115-18.
Author feels that adult performances for children are far better than child actor performances, because of the detrimental effect on the child performer's spontaneous nature.

131 CHRISTENSEN, J. A. "School Drama: A Wind of Change." Media and Methods, 8 (January 1972), 32-33, 52-56.
The author puts forth a strong argument for the great versatility of well-nurtured creative informal drama as opposed to formal drama, and surveys works related to the discussion.

132 CLARK, ANNA MAY. "A Method of Recording Children's Overt Responses to Creative Dramatics Material and a Study of the Results." Master's thesis, Michigan State College [University], 1954.
Concludes that the success of creative dramatics depends upon the value of the materials used.

133 CLARK, BRIAN. Group Theatre. New York: Theatre Arts Books, 1972.
Designed as a practical handbook for adult group interaction and improvisation, however the information is comprehensive enough to apply to the theory and practice of creative dramatics.

134 COIT, DOROTHY. "Plays for Children." Players Magazine, 14 (May-June 1939), 7.
Suggests that the classics, such as Shakespearean drama, are more valuable to a child audience than material that intends only to entertain.

135 COMER, VIRGINIA LEE. "Children's Theatre: An Adventure for High School and College." Quarterly Journal of Speech, 32 (October 1946), 331-34.
Points out the value, to the high school actor, of performing plays for a child audience.

136 Community Drama: Suggestions for a Community Wide Program of Dramatic Activities. New York: Century Publishers, 1921.
A portion of the book evaluates the methods and techniques of educational dramatics; a bibliography of suitable material is included.

THEORY AND EVALUATION OF THE FIELDS

137   COOK, PAUL. "Miner Teachers College Experiments with
      Children's Plays." Journal of Theatre Education, 1
      (June 1950), 93-94.
           Discusses the initial program at Miner Teachers
      College and evaluates criteria for selecting children's
      plays.

138   COOK, WILTON W. "The Relation of Originality and Imitation
      in Dramatic Behavior." Master's thesis, University of
      Southern California, 1926.

139   CURTIS, ELNORA WHITMAN. "The Dramatic Instinct in Education."
      Pedagogical Seminary, 15 (September 1908), 299-346.
           Analyzes a broad spectrum of dramatic activities for
      children in 1908; discusses the advantages and disadvan-
      tages of the various types.

140   _____. The Dramatic Instinct in Education. Boston: Houghton
      Mifflin Company, 1914.
           Criticizes various aspects of formal and informal
      drama in the early part of this century.

141   DAVIS, JED AND MARY JANE LARSON WATKINS. Children's Theatre:
      Play Production for the Child Audience. New York: Harper
      and Row, 1960.
           Covers practically every aspect, both technical and
      aesthetic, of children's theatre; gives some brief
      attention to creative dramatics.

142   DIENESCH, MARIE. "Creative and Formal Dramatics." World
      Drama, 2 (Winter 1952), 30-36.
           A broad definition of the two fields; commentary,
      both pro and con, follows the article.

143   GOLDBERG, MOSES. Children's Theatre: A Philosophy and a
      Method. Englewood Cliffs, New Jersey: Prentice-Hall,
      1974.
           A thorough presentation of the state of, and need
      for, children's theatre today - covers history,
      directing, acting, designing and management for child-
      ren's theatre. Chapter VI, "Playwriting for Children's
      Theatre" is of particular value.

144   GRAHAM, KENNETH L. "An Introductory Study of Evaluation of
      Plays for Children's Theatre in the United States."

CHILDREN'S THEATRE AND CREATIVE DRAMATICS

(GRAHAM, KENNETH L.)
Ph.D. dissertation, University of Utah, 1947.
Concerned primarily with aesthetic criteria for choosing children's plays; gives seventy-six critical statements about writing plays for children.

145 _____. "Purposes of Children's Theatre Plays." Dramatics, 20 (March 1949), 11-12.
Summarizes the work in Dr. Graham's dissertation.

146 Guidelines for the English Program in the Middle School and in the Junior High School. Curriculum Bulletin No. 57. New Orleans: Division of Instruction, New Orleans Public Schools, 1972.
Work is particularly significant to theoreticians of child-related drama who are concerned with oral language experiences and vicarious language experiences.

147 HAYDON, LARRAE ALBERT. "Children's Theatre: A Practical Ideal." Master's thesis, University of Washington, 1940.

148 HENIGER, ALICE MINNIE HERTS. The Kingdom of the Child. New York: E. P. Dutton and Company, 1918.
Theorizes about techniques of formal and informal drama; a portion of the book is devoted to the use of creative dramatics in religious education.

149 HILE, FREDERIC W. "An Attempt to Correlate Psychological Factual Material Concerning Children With a Progressive Modus Operandi for a Modern Children's Theatre Project." Elementary-School Speech Magazine, 1 (December 1936-January 1937), 8-9.

150 HORTON, LOUISE C. "Children's Theatre and the Future." Players Magazine, 19 (May 1943), 34-35, 40.

151 HUNT, JEAN LEE. "Shall We Demand Efficiency in Play?" Progressive Education, 3 (October-November-December 1926), 305-11.
The author uses the word "efficiency" in the sense of productivity.

152 ISRAELS, BELLE LINDNER. "Another Aspect of the Children's Theatre." Charities and the Commons, 19 (January 4, 1908), 1310-11.
Points out the detrimental effects of young children as professional actors in plays for children.

CHILDREN'S THEATRE AND CREATIVE DRAMATICS

THEORY AND EVALUATION OF THE FIELDS

153 JOHNSON, SISTER MARY HENRIETTA. "Justification and
    Suggestions for Teaching Creative Dramatics in the
    Primary, Elementary, and the Junior High School."
    Master's thesis, Central Washington College of Education,
    1957.

154 JONES, CHARLES A. "An Evaluation of the Educational
    Significance of the Children's Theatre of Evanston."
    Ph.D. dissertation, Northwestern University, 1953.

155 KLEIN, ESTHER JEANETTE. "A Program for a Children's
    Community Theatre." Master's thesis, University of
    Denver, 1949.

156 KLEIN, RUTH C. "A History of Children's Theatre in America."
    Master's thesis, Northwestern University, 1926.
        A critical history of children's theatre in general,
    with special attention given to the Children's Theatre
    of Evanston and the work of Winifred Ward.

157 KNUDSON, RICHARD LEWIS. "The Effect of Pupil-Prepared
    Videotaped Dramas on the Language Development of
    Selected Rural Children." Ph.D. dissertation, Boston
    University School of Education, 1970.
        Examines work with a group of forty selected ninth
    graders who produced short dramas for videotape produc-
    tions. "The study showed that the Specialized Language
    Activities Program did have a significant positive
    effect on the language growth of students."

158 KOZELKA, PAUL. "Children and the Theatre." Teachers
    College Record, 51 (November 1949), 106-09.
        Gives criteria for evaluating the child audience's
    response to theatre.

159 KRAUS, JOANNA HALPERT. "Taking Children's Theatre to the
    Moon." Players Magazine, 45 (April-May 1970), 186-89.
        A report on and assessment of children's theatre
    today; gives a statement on what the future of
    children's theatre could and should be.

160 KREMER, LESTER ROLAND. "Children's Theatre as Produced by
    High Schools." Master's thesis, University of South
    Dakota, 1956.
        Evaluates the effectiveness of the major high schools
    in this country producing plays for children.

CHILDREN'S THEATRE AND CREATIVE DRAMATICS

161 KUPPER, HERBERT. "Fantasy and the Theatre Arts." Educational Theatre Journal, 4 (March 1952), 33-38.
Analyzes the intrinsic need for fantasy in childhood,
and children's theatre's role in supplying it.

162 KWIAT, CHARLOTTE A. "Values of Dramatization." Elementary
English, 27 (November 1950), 465-66.
Summarizes the aesthetic and educational values of
informal drama in the classroom.

163 LAZIER, GIL. Comp. "Systematic Analysis of Developmental
Differences in Dramatic Improvisational Behavior:
Inventory of Dramatic Behavior." Speech Monographs,
38 (August 1971), 155-65.
Analyzes a pre-post test for determining the effective-
ness of various creative dramatics approaches.

164 ____. AND BRIAN SUTTON-SMITH. Assessment of Role Induction
and Role Involvement in Creativity. Washington, D.C.:
Office of Education, Department of Health, Education
and Welfare, 1970.
This project, conducted at the Teachers College of
Columbia University, is a descriptive analysis of the
teaching of creative dramatics, and develops scales for
analyzing child involvement in improvisation, role-
playing and inter-related disciplines.

165 LEWIS, GEORGE L. "Children's Theatre by High School
Students." Players Magazine, 33 (March 1957), 131.
Comments on the values reaped by the high school
student who performs in plays for children.

166 LINDQUIST, FRANKLIN R. "Communication Through the Arts:
Dramatization." Childhood Education, 27 (February 1951),
269-71.
Stresses the values, both aesthetic and educational,
of creative dramatics over formalized dramatic
activities.

167 MAJOR, CLARE TREE. "The Children's Theatre." New York
State Education, 22 (October 1934), 45-47.
Concerned with the "menace" of motion pictures;
advocates good children's theatre as a substitute.

168 ____. "Playing Theatre." Columbia University Institute
of Arts and Sciences Institute Magazine, 3 (February
1931), 9.
Gives the objectives of good children's theatre.

18

THEORY AND EVALUATION OF THE FIELDS

169   MALMGREN, DONALD E. "The Never-Never Land of the Here and
      Now." Speech Teacher, 16 (January 1967), 74-78.
         Advocates reality rather than fantasy in children's
      plays.

170   McCASLIN, NELLIE. "Philosophy of Children's Theatre."
      Education, 83 (February 1963), 350-52.

171   _____. Theatre for Children in the United States: A History.
      Norman, Oklahoma: University of Oklahoma Press, 1971.
         A comprehensive and scholarly assessment of the
      field; more synthetic than innumerative, therefore more
      valuable as a history and criticism.

172   McINTYRE, BARBARA M. "A Preliminary Study and Evaluation of
      Suitable Stories for Creative Dramatics." Master's
      thesis, University of Minnesota, 1950.
         Evaluates thirty-two stories suitable for use in
      creative dramatics for children nine through eleven
      years old.

173   MEARNS, HUGHES. Creative Power: The Education of Youth in
      the Creative Arts. 2nd rev. ed. New York: Dover
      Publications, 1958.
         A seminal work for advocacy in creative teaching and
      learning.

174   MILNE, A. A. If I May. New York: E. P. Dutton and Company,
      1921.
         A portion of the book is devoted to a criticism of
      children's plays and pantomime.

175   MORENO. J. L. The Theatre of Spontaneity. New York: Beacon
      House, 1947.
         An outgrowth of Dr. Moreno's work in psychodrama, the
      book presents techniques for implementing therapeutic,
      creative dramatic activities with children from four
      through sixteen.

176   MORRIS, LISABETH A. "The Formulation of a Philosophy of
      Theatre for Children." Master's [Speech] thesis,
      Eastern Texas State University, 1966.

177   MORTON, BEATRICE KERR. "A Descriptive Study of Drama and
      Its Effect on the Creative Potential of a Group of
      Ninth Grade Students." Ph.D. dissertation, University

CHILDREN'S THEATRE AND CREATIVE DRAMATICS

(MORTON, BEATRICE KERR)
of Utah, 1971.
Results were generally inconclusive, with the exception of the fact that "drama does release creativity."

178 MOSES, MONTROSE. Another Treasury of Plays for Children. Boston: Little, Brown and Company, 1926.
The appendix of this book evaluated dramatic experiences in educational situations.

179 _____. Concerning Children's Plays. New York: Samuel French, 1931.
Suggests that playwrights stress education and morals less, and entertainment more, in their plays.

180 _____. "Forgive Us Our Children's Plays." New York Herald Tribune Books, March 7, 1926, p. 8.
The author is disgusted with the patronizing tone of most children's plays.

181 _____. "Let's Dramatize for Children." Theatre Arts, 8 (December 1924), 831-35.

182 _____. A Treasury of Plays for Children. Boston: Little, Brown and Company, 1921.
The author discusses his philosophy for selecting plays for children.

183 MURPHY, SISTER MARY HONORA. O.P. "An Introductory Study of Theory and Directorial Practices in Children's Theatre, USA." Master's thesis, Catholic University, 1955.

184 NADEL, NORMAN S. "The Drama Critic and Professional Children's Theatre." Children's Theatre Conference Newsletter, 14 (November 1965), 10-12.

185 OGLEBAY, KATE. "What is a Children's Theatre?" Theatre Magazine, 40 (September 1924), 41-42.

186 PALMER, LUELLA A. Play Life in the First Eight Years. Boston: Ginn and Company, 1916.
Gives a partial discussion of the values of dramatic play in the education and growth of the child.

187 PATTEN, CORA MEL. "The Children's Theatre Movement - A Resume." Drama, 18 (November 1927), 51.
Evaluates major, early theatre for children.

THEORY AND EVALUATION OF THE FIELDS

188 POPOVICH, JAMES E. "A Study of Significant Contributions to the Development of Creative Dramatics in American Education." Ph.D. dissertation, Northwestern University, 1955.

189 PRIVACKY, AUGUSTA. "The Dramatic Approach." Instructor, 64 (June 1955), 65.
       Analyzes the educational factors in creative dramatics.

190 PROBST, SISTER MARY HELENE. "An Analysis of the Educational Advantages of Creative Dramatics for Children." Master's thesis, Catholic University, 1940.

191 "Research Board: A Statement of Recommended Policy." Educational Theatre Journal, 2 (December 1950), 319-21.
       Discusses the "social function" of child-related dramatics.

192 RIBICOFF, ABRAHAM. "The Theatre as Teacher." Educational Theatre Journal, 13 (December 1961), 241-44.

193 ROWLAND, ELSI. "The Symbol and the Source." Players Magazine, 40 (May 1964), 243, 249.
       Assesses the contemporary [1964] scene in children's theatre and creative dramatics.

194 SAINT-DENIS, MICHEL. "Introduction," The Snow Queen. Adapted from the Story by Hans Christian Andersen by Suria Magito and Rudolf Weil. New York: Theatre Arts Books, 1951.
       The author discusses his philosophy for and about directing plays for children.

195 SANDS, MARY K. "Dramatics for the Few or the Many?" Players Magazine, 8 (November-December 1931), 2.

196 SCOTT, CHARLES LOUIS. "A Study to Determine the Feasibility of Producing Children's Theatre at the Warren County Fair." Master's thesis, Miami University of Ohio, 1967.
       The author shows why the venture was not feasible.

197 SCOVILLE, SHARON L. "The Rogue as a Children's Theatre Protagonist." Master's thesis, University of Kansas, 1966.
       The work concludes that there is definite need for the "Imperfect hero" in children's theatre.

21

CHILDREN'S THEATRE AND CREATIVE DRAMATICS

198   SEAGOE, MAY V. "Issues and Criteria for Children's Televi-
      sion." Educational Theatre Journal, 4 (October 1952),
      231-37.
            Precepts stated are generally good comments on the
      criteria necessary to please any child audience.

199   SEILER, CONRAD. "The Best Audience in the World." Players
      Magazine, 34 (March 1958), 129-30.
            Evaluates the child audiences' reaction to plays.

200   "Shaw Advises Children's Theatre Group to Give Plays with
      Themes of Adult Depth." New York Times, September 24, 1947,
      p.20.
            George Bernard Shaw comments on his own play for
      children-adults, Androcles and the Lion, and deprecates
      Barrie's Peter Pan, which he finds shallow and patronizing.

201   SHUMAKER, ANN. "Editorial." Progressive Education, 8
      (January 1931), 98-100.
            Theorizes about the value of informal dramatics in
      progressive education.

202   SIDE, RONALD. "Creative Drama." Elementary English, 46
      (April 1969), 431-35.
            The author advocates treating creative dramatics (as
      well as creativity) as a curricular subject, as opposed
      to a method, especially early in childhood training.
      "A Suggested Programme for Creative Drama at Various
      Levels" is included.

203   SIKS, GERALDINE B. "An Appraisal of Creative Dramatics."
      Educational Theatre Journal, 17 (December 1965), 328-34.

204   _____. "You, Too, Can Create Theatre Magic." Instructor,
      68 (June 1959), 21, 60.
            Gives a critical evaluation of the work of Dorothy
      Schwartz, Ann Shaw, and Ann Brown Pirtle.

205   _____. AND HAZEL BRAIN DUNNINGTON. Eds. Children's Theatre
      and Creative Dramatics. Seattle: University of
      Washington Press, 1961.
            The book reprints many articles significant to
      children's theatre; also included are a bibliography of
      child drama and an outline for teaching children's
      theatre and creative dramatics in college.

THEORY AND EVALUATION OF THE FIELDS

206 SIMPSON, GWEN HOLLY. "An Approach to Children's Theatre."
     Dramatics, 39 (June 1968), 16-17.
     Contains production theory and practicum for
     children's theatre.

207 SLOMMA, LILO. "Some Observations on the Young Spectator."
     ASSITEJ Quarterly Review, No. 2 (April-June 1967), 9-10.
     A translation of the article in French in the same
     issue (5-9); of concern is the child audiences' reaction
     to amoral characters.

208 SMITH, MARJORIE I. "Dramatic Activity Before 1800 in the
     Schools and Colleges of America." Master's thesis,
     Cornell University, 1948.

209 SOLLER, SARA THORNHILL. "The Attenuation of Evil Characters
     and Plot Elements in Children's Theatre Scripts Adapted
     from Five Fairy Tales." Master's thesis, University of
     Kansas, 1967.

210 SPENCER, BARBARA DOLMAN. "The Theatre for Children."
     Educational Outlook, 30 (January 1956), 41-47.
     Discusses theory of professional children's theatre
     and creative dramatics in this country.

211 STANISTREET, GRACE. "A Definition." Players Magazine,
     27 (November 1950), 36-37.
     Develops Stanislavski's statement that good
     children's theatre is the "same as for adults only
     still better."

212 _____. "What's in a Play?" Players Magazine, 31 (March
     1955), 134-36.
     Delineates various aspects of formal drama for
     children.

213 STEPHENS, LOUISE. "The Children's Theatre." Theatre and
     School, 13 (April 1935), 13-16.
     Gives definitions of good children's theatre and
     good children's plays.

214 _____. "A Purpose and a Plan." Players Magazine, 27
     (March 1951), 134-35.
     Theorizes about the benefits of good children's
     theatre, based on the author's experience at Mills
     College.

CHILDREN'S THEATRE AND CREATIVE DRAMATICS

215   STRAWBRIDGE, EDWIN. "Do Your Play For, Not To, the
      Children." Recreation, 47 (October 1954), 484-86.

216   TRAKTMAN, MAX. "For a More Complete Picture of Children's
      Theatre." Children's Theatre Review, 16 (February 1967),
      15.
          Distinguishes between regular college children's
      theatres and touring companies.

217   TURNER, PEARL IBSEN. "Far Better Than the Ready-Made Play."
      Instructor, 77 (December 1967), 47, 76.
          The author discusses her provocation for using
      creative dramatics rather than formalized plays with
      kindergarten and first grade children; after working
      ten years with written plays, she rejects them.

218   VAN DORN, KATHERINE. "Child Actors of the New Theatre."
      Green Book Album, 5 (February 1911), 382-88.
          Gives a psychological study of the child actor in
      plays for adults.

219   VAN TASSEL, WESLEY. "Differences in Contemporary Views of
      Theatre for Children." Educational Theatre Journal,
      21 (December 1969), 414-25.
          Dr. Van Tassel discusses the results of a 1965
      survey concerned with "the application of published
      Children's Theatre theory to actual stage practice."
      He concludes that "Children's Theatre is not widely
      respected as an art" although there is great potential,
      in the field, for revising this situation.

220   VIOLA, ANN. "Drama With and For Children: An Interpretation
      of Terms." Educational Theatre Journal, 8 (May 1956),
      139-42.

221   WAGNER, JEARNINE. "A Departure Point for Establishing a
      Children's Theatre Curriculum." Master's thesis,
      Baylor University, 1963.

222   WARD, MARY. "Our Theatre's Need." Child Education, 12
      (June 1936), 392-93, 423.
          Discusses aspects of the educated children's audience.

223   WARD, WINIFRED. "Children's Theatre: Help Wanted." Theatre
      Arts, 44 (August 1960), 53, 55.
          Comments on the pressing need for good scripts in
      children's theatre; compares and contrasts children's
      theatre to adult theatre along this line.

THEORY AND EVALUATION OF THE FIELDS

224   _____. "Creativity Versus Formal Dramatics." Southern Speech Bulletin, 2 (March 1937), 4-6.

225   _____. Drama With and For Children. Washington, D.C.: United States Department of Health, Education and Welfare, 1960. [Bulletin No. 30]
A critical evaluation of the state of children's theatre in this country.

226   _____. "The Next Act in Children's Dramatics." Drama, 18 (February 1928), 147-48.
Evaluates formal and informal dramatics in the educational system.

227   _____. "A Passport to Never Never Land." Dance Magazine, 21 (April 1931), 25-26.
Comments on the value of formal drama for the audience as well as the child actor.

228   _____. "The Place of Dramatics in the New Education." Theatre and School, 27 (May 1928), 13-17.

229   _____. "Two Kinds of Children's Theatres." Theatre Arts, 33 (September 1949), 55-56.
Makes a distinction between plays for children and plays by children.

230   WASHBURNE, CARLTON. A Living Philosophy of Education. New York: The John Day Company, 1940.
One chapter is devoted to the philosophy of elementary education as it applies to dramatics.

231   WEIDNER, JANICE M. "A Critical Re-Examination of the Criteria for Evaluating Children's Plays." Master's thesis, University of Pittsburgh, 1964.

232   WHEATON, PHILLIP. "Testing for Dramatic Ability in Young Children." Master's thesis, Clark University, 1945.

233   WHITING, FRANK M. "Values of Children's Theatre in a College or Community Program." Players Magazine, 23 (May-June 1947), 117-18.

234   WRIGHT, GEORGE W. AND NAOMI D. WRIGHT. "Humanizing Education Through Dramatization." Educational Screen, 8 (April 1934), 95-96.
Surveys the various needs of education for dramatic activities.

CHILDREN'S THEATRE AND CREATIVE DRAMATICS

235   WYATT, E. V. R. "Children Audiences." Catholic World, 124
      (February 1927), 669-70.
         Distinguishes between child and adult audiences.

236   YOUNG, HOWARD. "A Proposed One Year's Course of Study in
      Children's Theatre." Master's thesis, Texas Christian
      University, 1953.

237   ZIRBES, LAURA. Ed. "A Symposium of Dramatization." Child-
      hood Education, 5 (December 1928), 188-97.
         Surveys the attitudes of six educators on the issue
      of the value of drama in education.

238   ZOLOTOW, SAM. "Six Rules on Dramas for Children Seen."
      New York Times, September 1, 1949, p. 24.

      See also the following entries. 16, 398, 415, 424, 445, 659,
      686, 702, 713, 738, 961, 973, 1179, 1219, 1230, 1233, 1236,
      1247, 1259, 1292, 1295, 1309-10, 1316-17, 1350, 1541, 1546,
      1609, 1627, 1655, 1658, 1668, 1673-74, 1710-11, 1719, 1723,
      1727, 1759, 1799, 1800, 1814, 1816, 1841, 1913, 2007, 2134.

                         RELATED ACTIVITIES

239   ABBE, DOROTHY. The Dwiggins Marionettes: A Complete
      Experimental Theatre in Miniature. Boston: Plays, Inc.
      1970.
         Gives the story of William Addison Dwiggins (1880-
      1956) and his puppet theatre; includes a facsimile
      reproduction of "W. A. Dwiggins' Marionette in Motion"
      published 1939.

240   ABBOT, JULIA WADE. "Rhythmic Acitivity in the Kindergarten:
      Part I." Childhood Education, 12 (May 1936), 352-57.

241   _____. "Rhythmic Activity in the Kindergarten: Part II."
      Childhood Education, 12 (June 1936), 402-05.

242   AKER, SUZANNE. "Creative Dance for Primaries." Instructor,
      75 (December 1965), 39,103.

243   ALBERTS, DAVID. Pantomime: Elements and Exercises. Lawrence,
      Kansas: University Press of Kansas, 1971.
         A three part book which delineates the subject,
      illustrates exercises and gives suggestions for
      performances.

RELATED ACTIVITIES

244 ANDERSON, BENNY E. Let's Start a Puppet Theatre. Cincinnati: Van Nostrand Reinhold Company, 1973.
Introduces the uninitiated to a variety of puppetry techniques and shows their applicability to a theatre situation.

245 ANDO, TSURURO. Bunraku: The Puppet Theatre. Trans. Don Kenny. Philadelphia: John Weatherhill Company, 1970.
A comprehensive history of this particular aspect of Japanese Theatre.

246 ANDREWS, GLADYS. Creative Rhythmic Movement for Children. New York: Prentice-Hall, 1954.
Based on the author's master's thesis at New York University entitled "A Study to Describe and Relate Experiences for the Use of Teachers Interested in Guiding Creative Rhythmic Movement."

247 ARNOTT, PETER D. Plays Without People: Puppetry and Serious Drama. Bloomington, Indiana: Indiana University Press, 1964.
The author advocates the use of puppets/marionettes in serious drama, for a broad cross-sectional audience.

248 Art Teaching Guides: Puppets and Puppetry, Grades 2-6. Curriculum Bulletin 8H, 1968-69 Series. New York: Board of Education of the City of New York, 1969.
This pamphlet discusses puppet materials and provides methods for teacher use and student motivation.

249 ASHTON, DUDLEY. Rhythmic Activities: Grades K-6. Monograph of the American Association for Health, Physical Education and Recreation. Washington, D.C.: National Education Association, 1964.
Concerned primarily with classroom activities, and rhythm's application to language and literature.

250 BACMEISTER, RHODA W. "Things a Child Can Make and Do." Parent's Magazine, 22 (September 1947), 18-19, 136-45.
Included are suggestions for story telling, rhythm, puppet and dramatic activities.

251 BAIRD, BIL. Art of the Puppet. Boston: Plays, Inc., 1966.
An extensive definition and history (written as well as illustrated) of the puppet and puppet theatre.

CHILDREN'S THEATRE AND CREATIVE DRAMATICS

252   BATCHELDER, MARJORIE H. Puppet Theatre Handbook. New York:
       Harper and Row Publishers, 1947.
            An introduction to the use of puppets in plays,
       primarily for the child audience.

253   _____. AND VIRGINIA L. COMER. Puppets and Plays: A Creative
       Approach. New York: Harper and Row Publishers, 1956.
            Discusses the use of puppets in formal and informal
       drama; there is a bibliography related to Children's
       Theatre and Creative Dramatics.

254   BENARY, BLANCHE. "Puppetry - A Teaching Tool." Instructor,
       72 (April 1963), 29, 104.
            Emphasis is on creative expression in kindergarten.

255   BETHEA, KAY. "Musical Theatre for Children: A Growing
       Repertoire." ASSITEJ Quarterly Review, No. 2 (April-
       June 1967), 15-20.
            An outgrowth of the author's dissertation [see next
       entry].

256   BETHEA, SARA KATHRYN. "Opera for Children" An Analysis of
       Selected Works." Ph.D. dissertation, University of
       Kansas, 1971.
            A comprehensive and stimulating dissertation which
       surveys opera production for children in the United
       States and analyzes nineteen operas for children from
       Mozart through Menotti. A bibliography of scores and
       recordings concludes the work. To date, the most
       extensive work in the field.

257   BORTEN, HELEN. Do You Move As I Do? London and New York:
       Abelard-Schuman, 1963.
            Gives a series of tone poems related to children
       and movement; each can be used as a point of departure
       for creative dramatics activity.

258   BROADBENT, R. J. A History of Pantomime. 1901; rpt. New
       York: Benjamin Blom, 1964.
            An extended history of mime from early Greece through
       English pantomimes for children in the twentieth century.

259   BROWN, GRACE ANDERSON. Mime in Schools and Clubs. London:
       Macdonald and Evans, 1953.
            Explains mime techniques generally employed in
       British curricula and recreational clubs.

RELATED ACTIVITIES

260   BRUFORD, ROSE. Teaching Mime. London: Methuen and Company, 1958.
     Covers all aspects of individual and group mime; includes chapters on the use of mime with masks or music, and thirteen mime plays.

261   BUCKLEY, ROSE AND FLORENCE OWENS. "Interpretive Rhythms in the Kindergarten." Childhood Education, 19 (May 1933), 427-29.

262   CHRISTIANSON, HELEN MARGUERITE. Bodily Rhythmic Movement of Young Children in Relation to Rhythm in Music. New York: Bureau of Publications, Columbia University Teachers College, 1938.

263   "Close to Somebody; Children's Theatre: Workshop at the City Center of Music and Drama." New Yorker, 47 (October 23, 1971), 36-38.

264   COMPLO, SISTER JANNITA MARIE, I.H.M. "Drama Kinetics: A New Approach for Children in Creative Expression." Ph.D. dissertation, Wayne State University, 1971.
     The investigator has created a packet curriculum for uninitiated teachers to further their usage of creative drama techniques. The approach is equally applicable to "Language Arts, Music, Mathematics, Science, Social Studies, and Physical Education."

265   CORRETHERS, L. YOUNG. "Adventures with Puppets." Progressive Education, 5 (January-February-March 1928), 9-10.
     Discusses a puppet play about Sleeping Beauty which was created by sixth graders.

266   CRAWFORD, CAROLINE AND ELIZABETH ROSE FOGG. The Rhythms of Childhood: To the Little Children Who Dance for Joy. 8th ed. New York: A. S. Barnes and Company, 1935.
     Contents include many examples of music to be used in creative dance with small children.

267   D'AMICO, VICTOR E. Creative Teaching in Art. Rev. ed. Scranton, Pennsylvania: International Textbook Company, 1953.

268   DIXON, C. MADELINE. The Power of the Dance: The Dance and Related Arts for Children. New York: The John Day Company, 1939.
     A summary of modern dance techniques, slanted toward elementary school-aged children.

CHILDREN'S THEATRE AND CREATIVE DRAMATICS

269   DOING, RUTH. "Rhythm and Dramatic Expression." Progressive
      Education, 8 (January 1931), 54-57.
           Discusses basic movement and its relationship to
      creative expression.

270   DONHAM, NANETTE M. "The Adaptation of Children's Literature
      to Chamber Theatre." Master's thesis, Occidental College,
      1961.

271   DWYER, TERENCE. Opera in Your School. London: Oxford Univer-
      sity Press, 1964.
           Although the book is concerned primarily with opera
      produced by older children, the audience for this work
      would range from age five up.

272   DYSLINGER, WENDELL S. AND CHRISTIAN A. RUCKMICH. The
      Emotional Responses of Children to the Motion Picture
      Situation. New York: Macmillan Company, 1933.
           Findings, although dated, are relevant for comparison
      to the child's response to a theatre experience.

273   EASTMAN, MARCIA. Creative Dance for Children. Tucson:
      Mettler Studios, 1954.

274   EDMONDS, EDITH. "Fist Puppet Possibilities." Childhood
      Education, 15 (May 1939), 417-18.

275   ELLIS, MARY JACKSON. Finger Play Approach to Dramatization.
      Minneapolis: T. S. Denison, 1960.

276   "Equity Musical Theatre for Children." Children's Theatre
      Review, 17 (August 1968), 13.

277   EVAN, BLANCHE. The Child's World: Its Relation to Dance
      Pedagogy. New York: St. Marks Editions, 1964.
           Reprints ten articles from Dance Magazine.

278   EVANS, RUTH AND EMMA BATTIS. Childhood Rhythms: A Program of
      Rhythmic Activities for Children of Elementary School
      Age. New York: Chartwell House, 1955.

279   FIELDER, GRACE. The Rhythmic Program for Elementary Schools.
      St. Louis: C. V. Mosby Company, 1952.
           Covers work on all elementary grade levels.

280   FINLEY, WERDNA. "The Children's Theatre Conference."
      Educational Theatre Journal, 14 (December 1962), 356-57.

RELATED ACTIVITIES

(FINLEY, WERDNA)
States that the Eighteenth Annual Convention of the Children's Theatre Conference was devoted to rhythm and movement discussion and analysis.

281 FISK, MARGARET PALMER. The Art of the Rhythmic Choir: Worship through Symbolic Movement. New York: Harper and Brothers, 1950.

282 FLURRY, RUTH. "Interpretative Rhythm." Creative Schools. Ed. Department of Elementary School Principals. Washington, D.C.: National Education Association, 1944. Pp. 75-78.

283 FOX, LILLIAN MOHR. "Rhythmic Self-Expression by Third-Grade Pupils." Creative Schools. Ed. Department of Elementary School Principals. Washington, D.C.: National Education Association, 1944. Pp. 79-85.

284 GARDNER, JANE C. "Try Puppetry." Instructor, 69 (February 1960), 29, 76.
Discusses improvisational work in the kindergarten.

285 GEHMAN, ROBERT B. "Mr. Oliver J. Dragon ... and Friends." Theatre Arts, 34 (October 1950), 26-30.
Evaluates professional puppetry and its effect on child audiences.

286 GIDLEY, ROSE KENNEDY. "Living Marionettes." Instructor, 58 (January 1949), 23.
Discusses the work of Hazel Robertson in Palo Alto.

287 GOODLANDER, MABEL R. "Puppets and Pantomimes." Progressive Education, 8 (January 1931), 31-32.
Explores dramatic activities and improvisation in education.

288 GOODRIDGE, JANET. Creative Drama and Improvised Movement for Children. Boston: Plays, Inc., 1973.
The handbook "aims to provide some suggestion for Creative Drama in schools and in particular to assist teachers in the selection of appropriate material for improvised movement." Published originally in Great Britain as Drama in the Primary School, 1970.

289 GRAUBARD, PAUL S. "Pantomime: Another Language." Elementary English, 37 (May 1960), 302-06.
Advocates the use of mime in the study of language arts.

CHILDREN'S THEATRE AND CREATIVE DRAMATICS

290   HAYES, ELOISE. "Expanding the Child's World through Drama
      and Movement." Childhood Education, 47 (April 1971),
      360-67.
         A description and discussion of work with fifth
      graders in Hawaii in a Language Arts Program [essentially
      Creative Drama]. See Eloise Barclay DuBois' article
      "Values and Techniques of Creative Dramatics," which is
      the companion piece.

291   HAZELTINE, ALICE I. "The Children's Play Movement and the
      Public Library." Drama, 19 (December 1919), 112-13.

292   HEIDT, ANN. "Hand Puppets." School Arts, 72 (June 1973),
      12-13.
         Concerned with the creation of papier maché puppets
      and the ultimate staging of a play.

293   HETZER, MARGUERITE. "Rhythm Band Tells a Story." Instructor,
      61 (February 1952), 17, 69, 77.
         Describes how to convert well-known children's
      stories to rhythm and movement exercises; examples
      are given.

294   HUNT, DOUGLAS AND KARI HUNT. Pantomime: The Silent Theatre.
      New York: Atheneum, 1964.

295   JAQUES-DALCROZE, EMILE. Rhythm, Music and Education. Trans.
      Harold F. Rubenstein. New York: G. P. Putnam's Sons,
      1921.
         A seminal work in the field of eurythmics.

296   JERSILD, ARTHUR AND SYLVIA F. BIENSTOCK. Development of
      Rhythm in Young Children. New York: Bureau of Publica-
      tions, Columbia University Teachers College, 1935.
         The purpose of this monograph is to "study by objective
      methods the development from two to six years of the
      ability to sing and to keep time to music and the
      influence of various factors on this development."
      Results provide a basis for improving the child's
      musical, improvisational and motor activities in a
      musical context.

297   KATZ, ALEXANDRA ARONOFF. "A Production Analysis for the
      Dance Pantomime of Snow White and the Seven Dwarfs."
      Master's thesis, Baylor University, 1965.
         Observes that children "enjoy actions more than
      words."

CHILDREN'S THEATRE AND CREATIVE DRAMATICS

RELATED ACTIVITIES

298   KELIHER, ALICE V. "Creative Rhythms." Grade Teacher, 75
      (November 1957), 129.
      Concerned with the use of music in elementary
      education.

299   LEPESCHKIN, JULIE WILSON. "Rhythms and Dance in Creative
      Education." Childhood Education, 31 (November 1954),
      130-36.
      The emphasis is on movement, dance and music in the
      primary grades.

300   LOWNDES, BETTY. Movement and Creative Drama for Children.
      Boston: Plays, Inc., 1971.
      Explores the concept of "movement thinking" and the
      way children learn about and react to creative movement,
      mime, improvisation and sensory awareness.

301   MAHLMANN, LEWIS AND DAVID JONES. Puppet Plays for Young
      Players. Boston: Plays, Inc., 1973.

302   MAIER, LUCILLE S. "Bodily Activity and Creative Dramatics."
      Elementary English Review, 19 (February 1942), 70-71.

303   MALONE, MARJORIE. "Yes, You Can Teach Creative Music."
      National Education Association Journal, 40 (November
      1951), 536-37.
      Concerned with using music in the elementary school
      curriculum.

304   MARASH, JESSIE G. Mime in Class and Theatre. London:
      Harrap, 1950.

305   MARSH, AGNES LEWIS AND LUCILE MARSH. The Dance in Education.
      New York: A. S. Barnes and Company, 1930.
      Numerous approaches to dance and mime in the
      elementary school are given.

306   MAYNARD, OLGA. Children and Dance and Music. New York:
      Charles Scribner's Sons, 1968.
      Gives creative dance technique for very young
      children, based on a project at Adelphi University.

307   McPHARLIN, PAUL. Puppet Theatre in America: A History
      1524-1948. 1949; rpt. Boston: Plays, Inc., 1969.
      Contains a supplement by Marjorie B. McPharlin
      entitled "Puppets in America Since 1948."

CHILDREN'S THEATRE AND CREATIVE DRAMATICS

308   McSWAIN, E. T. "The Art Experience in the Development of the
      Child's Personality." Educational Theatre Journal, 5
      (May 1953), 125-27.
          Stresses the value of the arts as a personal experience
      rather than a performance.

309   McVICKAR, OLIVE B. "Music in the Kindergarten." Instructor,
      60 (April 1951), 28, 70.
          Discusses some sophisticated uses of music and
      rhythmic movement for kindergarten-aged children.

310   MEADER, DEBORAH. "The Revival of the Art of the Chinese
      Shadow Theatre." School Arts, 38 (November 1938), 85-87.

311   MORGAN, ESTHER AND HAZEL GRUBBS. "An Approach to Rhythms
      for Children." Childhood Education, 29 (April 1953),
      383-88.
          Gives rhythmic techniques for the uninitiated teacher.

312   MOSES, IRENE E. PHILLIPS. Rythmic Action Plays and Dances:
      A Book of Original Games and Dances, Arranged Progressive-
      ly, to Mother Goose and Other Action Songs with a
      Teaching Introductory: For Kindergarten, Primary School,
      Playground and Gymnasium. Springfield, Mass.: Milton
      Bradley, 1928.

313   MURRAY, RUTH LOVELL. Dance in Elementary Education: A
      Program for Boys and Girls. 2nd ed. New York: Harper
      and Row, 1953.

314   "Music and the Theatre for American Children." Recreation,
      32 (October 1938), 396-97.
          Discusses early work of the Junior Programs, Inc., of
      Maplewood, New Jersey.

315   MYERS, SUSANNA. Three Nursery Song Pantomimes for Young
      Children. New York: The Drama Bookshop, 1933.
          Contains "Polly Put the Kettle On", "The Man in the
      Moon", and "Simple Simon."

316   NEWTON, ROBERT G. Exercise Improvisation. London: J.
      Garnet Miller, 1960.

317   _____. Improvisation: Project and Practice. London: J.
      Garnet Miller, 1972.
          A very brief handbook, concerned with improvisational
      techniques.

Children's Theatre and Creative Dramatics

RELATED ACTIVITIES

318   NORTH, MARION. Body Movement for Children. Boston: Plays,
       Inc., 1972.
           Materials and ideas well-presented for teachers not
       overly familiar with the Laban method.

319   OLWELL, GEORGIANA P. "The Role of Puppetry in the Speech
       Improvement Program of New York City in Grades One to
       Six." Master's thesis, Queen's College, 1961.
           Emphasis is on puppetry in a language arts program.

320   OSBORN, D. KEITH AND DOROTHY HAUPT. Creative Activities for
       Younger Children. Rev. ed. Detroit: Merril-Palmer
       Institute of Human Development and Family Life, 1964.
           Of particular note are Chapter VI "Rhythm Instruments,"
       and a five page list of readings and resources related
       to children's creative activities.

321   POLSKY, MILTON. "Allan Albert Talks about Improvisation."
       Dramatics, 45 (April 1974), 16-19, 29.
           Discusses The Proposition Circus and The Proposition,
       and its conceiver and director, Allan Albert, concerning
       his work for and with children.

322   _____. "Nonverbal Games for Creative Dramatics." Instructor,
       81 (February 1972), 135.
           Advocates the use of nonverbal techniques, such as
       theatre games and improvisation, to initiate and
       augment creative drama. Six techniques are given.

323   _____. "You Can Play Many Parts in Bag-o'-Drama and
       Sociodrama." Dramatics, 45 (February 1974), 13-17, 29.
           A lucid discussion of techniques for role playing.

324   PURSLEY, MONA STILES. "Developing Creativity in the Child
       Through Movement." Master's thesis, Baylor University,
       1963.

325   RASMUSSEN, CARRIE. "Rhythm in Bodily Action and Creative
       Dramatics." Quarterly Journal of Speech, 22 (April
       1936), 291-94.

326   _____. "Rhythm in Bodily Language and Creative Dramatics."
       Southern Speech Bulletin, 6 (March 1941), 84-85.

327   _____. "Verse Speaking and Bodily Activity." Quarterly
       Journal of Speech, 20 (April 1934), 282-86.

CHILDREN'S THEATRE AND CREATIVE DRAMATICS

328   REDDY, IDA. Ed. Programmes for Children. Hamilton, Ontario:
      South Central Regional Library System, 1972.
          Concerned with creative drama, puppetry and story-
      telling as well as other arts for children in a library
      program.

329   REED, FRIEDA. "Theatre for Children." Dramatics, 27
      (January 1956), 14-15, 27.
          A dance-pantomime program at the Children's Theatre in
      Upper Darby, Pennsylvania, is discussed.

330   _____. "Theatre for Children." Dramatics, 30 (January 1959),
      22-23.
          Defines dance-pantomime and discusses its applicability
      to children's theatre.

331   _____. "Theatre for Children." Dramatics, 31 (February
      1960), 22-23.
          Discusses the activities of the Children's Theatre
      and Puppet Theatre of Temple, Texas.

332   ROGERS, FREDERICK RAND. Ed. Dance: A Basic Educational
      Technique. A Functional Approach to the Use of
      Rhythmics and Dance As Prime Methods of Body Development
      and Control, and Transformation of Moral and Social
      Behavior. New York: Macmillan Company, 1941.

333   ROOT, LAWRENCE T. "Speech Improvement through Puppetry."
      Instructor, 59 (Feburary 1950), 8.

334   ROWLANDS, DAVID. A Puppet Theatre for Language Teaching.
      Leeds, England: Nuffield Foundation, 1965.
          Instructions for making puppets and a puppet theatre
      are given, and dialogues of plays suitable for
      curricular use are included.

335   SALZMAN, MICHAEL MARK. "Creative Dramatics: A Means Toward
      Greater Understanding and More Meaningful Appreciation
      of 19th Century Program Music Taught to a Sixth Grade
      General Music Class." Master's [Music] thesis, North-
      western University, 1965.

336   SCHULHOFF, HELEN. "Creative Dramatization Through Music."
      Instructor, 45 (May 1936), 36, 72.
          Describes an assembly program, developed creatively,
      about the lives of major composers.

RELATED ACTIVITIES

337   SCOTT, LOUISE BINDER. "What Values, Puppetry?" Elementary
      English, 30 (April 1953), 210-13.
         Introduces the value of puppetry to the classroom
      teacher.

338   _____. AND J. J. THOMPSON. Rhymes for Fingers and Flannel-
      boards. St. Louis: Webster Publishing Company, 1960.

339   SEATTER, ELIZABETH. "Growth in Rhythm." Instructor, 54
      (October 1945), 22.
         Mental and creative growth of a kindergarten class
      is discussed.

340   SEAVER, MARGARET C. "Rhythms - A Creative Expression."
      Childhood Education, 4 (September 1927), 27-31.
         Explains the learning process involved in the use of
      movement and music.

341   SEEDS, CORRINE. "Rhythmic Expression: An Outgrowth of
      Learning." Progressive Education, 11 (November 1934),
      398-406.
         An extended discussion of rhythmic activities and
      mime with third graders.

342   SEHON, ELIZABETH L. AND EMMA LOU O'BRIEN. Rhythms in
      Elementary Education. New York: A. S. Barnes and
      Company, 1951.

343   SEIPP, KENNETH F. "Artistic Musical Theatre Needs the
      CTC!" Children's Theatre Review 16 (February 1967),
      7-9.

344   SHIRLEY, MARY K. "Tschaikovsky's 'Nutcracker Suite'."
      Instructor, 59 (December 1949), 20, 89.
         Shows the development of a musical play, with
      puppets and fifth grade children.

345   "Show: Punchinello Puppet Theatre in Central Park." New
      Yorker, 45 (September 6, 1969), 27.

346   SIES, ALICE CORBIN. "Play Activities in the Kindergarten
      and Primary Grades: How to Create Rhythmic Activities
      from Life Situations." Childhood Education, 2
      (December 1925), 169-74.

347   SIMON, JOSEPHINE M. "Creative Dramatics as a Basis for
      Aesthetic Education." Ph.D. dissertation, Boston
      University School of Education, 1971.

CHILDREN'S THEATRE AND CREATIVE DRAMATICS

(SIMON, JOSEPHINE M.)
The purposes of the dissertation are (1) to "articulat for the writer as well as the reader the philosophic basis for the use of the arts in education," and (2) "to make a case for the particular value of drama in the restrictive environment of our traditional educational system." Examples of creative dramatic practicum are included.

348 SIVINSKI, ETHEL R. "Using Puppets in Creative Work." Instructor, 58 (March 1949), 17, 84.
Discusses a first grade project with puppets.

349 SMITH, IRENE. "Puppetry in the Classroom." Elementary English Review, 10 (November 1933), 219-222.
Gives instructions for constructing simple puppets and using them in improvisational plays.

350 SPEAIGHT, GEORGE. History of the English Toy Theatre. Rev. ed. Boston: Plays, Inc., 1969.

351 STANISTREET, GRACE M. "Creative (Folk) Arts in Action at Adelphi University." Children's Theatre Review, 16 (February 1967), 6-7.
Discusses weekly programs in art, music, dance and dramatics.

352 _____. "Pantomime is Easy. Part I." Recreation, 38 (May 1944), 92-94.
Explores the use of pantomime in formal drama.

353 _____. "Pantomime is Easy. Part II." Recreation, 38 (June 1944), 137-38, 156.
A companion piece to above; concerned with mime and informal drama.

354 STEVENS, RUTH FULLER. "Rhythmic Expression." Childhood Education, 7 (December 1931), 200-05.
Discussion of a UCLA program in the arts for children; stresses rhythmic activity and elementary musical forms.

355 STEWIG, JOHN WARREN. "Instructional Strategies." Elementary English, 50 (March 1973), 393-96, 403.
The author is concerned with visual stimuli and their effect on Creative Dramatics.

356 _____. "Pictures: Impetus to Dramatize." Elementary English, 50 (March 1973), 393-6.

RELATED ACTIVITIES

(STEWIG, JOHN WARREN)
States that pictures, which stimulate dramatic play, should be open-ended, and exhibit conflict meaningfulness; also, they should lend themselves to questioning techniques and character addition. Session plans are given.

357 STINCHCOMB, MRS. HOGUE. "Art Education and Dramatic Expression Through Children's Plays." Playground and Recreation, 19 (June 1925), 159.
Discusses the play program at Highland Park, Michigan.

358 STINE, JOHN. "Dramatization Through Pantomime." Instructor, 49 (March 1940), 18, 61-63.
Author advocates the use of informal drama in the educational system, as opposed to controlled and formal drama.

359 STRAWBRIDGE, EDWIN. "The Child and Art." Players Magazine, 21 (December 1944), 22-23.
Includes a discussion of the author's dance-drama programs and a bibliography of new and appropriate plays for children.

360 SZWED, EDWIN. "Integrating Physical Activities and Reading Readiness." Instructor, 79 (August-September 1969), 103.
Explores the use of storytelling and rhythmic activities for kindergarten and primary children.

361 TAUB, EVA POLLOCK. "Folk Songs for Little Folk." Instructor, 67 (June 1958), 28, 58.
Shows how to integrate folk songs, finger play, song, dance and creative dramatics into the kindergarten.

362 TAYLOR, LOREN E. Choral Drama. Minneapolis: Burgess Publishing, 1965.
The author discusses the basic techniques of conducting choral speaking with children; includes three choral plays, and a long list of relative source material.

363 _____. Informal Dramatics for Young Children. Minneapolis: Burgess Publishing, 1965.
Concerned primarily with rhythmic activities in dramatic situations; includes a list of useful books which is annotated.

364 _____. Pantomime and Pantomime Games. Minneapolis: Burgess Publishing, 1965.

CHILDREN'S THEATRE AND CREATIVE DRAMATICS

(TAYLOR, LOREN E.)
Work covers individual, dual and group pantomime activity suitable for young children. Numerous pantomime games and several plays are included.

365 UBHOFF, VIRGINIA. "Correlation of Art and Drama." Platoon School, 8 (September 1939), 8-9.
Discusses an informal drama production by fourth graders on the Vikings.

366 WALSH, ROSALIA. Creative Activities for Every School. Cullowee, North Carolina: Western Carolina College, 1962.
Activities and materials for creative art, drama, math, thinking, and writing in the elementary schools are presented in mixed-media fashion.

367 WALTERS, HELEN. "Three Billy Goats Gruff." Grade Teacher, 52 (June 1935), 36.
Discusses a first grade puppet demonstration.

368 WALTERS, MAUDE OWENS. Puppet Shows for Home and School. New York: Dodd, Mead and Company, 1929.

369 WEILER, VIRGINIA BRYANT. "Rhythms in the Elementary School." Instructor, 56 (June 1947), 28, 65.

370 WHITLOCK, VIRGINIA BENNETT. Come and Caper: Creative Rhythms, Pantomimes and Plays with Music by Various Composers. New York: G. Schirmer, Inc., 1932.
A thematic approach to creative music, dance and dramatics.

371 WILDE, EVA LOUISE. "Adventures with Puppets." Progressive Education, 5 (January-February-March 1928), 10-14.
Explains how to build a puppet theatre and hand puppets, and how to use them with third graders.

372 YOUNG, BRUCE F. AND MORRIS ROSENBERG. "Role-Playing As a Participation Technique." Journal of Social Issues, 5 (Winter 1949), 42-45.
Discusses types of resistance, on the students' part, to role-playing.

373 ZELIFF, J. S. "Magic of Puppetry: Project in Bridgeport, Connecticut, Inner-City Schools. Parents' Magazine, 45 (July 1970), 46-47.

Children's Theatre and Creative Dramatics

RELATED ACTIVITIES

374 ZINAR, RUTH. "Creative Dramatics and Music." School
      Activities, 24 (December 1952), 121-22.
          Suggests that music and other rhythmic activities are
      good warm-ups for beginning children in creative
      dramatics.

      See also the following entries. 43, 117, 124, 126, 157, 167,
      186, 198, 239, 387, 394-96, 484, 498, 509, 567, 619, 622, 673,
      686, 743, 762, 772, 923, 1178, 1190-91, 1197, 1206-07, 1217,
      1239, 1250, 1253, 1255, 1265, 1285-86, 1293-94, 1297, 1306,
      1312, 1383, 1407, 1412, 1465, 1507, 1514, 1516, 1518, 1522,
      1537-38, 1546-47, 1569, 1587-88, 1591, 1594, 1602, 1615,
      1625, 1629, 1648, 1651-52, 1657, 1664, 1678, 1688, 1693-95,
      1711, 1728, 1739, 1769, 1772-74, 1784, 1802, 1885, 1889, 1908,
      1929, 1931-33, 1938, 1978, 2025, 2032, 2044, 2050, 2092, 2113,
      2122, 2178, 2184, 2193, 2201, 2207, 2214, 2234, 2258.

RECREATIONAL ACTIVITIES

375 ADAMS, WINONA. "Recreational Dramatics Can Teach, Too."
      Instructor, 63 (June 1954), 55, 80.
          Discusses creative dramatics activities of third and
      fourth grade boys in a settlement house.

376 BOLTE, DENSLOW E. "Summer Camp Programs." Players Magazine,
      30 (May 1954), 188-89..
          Shows how to work with formal dramatics in a children's
      summer camp.

377 BRAUCHER, HOWARD S. "Tendencies and Developments in the
      Field of Recreation." Playground, 5 (July 1911), 127-43.
          One aspect of the article is a discussion of dramatic
      activities in recreational programs of some major cities
      in the United States.

378 CASWALL, MARGARET. "Boston Revives the Medieval Pageant
      Wagon." Recreation, 28 (July 1934), 204-05.

379 CHAMPLIN, W. D. "An Experiment in Drama." Recreation, 25
      (February 1932), 617, 640
          Discusses Elizabeth Hanley's work in formal dramatics
      out of the Philadelphia Playgrounds Association.

380 "Children's Drama in Park and Playground." Playground, 22
      (December 1928), 517-19.

Children's Theatre and Creative Dramatics

CHILDREN'S THEATRE AND CREATIVE DRAMATICS

("Children's Drama ...")
    Reviews the founding of the Van Courtland Park Theatre
    in New York and the Port Chester Children's Theatre, also
    in New York State.

381 "A Children's Folk Theatre." Recreation, 25 (April 1962),
     4-5.

382 CHURCHYARD, MIRIAM. "The Play's the Thing!" Recreation, 26
     (January 1933), 473-75.
         Discusses a program in formal dramatics at Douglas,
     Arizona.

383 DANFORD, HOWARD GORBY. Creative Leadership in Recreation.
     Boston: Allyn and Bacon, 1964.
         A college text book, related to all aspects of
     dramatic activities in the recreational program.

384 "Drama Comes to the Playground." Recreation, 26 (July 1932),
     202-03.
         Discusses the activities of the Children's Playground
     Theatre in Bloomfield, New Jersey, and the use of child
     actors.

385 "Drama in the Recreation Program." Recreation, 41 (January
     1948), 476.
         Gives excerpts of speeches from the Twenty-Ninth
     National Recreation Congress related to materials and
     techniques in formal drama and creative dramatics.

386 "Dramatics in Camp." Playground, 19 (June 1925), 154-58.
         A variety of camp dramatic activities is discussed.

387 EICHSTEADT, NANCY. "Dramatics on the Playground." Recreation,
     53 (April 1960), 176.
         Discusses a very informal approach to creative
     dramatics and puppetry using an uninitiated, but
     interested, adult.

388 FERREIRA, MARGARET B.; FRANCES P. ARNOLD; DORIS V. WILSON.
     How Girls Grow, Interpreted Through Creative Dramatics.
     New York: The Girl's Friendly Society, n. d.
         Concerned primarily with recreational dramatic
     activities and their effect on maturation and socializa-
     tion.

RECREATIONAL ACTIVITIES

389   FINK, GEORGINE. "Story Play." Playground, 23 (November
            1929), 511-12.
            Defines "story play" and its relationship to creative
            dramatics in the recreational program of the San Francisco
            Recreational Department.

390   GOODALL, GRACE M. "Drama in the Parks: An Experiment."
            Recreation, 45 (March 1952), 545-47.
            A production of Charlotte Chorpenning's Cinderella
            is reviewed; this was a joint venture of the Metropolitan
            Park District and the Junior Programs, Inc., of Yakima,
            Washington.

391   GUDGELL, J. A. "How to Use Drama Effectively: For Your
            Campers; For Your Camp." Camp Magazine, 40 (September
            1968), 16-17.

392   HAAGA, AGNES. "Creative Dramatics in the Recreation Program."
            Recreation, 45 (May 1951), 77-80.
            Advocates the use of an educated leader to handle
            creative dramatics in a recreational program.

393   HALL, KATE. "Dramatics for the Camp Community, Part I."
            Recreation, 33 (April 1939), 21-24, 48-49.
            Covers a variety of dramatic-related subjects in a
            camp environment; a brief bibliography is included.

394   _____. "Dramatics for the Camp Community, Part II."
            Recreation, 33 (May 1939), 91-94, 114.
            A continuation of the above.

395   HANEY, JOHN BENJAMIN. "Dramatic Materials for Summer Camps."
            Master's thesis, University of Michigan, 1954.
            This thesis is concerned with aspects of both formal
            and informal drama in summer camps; techniques of each
            are discussed at length.

396   HARRISON, GLORIA. "Recreation Goes Dramatic." Physical
            Educator, 2 (June 1942), 224.
            Emphasis is on informal dramatics and its socializing
            benefits.

397   _____. "Recreation Goes Dramatic." Recreation, 37 (May
            1943), 66-69.
            A reprint of the above.

CHILDREN'S THEATRE AND CREATIVE DRAMATICS

398   HENKEL, DONALD DALE. "Assessment of Effects of an Acting
      Experience upon Participants in a Public Recreation
      Department Children's Dramatic Program." Ph.D. disserta-
      tion, University of Illinois, 1967.
         The work concludes that personality and social
      behavior of child participants were not particularly
      modified by a program in dramatics.

399   HENRY, DONALD R. "Recreational Use of Drama." Players
      Magazine, 37 (January 1961), 78.
         Comments on college curricula which offer courses in
      creative dramatics and formal drama, related to drama.

400   HINES, A. B. "Boy's Club Dramatics." Playground and
      Recreation, 22 (April 1920), 38-41.
         Discusses activities at the Madison Square Boy's Club
      Foundation.

401   HOBBS, MABLE FOOTE. "The Children's Playground Theatre."
      Playground, 21 (March 1928), 663-70.
         Emphasis is on formal dramatics, but some creative
      dramatics techniques are covered.

402   _____. "The Place of Drama in Recreation." Recreation,
      29 (July 1935), 211.
         See Milton Smith, "The Place of Drama in Leisure
      Time," for companion article.

403   KAMPMANN, LOTHAR. Creating with Puppets. New York: Van Nos
      Reinhold, 1972.
         A comprehensive, although brief, and well-illustrated
      introduction to puppet making and its use in formal
      plays as well as improvised ones.

404   KASE, JUDITH B. "Informal Theatre: Camp Activity for
      Everybody." Camp Magazine, 42 (March 1970), 16-17.

405   KENNEDY, H. S. "The Children Need Recreation in Wartime."
      American City, 57 (July 1942), 64.
         Discusses the Children's Traveling Theatre of
      Summit, New Jersey, which is a trailer theatre.

406   _____. "Summit's Trailor Theatre." Recreation, 36 (May
      1942), 78, 110.
         Comments upon the fact that the trailor theatre was
      built for $73.69.

RECREATIONAL ACTIVITIES

407   KOGAN, JAY. "Story-Playing Kits." Recreation, 51 (June
      1958), 212.
          Discusses the program of the Philadelphia Drama
      Library and its involvement with creative dramatics,
      puppetry and children's formal theatre; the kits are
      canvas bags, used for creative dramatics, and based on
      the Paper Bag Player's concept.

408   KOGELMAN, DORTHIE R. "Exploring the Possibilities: Student's
      Programs in Puppetry and Children's Theatre." Dramatics,
      44 (April 1973), 23-25.
          Shows ways to expand a Children's Theatre program
      using muppets, Banraku, and so forth.

409   LIES, EUGENE T. The New Leisure Challenges the Schools:
      Shall Recreation Enrich or Impoverish Life? Washington,
      D.C.: National Education Association, 1933.
          Emphasizes the educational value of creative
      dramatics; includes a list of cities using trained
      leaders in their recreational drama programs.

410   _____. "The New Leisure Challenges the Schools: Dramatics."
      National Education Association Journal, 23 (February
      1934), 58-60.
          An outgrowth of the author's book; see above.

411   MARTIN, HELEN FLORENCE. "Creative Dramatics in Girl Scout
      Established Camps." Master's thesis, University of
      Washington, 1952.

412   MARTIN, MARGARET CLEMEN. "On the Playgrounds." Recreation,
      39 (August 1945), 232.
          Formal drama, performed on a trailor theatre owned
      by the Children's Theatre of Portland, Maine, is
      discussed.

413   McCASLIN, NELLIE. "The Why's of Creative Drama." National
      Camp Directors Guide. New York: Girl Scouts of America,
      Inc., 1962. Pp. 18-19, 21-22, 24.
          Stresses the value of creative dramatics in a camp
      situation, rather than the tedious and time-consuming
      process of formal drama.

414   McCLINTOCK. R. B. "Omaha Park and Recreation Department
      Gets Mobile Show Wagon." American City, 67 (April
      1952), 153.

CHILDREN'S THEATRE AND CREATIVE DRAMATICS

415   MITCHELL, ELMER D. AND BERNARD S. MASON. The Theory of Play.
      Rev. ed. New York: A. S. Barnes and Company, 1948.
          Gives a history of play in the recreational
      situation; stresses the benefits of informal drama.

416   MUSSELMAN, VIRGINIA AND SIEBOLT H. FRIESWYK. "Drama in
      Recreation." Recreation, 55 (February 1962), 75-90.
          An extensive application of all forms of drama to the
      recreation program.

417   NEUMEYER, MARTIN H. AND ESTHER S. NEUMEYER. Leisure and
      Recreation: A Study of Leisure and Recreation in Their
      Sociological Aspects. New York: A. S. Barnes and
      Company, 1936.

418   ODOM, HELEN B. "Creative Play for the Activity Program."
      Master's thesis, Sul Ross State College, 1951.
          Concerned primarily with the educational values of
      dramatic play.

419   "Outdoor Matinees for Children." Recreation, 34 (March 1940),
      99-100.
          Discusses the 1938 program of eight outdoor theatres
      in the Los Angeles area.

420   PEIXOTTA, SIDNEY S. "The Ideal Dramatics for a Boy's Club."
      Charities and Commons, 21 (October 3, 1908), 64-66.

421   "Playground Drama Through the Institute." Recreation, 26
      (August 1932), 246-48.
          Discusses a Brooklyn Recreational Association's class
      in recreational dramatics.

422   PREECE, MARIAN. "Playground Drama." Recreation, 39
      (August 1945), 244-45.
          Discusses formal and informal drama on the play-
      grounds; emphasizes the fact that an untrained leader
      should not work with formal drama.

423   RAMSTEAD, EDITH WINCHESTER. "Methods to Be Used in
      Recreational Dramatics for Children, Derived from a
      Comparative Study of Existing Procedures." Master's
      thesis, Stanford University, 1940.
          Thesis is concerned primarily with the techniques of
      formal Children's Theatre, but states that creative
      dramatics is also vital to a recreational program.

RECREATIONAL ACTIVITIES

424 SAPORA, ALLEN V. AND ELMER D. MITCHELL. The Theory of Play
     and Recreation. 3rd ed. New York: The Ronald Press
     Company, 1961.
        A text book concerned with a variety of dramatic
     activities and storytelling.

425 "The Season in the Playground Theatre." Players Magazine,
     25 (September 1931), 337-40.
        Surveys major dramatic programs in recreation during
     1930.

426 SIMON, S. SYLVAN. Camp Theatricals. New York: Samuel French,
     1934.
        Handbook contains directions for producing formal
     dramatic work in camps; a list of suitable plays is
     included.

427 SMITH, MILTON. "The Place of Drama in Leisure Time."
     Recreation, 27 (January 1934), 462.
        See Mable Foote Hobbs, "The Place of Drama in
     Education," for companion article.

428 STANISTREET, GRACE. "The Case for Creative Arts in
     Recreation." Recreation, 48 (March 1955), 117-18.
        Advocates the use of all creative arts, spontaneously,
     in the recreation program.

429 SULLIVAN, DAN. "'Camp' and Children's Theatre." Children's
     Theatre Review, 16 (August 1967), 7-9.
        Concerned with the lack of sincerity in many
     professional children's theatre productions.

430 TELLEEN, R. "Informal Dramatics Can Provide the Means:
     Expression of Individuality." Camp Magazine, 43
     (May 1971), 12-13.

431 WHITE, ALICE M. G. Dramatic Cues for Girl Scout Leaders.
     New York: Girl Scouts of America, Inc., 1937.
        Discusses informal and formal drama in terms of
     Girl Scouting.

432 YODER, UNA RING. "Drama for the Youth in City Recreation."
     Master's [of Science] thesis, Kansas State Teacher's
     College - Emporia, 1959.
        A two part thesis concerned primarily with formal
     drama for children in fourth grade and older; the
     second part contains seven plays suitable for students
     in a recreational program.

Children's Theatre and Creative Dramatics

CHILDREN'S THEATRE AND CREATIVE DRAMATICS

See also the following entries. 67, 747, 819, 989-90, 1043, 1117, 1135, 1177, 1270, 1314, 1348, 1396, 1512, 1514, 1594, 1622, 1915, 2225.

OUTSIDE THE USA

433   ALLEN, JOHN. "The Theatre in Australia." Educational Theatre Journal, 13 (May 1961), 99-102.
        Comments on the dearth of creative dramatics and improvisation in Australian schools, and states that in 1961, creative dramatics was not taught to prospective teachers.

434   ANSORGE, PETER. "From Hook to Humperdinck." Plays and Players, 15 (February 1968), 44-46.
        Discusses several Christmas performances in London, and gives a British audience reaction to the Paperbag Players.

435   _____. "Tomorrow's Sun." Plays and Players, 14 (March 1967), 56-57.
        Evaluates the work of Brian Way, Caryl Jenner, Michael Croft, and Ronald Chenery, and the future of children's theatre in England.

436   BORK, KURT. "Introduction." World Theatre, 14 (August 1965), 333.
        Discusses major aspects of children's theatre in East and West Germany.

437   "British Theatre for School Children." School and Society, 42 (August 1935), 282.
        Gives the details about several productions of Oscar Ebelsbacker for British children.

438   BULOW-HANSEN, TAGE. "Their Own Theatre." Danish Foreign Office Journal, No. 9 (1953), 1-4.
        Comments on the work of Thomas P. Hejle at the Danish Theatre School, and his productions for children.

439   BURGER, ISABEL. "Discovery - Children's Theatre - 1819." Player's Magazine, 34 (December 1957), 54-55, 65.
        Comments on the work in children's theatre at the Stadt Theatre in Biberach an der Riss, Germany, which has been ongoing since 1819.

Children's Theatre and Creative Dramatics

OUTSIDE THE USA

440 <u>Canadian Child and Youth Drama Association Brochure.</u> Calgary, Alberta: Calgary Allied Arts Council, 1969.
Lists professional children's theatre companies in Canada, and discusses work in Alberta in detail.

441 <u>Canadian Child Drama Association: Annual Report for 1962-63.</u> Ottawa, Canada: Dominion Drama Festival, 1963.
A major portion of this document is devoted to the twenty-six children's theatres in Canada in 1962.

442 "Canadian Theatres for Youth: A Check List." <u>Canadian Theatre Review</u>, 2 (Spring 1974), 138-39.
Twenty-six theatres are cited.

443 CARTER, HUNTLEY. <u>The New Theatre and Cinema of Soviet Russia.</u> London: Chapman and Dodd, 1924.
A comprehensive survey of theatre and film in Russia from 1917-23; some attention is given to the Children's State Theatre of Moscow.

444 _____. "Notes on the Newest Russian Theatre." <u>Drama</u>, 14 (May-June 1924), 248-50.
Describes the work of Henriette Pascar at the Children's State Theatre in Moscow.

445 CHAKH-AZIZOV, KONSTANTIN. "Our Work." <u>ASSITEJ Quarterly Review</u>, 2 (October-December 1968), 8-9.
Lists the objectives of the Soviet Center of ASSITEJ and pleads for more international exchange programs in children's theatre.

446 CHERNIAVSKY, L. N. Ed. <u>The Moscow Theatre for Children.</u> Moscow: Cooperative Publishing Society of Foreign Workers in the U.S.S.R., 1934.
Illustrates the Moscow Theatre for Children and the work of Natalia Satz.

447 <u>Child and Youth Drama Activity in the London Area.</u> London, Ontario: Canadian Child and Youth Drama Association, 1967.
Concerned with Canadian Children's Theatre in the London, Ontario, area.

448 "The Child Theatre in the Soviet Union." <u>School Arts</u>, 33 (February 1934), 372-75.

Children's Theatre and Creative Dramatics

CHILDREN'S THEATRE AND CREATIVE DRAMATICS

449   "Children's Theatre in Israel." World Theatre, 14 (May-June 1965), 224.

    Cites the beginning work of the Cameri Theatre and the Haifa Municipal Theatre.

450   CLARKE, TOM. "I've Got the Best Job on Earth." National Parent-Teacher, 49 (November 1954), 16-19.

    The author shows how he established a London-based children's theatre which toured throughout Great Britain.

451   COREY, ORLIN. "On a Fox Chase in South Africa: A Report, an Analysis and Conclusions." Children's Theatre Conference Newsletter, 14 (November 1965), 4-9.

    Comments on children's theatre in South Africa through the vehicle of two productions: Reynard the Fox and The Book of Job.

452   CRAMPTON, ESME. Comp. Drama Canada: Trends in Drama in Education During the Past Twenty-Five Years. Toronto: University of Toronto Press for the College of Education Guidance Center, 1972.

    A portion of the booklet is devoted to the study of play-acting in the elementary classroom.

453   CRAWFORD, DOROTHY AND JEANNE HALL. "Report on the British National Festival of Theatre for Young People, Summer 1973." Children's Theatre Review, 22:4 (1973), 6-8.

454   DANN, NEVA F. "Dramatics in Amsterdam." Drama, 21 (April 1931), 28.

455   DASTÉ, CATHERINE. "Room for Imagination!" International Theatre Informations, Winter/Spring 1974, pp. 23-25.

    The author's involvement with children's theatre in general and the Saint-Étienne Theatre [France] in particular are discussed.

456   DEVINE, GEORGE. "Theatre for Children, Art That Is Different." World Theatre, 2 (Winter 1952), 9-21.

    Gives an extended discussion of the objectives and products of the Young Vic Theatre from 1946-51.

457   DODD, NIGEL AND WINIFRED HICKSON. Comps. Drama and Theatre in Education. London: Heinemann Educational Books, 1971.

    A thorough cross-section of essays on British drama from the infant schools through the universities; there is editorial commentary on each page.

Children's Theatre and Creative Dramatics

OUTSIDE THE USA

458 DOUGLAS, ELIZABETH. "Canadian Theatre: Experiment with Child Drama." Players Magazine, 31 (March 1955), 131.
Comments on work in the Nova Scotia Summer School programs based on Peter Slade's theories on educational drama.

459 DOWNS, S. W. "Notes on Children's Theatres in Germany and Denmark." Theatre and School, 13 (October 1934), 10-11.

460 ELVGREN, GILLETTE, JR. "Children's Documentary Theatre in Nottingham." Children's Theatre Review, 22:1 (1973), 11-13.
Reviews a British children's theatre performance in the Joan Littlewood tradition, and comments on the potential of this format as "an entertainment and educational vehicle."

461 "The English School Theatre." New Statesman and Nation, 11 (February 8, 1936), 185.
Describes a proposed professional theatre company, in its own theatre, which would give daily performances for British school children, based primarily on the classics.

462 FARJEON, HERBERT. "Entertainment for Children." New Statesman and Nation, 9 (January 5, 1935), 12-13.
The author is concerned with the inauthenticity of Christmas pantomimes, especially as they are concerned with classic, children's fairy tales.

463 FAULKES, MARGARET. "Creative Drama in England." Children's Theatre Conference Newsletter, 15 (February 1965), 7-10.
Author makes a distinction between the British terms drama (experiencing and creating), and theatre (viewing).

464 "For Children (And Adults) at Christmas: Some of the Shows." Illustrated London News, 242 (January 1963), 29.
Illustrates six Christmas pantomimes.

465 GOLDBERG, MOSES HAYM. "The Pedagogue in the Eastern European Children's Theatre." Educational Theatre Journal, 24 (March 1972), 5 12.
An outgrowth of Dr. Goldberg's dissertation, see below.

466 _____. "A Survey and Evaluation of Contemporary Principles and Practices at Selected European Children's Theatres." Ph.D. dissertation, University of Minnesota, 1969.

CHILDREN'S THEATRE AND CREATIVE DRAMATICS

(GOLDBERG, MOSES HAYM)
Analyzes children's theatres in Birmingham, Nancy, Brussels, Munich, Vienna, Milan, East Berlin, Bucharest, Prague, Sofia, Moscow and Leningrad. He concludes that "the more theatre for children is regarded philosophically as an entertainment art form, the more effective it seems at achieving social, psychological, or pedagogical goals. Conversely, the more it is regarded as a developmental tool for the instruction of the next generation, the less effective it seems at accomplishing this very purpose."

467   GOURFINKEL, NINA. "Opera for Children in Moscow." ASSITEJ Quarterly Review, 1 (January-March 1967), 9-10.

468   GREIN, J. T. "The Children's Theatre." Illustrated London News, 172 (March 10, 1928), 382.
Describes initial work at the Children's Theatre of London.

469   _____. "The Children's Theatre - and Another." Illustrated London News, 172 (August 27, 1927), 348.
Comments on two children's theatre projects in London; one lasted a year [1924], the other has just opened and looks promising.

470   _____. "The Young Generation." Illustrated London News, 173 (September 22, 1928), 516.
The critic gives a favorable evaluation of the work of Joan Luxton and Agnes Lowson at the Children's Theatre of London.

471   GUSTAFSON, ALRIK. "Children's Theatre in Sweden." Educational Theatre Journal, 3 (March 1951), 40-44.

472   HAGGERTY, JOAN. Please Can I Play God?: Notes and Sketches Based on an Adventure in Dramatic Play. New York: Bobbs-Merrill, 1967.
The author discusses her work in an economically and culturally deprived section of London's East End.

473   HAINAUX, RENE. "The East Berlin International Festival of Children's and Young People's Theatre." World Theatre, 15 (May-July 1966), 296-98.

474   "Hansel and Gretel and Treasure Island." Illustrated London News, 243 (December 28, 1963), 1086.
Illustrates two Christmas pantomimes.

Children's Theatre and Creative Dramatics

475   HEJLE, THOMAS P. "School Performances in Denmark." World
       Theatre, 2 (Summer 1952), 48-52.

476   HILL, ANN STAHLMAN. European Children's Theatre and the
       Second Congress of the International Children's Theatre
       Association. Nashville, Tennessee: Nashville Banner,
       1968. p.24.

477   _____. "Productions Are Highlight of International Meeting."
       Children's Theatre Review, 17 (August 1968), 5-8.
          Comments on children's theatre productions during
       the International Assembly of ASSITEJ in The Hague.

478   HOLLAND, BERTRAM H. Beginners on Stage: The Story of the
       Stretford Children's Theatre. London: Faber and Faber,
       1968.

479   HOUGHTON, NORRIS. "The Children's Theatre in Russia." Horn
       Book, 71 (August 1936), 54-55, 98, 100.

480   HOWARD, RHENA. "Report to Canadian Child Drama Association."
       Regina, Saskatchewan: By the author and the Regina
       Theatre for Children, 1968. [Typescript]
          Discusses the nine years of production of the Regina
       Theatre for Children.

481   HUMPHREY, GRACE. "A Children's Theatre in England." Drama,
       16 (May 1926), 294.
          Comments on the Kyrle Hall Theatre in Birmingham,
       which was the first theatre for children in England.

482   HURN, H. S. "Children's Theatre in Victoria." Players
       Magazine, 31 (October 1954), 17.
          Covers the initial work of the Holiday Theatre in
       Vancouver.

483   INTERNATIONAL THEATRE INSTITUTE. Theatre for Youth: An
       International Report on Activities for and by Children
       in Twenty-Seven Countries. London: The International
       Theatre Institute, 1956.

484   JACKSON, ALLAN STUART. "Production and Staging of the
       English Pantomime as Illustrated by Harlequin and the
       Red Dwarf; or, The Adamant Rock, Performed at Covent
       Garden Theatre, December 26, 1812." Master's thesis,
       Ohio State University, 1959.

CHILDREN'S THEATRE AND CREATIVE DRAMATICS

485 JENNER, CARYL. "Here Lies the Audience." Drama, New Series,
No. 65 (Summer 1962), 34-37.
Comments on economic, aesthetic and educational
problems in British Children's Theatre.

486 JODER, ANNA BEST. "Children's Theatre in England." Players
Magazine, 22 (January-February 1946), 10.
Discusses the work of Bertha Wadell at the Children's
Theatre of Lanarkshire, Scotland; there is also some
brief commentary on the West County Children's Theatre
Company of Bristol, England.

487 JONES, CARLESS. "Europe Points the Way to a Children's
Theatre." Players Magazine, 11 (November-December 1934),
9-10.
Compares Children's Theatre in the United States to
work in Moscow, Copenhagen and Leipzig.

488 "The Juri Wolker Theatre in Prague." World Theatre, 14
(March-April 1965), 180.

489 KENNEDY, H. S. "Theatre des Enfants." Players Magazine, 21
(May 1945), 32-33.
The author comments on a children's theatre that he
established while he was on duty in France.

490 KING, BEATRICE. "The Children's Theatre." Drama, New
Series, No. 5 (Summer 1947), 20-25.
The Director of the English School Theatre discusses
various aspects of children's theatre in England.

491 LATURELL, VOLKER D. "Theatres for Youth in the Federal
Republic of Germany." ASSITEJ Quarterly Review, 2
(January-March 1968), 33-34.

492 LEACH, ROBERT. Theatre for Youth. Oxford: Pergamon
Publishers, 1970.
Concerned primarily with the operation of a youth
"theatre workshop" and its application to British
Children's Theatre.

493 LOGAN, VIRGIL G. "Speech Education in Mexico." Speech
Teacher, 11 (September 1962), 227-32.
The author states that in pre-school and elementary
education there is emphasis on creative dramatics.

OUTSIDE THE USA

494 _____. "Speech Training in Mexico's Kindergarten and
Elementary Schools." Speech Teacher, 1 (November 1952),
271-76.
Shows how creative dramatics, rhythmic activities
and puppetry are used in early education in Mexico.

494 LONDON, DURT. The Seven Soviet Arts. Eric S. Bensinger,
trans. New Haven: Yale University Press, 1938.
A portion of this book is devoted to the work of
Natalia Satz and the Moscow Children's Theatre.

496 LONEY, GLENN. "The Children's Hour in Stockholm." Players
Magazine, 40 (May 1964), 241-42, 249.
Describes the activities of three children's theatres
in Sweden and comments on the country's attitude toward
drama for children.

497 LIONGO, GIUSEPPE. "Youth Theatre." World Theatre, 11
(Summer 1962), 179-80.
The Director of the Teatro per gli Anni Verdi comments
on Italian Children's Theatre.

498 MACAULAY, ROSE. "Age of Reason." New Statesman and Nation,
35 (January 10, 1948), 27.
The author states her objection to Christmas pantomimes because they make a farce of their original
children's stories.

499 MACKAY, CONSTANCE D'ARCY. "Children's Plays in England."
Theatre Magazine, 46 (August 1927), 43-45.
Analyzes the state of British theatre for children in
1927.

500 _____. "Children's Plays in France." Outlook, 117 (November
13, 1926), 558-59.
Traces the history and development of children's
theatre in France.

501 _____. "Children's Plays in Italy." Drama, 18 (October
1927), 15-16.
Emphasizes the use of puppetry to entertain children
in Italy.

502 MacKINNON, SISTER THERESA. "Theatre for Young Audiences in
Canada, 1950-1970." Master's thesis, New York University, 1973.

CHILDREN'S THEATRE AND CREATIVE DRAMATICS

503 MESERVE, WALTER J. AND RUTH I. MESERVE. "China's Children's
     Theatre: Education and Propaganda." Children's Theatre
     Review, 22:2 (1973), 3-10.

504 MILLER, IRVIN BENNETT. "Creative Drama in Britain."
     Elementary English, 36 (January 1959), 25-27.
          Evaluation of child's development and progress
     through creative dramatics, as it occurs in Great
     Britain.

505 MLAKAR. DUSAN. "Report from the Yugoslavia Center of
     ASSITEJ." ASSITEJ Quarterly Review, 2 (October-December
     1968), 21-23.
          Traces the history of theatre for children in
     Yugoslavia, and gives his attitude toward the philosophy
     of children's theatre.

506 MORTON, MIRIAM. "The Birth of Peter and the Wolf." Children's
     Theatre Review, 22:3 (1973), 1-4.
          An excerpt from the author's book on Soviet Children's
     Theatre; gives particular attention to major Soviet
     directors.

507 "The Moscow Children's Theatre." Theatre Arts Magazine, 22
     (April 1938), 304-05.
          Describes Alexei Tolstoi's play The Golden Key and its
     production at the Moscow Children's Theatre.

508 MOTTER, T. H. VAIL. School Drama in England. 1929; rpt.
     Port Washington, New York: Kennikat Press, 1968.
          An history of school plays and boy performances in
     England from 1400-1914; provides rich historical back-
     ground material for children's theatre.

509 "A Mouse and Blond Princess on Stage." Music and Dance, 51
     (March 1961), 22.
          Comments briefly on Australian Children's Theatre
     [A.C.T.] and the songbooks published from the plays it
     produces.

510 PORAT, ORNA. "The Cameri Theatre." ASSITEJ Quarterly
     Review, No. 1 (January-March 1967), 30-31.
          Describes the goals and initial work of the Cameri
     Theatre in Tel Aviv.

511 PRIVAT, ROBERT. "The Geneva Company of the Four Thursdays."
     ASSITEJ Quarterly Review, No. 11 (April-June 1967), 14.

OUTSIDE THE USA

(PRIVAT, ROBERT)
   Comments on the founding of the Geneva Children's
   Theatre.

512   ROSENBERG, HELANE S. "The Actor/Teacher at the Belgrade."
      Children's Theatre Review, 22:2 (1973), 11-13.
         Evaluates the Theatre in Education [TIE] movement,
      initiated at the Belgrade Theatre, Coventry, England, in
      1964.

513   SATZ, NATALIA. "Children Go to the Theatre." Elizabeth Hap-
      good, trans. Players Magazine, 39 (March 1963), 166-70.
         Contains excerpts from the author's book, Children
      Go to the Theatre; the excerpts are concerned primarily
      with Miss Satz attitude toward and philosophy concerning
      children's theatre.

514   "The School Theatre in Denmark." School and Society, 36
      (July 9, 1932), 45.
         Comments on the work of Thomas P. Hejle to establish
      and operate the Danish School Theatre's children's
      program.

515   SEGREDI, IRINA. "Theatre for the Young Audience." World
      Theatre, 16 (January 1967), 55-61.
         Analyzes Soviet commitment to children's theatre,
      and comments on the forty-two theatres for children or
      young people which are totally supported.

516   SHARON, MURIEL. "Report from England." Educational Theatre
      Journal, 5 (March 1953), 20-23.
         Evaluates the varying support creative dramatics and
      formal drama receive in England.

517   SHARPMAN, JOHN R. "Creative Drama: Observations in Four
      Countries." Canadian Speech Communication Journal, 4
      (December 1972), 77-81.
         Australian, Canadian, British and American children's
      theatres are discussed.

518   SIKS, GERALDINE B. "Children's Theatre in England."
      Educational Theatre Journal, 15 (May 1966), 8-9.
         Lists children's theatre productions in England in
      the Spring of 1966; particular attention is given to
      Robert Bolt's The Thwarting of Baron Ballingrew.

CHILDREN'S THEATRE AND CREATIVE DRAMATICS

519   SIKS, GERALDINE B.   A Research Study to Seek New Theatre Arts'
       Materials in European Countries and to Develop These
       Materials for Use in Theatre Education at Elementary and
       Teacher Training Levels: Summary, Theatre Arts' Materials
       Research.   Seattle, Washington: University of Washington
       Press, 1966.
           A pamphlet which discusses children's drama throughout
       Europe and the United States, and compares and contrasts
       fundamentals, concepts, techniques and traditions.

520   _____. "A View of Current European Theatres for Children and
       a Look Ahead in the U.S.A." Educational Theatre Journal,
       19 (May 1967), 191-97.
           A preface to the longer work annotated above.

521   SOSIN, GENE. "Art for Marx' Sake." Theatre Arts, 34
       (February 1950), 28-31.
           A summary of the author's dissertation work, completed
       in 1958. See 523.

522   _____. "Children's Theatre and Drama in Soviet Education."
       Through the Glass of Soviet Education: Views of Russian
       Society. E. J. Simmons, ed. 1953; rpt. New York:
       Columbia University Press, 1973.
           Summarizes the history of children's theatre in
       Russia; gives particular attention to the work of
       Henrietta Pascar and Natalia Satz.

523   _____. "Children's Theatre and Drama in the Soviet Union
       (1917-53)." Ph.D. dissertation, Columbia University,
       1958.
           Traces the history of theatre for children from its
       beginning in Moscow with Henrietta Pascar through its
       Natalia Satz regime.

524   SPENCER, SARA. "Children's Theatre in England." Education-
       al Theatre Journal, 3 (December 1951), 329-34.
           Recounts the experiences the author had during a
       three week tour of children's theatre in England;
       comments on the Slade controversy centered around his
       statement that children under twelve should not go to
       the theatre.

525   SUMMERFIELD, GEOFFREY. "About Drama in England." Elementary
       English, 47 (January 1970), 17-21.
           Shows the relationships between teacher and taught
       through the use of creative dramatics activities.

Children's Theatre and Creative Dramatics

OUTSIDE THE USA

526 "Theatre for Children and Youth in Bulgaria." ASSITEJ
     Quarterly Review, 2 (January-March 1968), 31.
         Briefly surveys the work of the fifteen theatres
     doing plays for children in Bulgaria by 1966; the
     Theatre for Children in Sofia is stressed.

527 TREWIN, J. C. "Pantomimes of Yesteryear." Illustrated
     London News, 243 (Special Christmas Number 1963), 23-29.
         Illustrates pantomimes from 1814 through 1963;
     includes some nineteenth century drawings.

528 TRUSSLER, SIMON. "Reworking Those Myths." Plays and Players,
     13 (February 1966), 24-25, 27.
         The critic gives his criteria for good children's
     theatre, as an outgrowth of his reviews of current
     children's theatre activity at Christmas in London.

529 TWOMEY, ROSEMARY. "A Visit to the Ion Creanga Theatre."
     Children's Theatre Review, 22:3 (1973), 15-17.
         States that the policy of this Romanian theatre in
     Bucharest "is to put the best talent and well conceived
     scripts before all children on a regular basis."
     [author's italics]

530 TYLER, GERALD. "Youth Drama in England." Dramatics, 24
     (January 1953), 8-9.
         Concerned with formal and informal drama as they
     relate to education in England.

531 "The Unicorn Theatre Club." Theatre World, 59 (September
     1963), 10.
         Comments on the work of Caryl Jenner at the Unicorn
     Theatre in London.

532 VAN GYSEGHEM, ANDRÉ. Theatre in Soviet Russia. London:
     Faber and Faber, 1943.
         One chapter of this book is devoted to the Moscow
     Theatre for Children.

533 "Views from the Christmas Shows." Illustrated London News,
     244 (January 1964), 66-67.
         Illustrations for twelve Christmas pantomimes are
     given.

534 VLAENDEREN, MICHEL VAN. "A Children's Theatre in Flanders."
     World Drama, 9 (Spring 1960), 58-61.

CHILDREN'S THEATRE AND CREATIVE DRAMATICS

535   WADDELL, BERTHA. "The Scottish Children's Theatre."
       Players Magazine, 23 (September-October 1946), 13-14.
           The founder and director of the Children's Theatre of
       Glasgow comments on work there from 1927 to 1946.

536   WARD, WINIFRED. "The Theatre According to the Russians."
       Drama: Northwestern University Drama Service Guild,
       November 6, 1936, pp. 4, 6, 24.
           Makes a comparison and contrast between theatre for
       children in Moscow and the United States.

537   WELTY, SUSAN. "In the Children's Theatres." Players
       Magazine, 15 (May-June 1939), 18-19.
           Major attention is given to the Juvenile's Theatre
       and the Children's Theatre in Toronto, and two children's
       theatres in Quebec and St. Johns, New Brunswick.

538   What's Going on in Canada in Child Drama and Theatre for
       Children and Youth. Ottawa, Canada: Canadian Child and
       Youth Drama Association, 1963. [typescript]
           An annotated bibliography of organizations working
       in formal or informal drama for children, or both.

539   WILSON, A. E. King Panto. New York: E. P. Dutton, 1935.
           Traces the history of the English pantomimes from
       commedia to 1934.

540   _____. The Story of Pantomime. London: Home and Van Thal,
       1949.
           Concerned with the history of the English Christmas
       pantomimes.

541   WOLFSON, MARTIN. "A Leningrad Theatre for the Young
       Spectator." Theatre Arts Monthly, 15 (May 1931), 420-25.
           A statistical survey of the technical operation of
       the Theatre of the Young Spectator in Leningrad.

See also the following entries. 259, 288, 611, 678, 691-95,
697, 726, 742, 807, 903, 955, 984, 1004, 1091, 1115, 1123,
1424, 1490, 1514, 1537, 1616, 1621, 1630, 1806, 1940, 2007,
2029, 2112.

CHILDREN'S THEATRE - HISTORY, PRE-1950

542   "Accent on Youth." Theatre Arts, 32 (June 1948), 59.
         Results of a survey show that there were over 1,500
      children's theatre projects in the United States in
      1948; the work of Winifred Ward and Charlotte Chorpenning
      is surveyed.

543   ADAMOWSKA, HELEN. "A Junior League Children's Theatre."
      Drama Magazine, 21 (April 1931), 37, 40.
         Surveys the activities of the Junior League and its
      relationship to children's theatre; some attention is
      given to the work of Mrs. James Rogers of the Chicago
      Junior League and a production of The Blue Bird.

544   ADDAMS, JANE. The Second Twenty Years at Hull House. New
      York: Macmillan Company, 1930.
         Discusses the arts program at Hull House, and gives
      special attention to a dramatic school that was
      established there.

545   _____. The Spirit of Youth and the City Streets. New York:
      Macmillan Company, 1909.
         Both creative dramatics and formal children's theatre
      activities are discussed, and shows how they meet the
      needs of city children.

546   _____. "Stage Children." Survey, 25 (December 3, 1910),
      342-43.
         Defends child actors in the theatre at Hull House;
      the article is a reply to a controversy in New York
      newspapers about children on the stage.

547   _____. Twenty Years at Hull House. New York: Macmillan
      Company, 1911.
         Mentions early theatre productions in the gymnasium
      of Hull House.

61

CHILDREN'S THEATRE

548   ALLEN, ARTHUR BRUCE. Drama Through the Centuries and Play
      Production Today. London: Allman and Son, 1936.
          Chapter one is concerned with formal play production
      using child actors; the rest of the book is devoted to
      dramatic play activities.

549   "American Children's Theatre." Literary Digest, 117 (June
      1934), 32.
          A brief history of the aims and goals of children's
      theatre is given.

550   ARNOLD, FRANK. "Play Service in Utah." Education, 39
      (December 1918), 244-48.

551   "At Burlingame's Play Centers." Recreation, 37 (May 1943),
      68-69, 72.
          Describes the activities of the Children's Playhouse
      in Burlingame, California.

552   BARTY, MARGARET. "Children and the Post-War Theatre."
      Theatre World, 39 (August 1943), 7-8.

553   BEST, MRS. A. STARR. "The Drama League at Twenty-One."
      Drama, 21 (May 1931), 35-39.

554   BLACK, DONALD AND ROSE KENNEDY. "Footlights on Small Fry."
      Colliers, 121 (February 7, 1948), 54.

555   BLANCHARD, DOROTHY. "The Children's Theatre in Postwar
      America." Dramatics, 16 (March 1945), 3-4.
          Concerned primarily with the role of children's
      theatre in the educational system.

556   "Boys and the Theatre." Atlantic Monthly, 107 (March 1911),
      350-54.

557   BRADEN, GEORGE. "Municipal and School Outdoor Theatres in
      California." American City, 38 (March 1920), 98-100.

558   CAMPBELL, WAYNE. Amateur Acting and Play Production. New
      York: Macmillan Company, 1931.
          Chapter I, Part III "A Theatre in a Class Room", is of
      special interest.

559   "Children's Educational Theatre." Atlantic Monthly, 100
      (December 1907), 798-806.
          Deals with both formal and informal dramatics.

CHILDREN'S THEATRE AND CREATIVE DRAMATICS

HISTORY, PRE-1950

560 "The Children's Theatre Builds for Art and Americanism."
Curtain Rises, 2 (June 1939), 8-9, 26.
The Children's Theatre at Navy Pier, Chicago is
discussed.

561 "Children's Theatre Cooperates with Bookstores." Publisher's
Weekly, 134 (August 27, 1938), 379.
Discusses the promotion of Clare Tree Major's
productions.

562 "Children's Theatre - 1945." Recreation, 40 (October 1946),
388.
The 1945 annual report on the Children's Theatre of
the Recreation Department of Austin, Texas
also summarizes the third season's program.

563 CHIPMAN, SANDS. "Stories Come to Life in a Children's
Theatre." Drama, 21 (April 1931), 27-31.

564 CHORPENNING, CHARLOTTE E. "Arts and the Child in Wartime."
Paper read at the Association of the Junior Leagues of
America, Inc., Kansas City Conference, Kansas City,
Missouri, April 28, 1942. [Available from AJLA, 825
Third Avenue, New York, New York 10022.]
Author gives her philosophy concerning children's
theatre and creative dramatics, as an outgrowth of her
work at Goodman Children's Theatre.

565 COMER, VIRGINIA LEE. "A Children's Theatre Takes to the
Road." Recreation, 34 (September 1940), 363-65, 402.
Activities of the 1938 Junior League are summarized;
statistics showed that 826 performances were given to
approximately 350,000 children.

566 DICKINSON, THOMAS HERBERT. Insurgent Theatre. New York:
B. W. Huebsch, 1917.
Chapter VII deals with children's theatre; the
author feels that great improvements are necessary in
the field, but feels confident that they will be
forthcoming.

567 DOYLE, KATHLEEN. "Children Tell the Christmas Story by
Movies." Parents' Magazine, 22 (December 1947), 26-27.
Discusses a Christmas production of the Palo Alto
Children's Theatre; illustrations are included.

CHILDREN'S THEATRE

568   DRENNAN, BERTHA. "Plays for Children." Commonweal, 14
          (June 24, 1931), 205-06.
             Reviews the history of children's theatre in the
          United States to 1930.

569   DUNHAM, MYRNA A. "A Children's Theatre in a Great Store."
          Emerson Quarterly, 10 (November 1929), 9-10.
             Discusses productions at Filene's Restaurant in
          Boston; because tea is served throughout the production,
          the actors must rely almost entirely on music, pantomime
          and dance.

570   EATON, WALTER PRICHARD. "The Theatre: Where Do the Children
          Come In?" American Magazine, 75 (December 1912), 53-59.
             Author reminisces about his childhood experiences in
          theatre, and urges more productions like Peter Pan; the
          next season in children's theatre is surveyed.

571   FIELDING, CYNTHIA. "Children at the Play." Stage, 11
          (December 1933), 40-42.
             Recounts humorous experiences related to children's
          theatre.

572   FITZGERALD, BURDETTE. "Choosing the Children's Theatre
          Play." Dramatics, 20 (December 1948), 11-13.
             A list of recommended plays is included.

573   _____. "Commercializing Children's Theatre." Players
          Magazine, 24 (April 1948), 160-61.
             Author feels that commercial theatres are not
          designed to cope with the complexity of good children's
          theatre, and consequently their productions are failures.

574   _____. "Oaks from Acorns." Players Magazine, 24 (March
          1948), 135-36.
             Summarizes the activities at the American Educational
          Theatre Association's convention in Salt Lake City; the
          use of creative dramatics and children's theatre in the
          Mormon Church is discussed.

575   _____. "Report on the Fourth Annual Children's Theatre
          Conference." Educational Theatre Journal, 1 (October
          1949), 100-08.
             Reports on a panel-created list of six rules for
          writing for children's theatre; eighty-three plays are
          endorsed by the same panel.

Children's Theatre and Creative Dramatics

576 _____. "Reporting the Third Annual Children's Theatre
Conference." Players Magazine, 25 (October 1948), 17.
Summarizes the convention program, and evaluates the
three children's plays that were staged at the University
of Denver.

577 FORNER, MARJORIE M. "Children's Theatres for Personality
and Culture." Catholic School Journal, 49 (January 1949),
20-21.
Summarizes the history of children's theatre; a brief
bibliography is included.

578 FRIEDMAN, K. C. "Time Concepts of Elementary School
Children." Elementary School Journal, 44 (February
1944), 337-42.
By implication, related to the attention span of
child audiences.

579 GERSTENBERG, ALICE. "The Chicago Junior League Theatre."
Drama, 18 (January 1928), 118.

580 GLAGOLIN, BORIS S. "The Theatre of American Youth."
Drama, 20 (March 1930), 170.
A brief discussion of child-related dramatic
activities.

581 GORDON, DOROTHY. "Creating Audiences for the Future."
Drama Magazine, 21 (June 1931), 12.
Advocates a children's theatre in every city in the
country.

582 HARKEN, ANNE HOOD. Children in the Theatre. New York:
National Child Labor Committee, 1941.
Gives many statistics related to children working in
legitimate theatre.

583 HAUSER, BERTRAM. "Where Children Play at Giving Plays."
Literary Digest, 86 (August 1, 1925), 25-26.

584 HERENDEEN, ANNE. "Adults Not Admitted." Theatre Guild
Magazine, 8 (December 1930), 31-32.
Urges the building of theatres specifically scaled
to young audiences.

585 HERTS, ALICE MINNIE. "The Children's Educational Theatre."
Atlantic Monthly, 100 (December 1907), 798-806.

CHILDREN'S THEATRE

(HERTS, ALICE MINNIE)
Discusses the founding of the Children's Educational Theatre and its principles, from the point of view of its founder and director.

586 _____. The Children's Educational Theatre. New York: Harper and Brothers, 1911.
Elaborates the history of the Children's Educational Theatre from 1902-1909.

587 _____. "Dramatic Instinct - Its Use and Misuse." Pedagogical Seminary, 15 (December 1908), 550-62.
Describes the author's work with child actors at the Children's Educational Theatre in New York City.

588 _____. "Make-Believe." Good Housekeeping, 64 (March 1917), 22-23.
Tells how characterization is developed in child actors.

589 _____. "The Power of Dramatic Instinct." Outlook, 101 (June 1912), 492-95.
Discusses the child's imitative and dramatic instincts.

590 HILLIARD, EVELYN; THEODORA McCORMICK; KATE OGLEBAY. Amateur and Educational Dramatics. New York: Macmillan Company, 1917.
Many techniques and practices of formal and informal drama are discussed.

591 HOOTMAN, MARGARET ELIZABETH. "A Survey of Pupil Interests as a Basis for Evaluating Plays for Junior High School Audiences." Master's thesis, Iowa State University, 1942.

592 HORTON, LOUISE C. "Children's Theatre." Dramatics, 20 (October 1948), 10-11.
Introduces the materials that later become the Handbook for Children's Theatre Directors.

593 _____. "Children's Theatre and the Future." Players Magazine, 19 (March 1943), 34-35, 40.
Explores techniques for training young actors, and suggests a heavy reliance on creative dramatics.

594 _____. "Children's Theatre in Postwar America." Dramatics, 16, (May 1945), 6-7.
A companion article to Dorothy Blanchard's piece of the same name.

HISTORY, PRE-1950

595   ____. "Drama for Children." Dramatics, 18 (October 1946), 18-19.
The annual meeting of the Children's Theatre Conference in Seattle is summarized.

596   ____. "Drama for Children." Dramatics, 19 (October 1947), 18-19.
The meeting of the Children's Theatre Conference at the University of Illinois is discussed.

597   ____. "Drama for Children." Dramatics, 20 (October 1948), 22-23.
Summarizes the annual meeting of the Children's Theatre Conference held in Denver.

598   ____. "Drama for Children." Dramatics, 21 (October 1949), 18-19.
The annual Children's Theatre Conference meeting in New York City is discussed.

599 "How Much Children Attend the Theatre, the Quality of the Entertainment They Choose and Its Effect on Them." Pedagogical Seminary, 16 (September 1909), 367-71.

600 JODER, ANNE BEST. "Conference at Seattle." Players Magazine, 23 (November-December 1946), 36.
Summarizes the activities at the first conference of the Children's Theatre Conference.

601 JOHNSON, J. L. "Summer Theatre for Children." American Home, 23 (May 1940), 62.

602 JOHNSON, ROBERT. "Report from the South." Theatre Arts Monthly, 33 (September 1949), 56.

603 "Junior Drama League." Drama, 20 (October 1929), 28.
Catalogues some of the major activities of the Junior League and its involvement with children's theatre.

604 "The Junior League Theatre Conference." Drama, 20 (February 1930), 139-40.
A conference held in Chicago in 1929 is summarized.

605 KASE, C. ROBERT. "The International Theatre Institute and UNESCO." Educational Theatre Journal, 1 (October 1949), 2-4.

CHILDREN'S THEATRE

606   "A Kindergarten for Future Playgoers." Theatre Magazine,
      7 (June 1907), 154-56, x-xiii.

607   LAMPERT, JANE. "Children's Theatre in the Children's
      Hospital." Players Magazine, 26 (October 1949), 16.
          A touring group called the Story Tellers takes
      numerous dramatic related arts into the Children's
      Hospital of Los Angeles.

608   LEE, DORRIS AND J. MURRAY LEE. "Creative School Experiences."
      Creative Schools: Twenty-Third Yearbook. Department of
      Elementary School Principals. Washington, D.C.: National
      Education Association, 1944. 1-18.
          Shows the appropriateness of formal and informal drama
      in learning situations.

609   LIPPMAN, L. B. "Children's Theatre." Saint Nicholas, 51
      (February 1924), 427.

610   MACKAY, CONSTANCE D'ARCY. "American History Plays for
      Children." Horn Book, 21 (September-October 1945),
      368-73.
          Describes a production of Rosemary and Stephen
      Vincent Benet's A Book of Americans an annotated list
      of other patriotic plays is included.

611   _____. Children's Theatres and Plays. New York: Appleton-
      Century Company, 1927.
          An early source concerned with the operation of
      children's theatres in the United States and England.

612   _____. "Children's Theatres in America." Woman's Home
      Companion, 54 (July 1927), 22.
          Surveys several major children's theatre companies
      in the United States.

613   _____. The Little Theatre in the United States. New York:
      Henry Holt, 1917.
          A brief portion of the book is devoted to children's
      theatre and some of the major practitioners in 1917.

614   MAJOR, CLARE TREE. "Children's Theatre in Nine States."
      The American Magazine of Art, 26 (January 1933), 42.

615   McFADDEN, DOROTHY. "Children's Theatre on Television."
      Players Magazine, 25 (October 1948), 64-65.
          Mentions major network's involvement in children's
      theatre, which is minimal, and urges more work in this
      area.

HISTORY, PRE-1950

616   _____. "Europe Challenges American Parents." National
         Parent-Teacher Magazine, 21 (June 1937), 10-11.
             Emphasizes the value of children's theatre and its
         lack of volume in the United States.

617   _____. "The Future of Professional Children's Theatre."
         Players Magazine, 20 (February 1944), 9-11.
             Discusses future goals of children's theatre, and
         shows the Junior Programs' Inc. involvement.

618   MELCHER, MARGUERITE FELLOWS. Offstage. New York: Alfred
         A. Knopf, 1938.
             Stresses the materials and methods for creating good
         plays with children; much emphasis, however, is placed
         on creative dramatics as a vehicle for aiding formal
         productions.

619   "Moral from a Toy Theatre." Scribners, 58 (October 1915),
         405-12.
             Comments on what children like in theatre.

620   MORRISON, ADRIENNE. "Drama for the Youngest Set." Theatre,
         52 (September 1930), 40, 62.
             Summarizes some contemporary [1930] theatre activities.

621   "National Scope for Junior League Children's Theatre."
         Drama Magazine, 21 (April 1931), 29.
             Discusses the Junior League's "Exchange Program" for
         children's theatre.

622   NOBLE, HELEN S. "Plays and Dances for Children." Theatre
         Magazine, 30 (September 1919), 175, 200.
             An extended discussion of what the author thinks makes
         good children's theatre; many of the author's productions
         in the New York City area are surveyed.

623   PATTEN, CORA MEL. "The Children's Theatre Movement." Drama,
         18 (November 1927), 51.
             Gives a brief history of the movement.

624   _____. "Introduction." Index to Children's Plays. Aeola L.
         Hyatt, ed. 3rd ed. Chicago: American Library Association,
         1931.
             The values of children acting in plays for children
         are discussed; notes the necessity of a well-stocked
         library of good children's plays.

CHILDREN'S THEATRE

625 "Report of the Seventeenth Annual Convention of the Drama
League of America." Playground, 20 (July 1926), 237-41.

626 RESNICK, JACK. "Children's Theatre - New York." Federal
Theatre Magazine, 11 (December 1936), 3.

627 SAVAGE, MRS. GEORGE. "The Business Side of It." Theatre
Arts, 33 (September 1949), 54.
Traces the ten year history of the Seattle Junior
Programs, Inc.

628 SHOHET, MAX. "Scrapbook of WPA Children's Theatre."
Typescript, available in the Theatre Collection of the
New York Public Library, n. d.

629 SPENCER, SARA. "A Moment of History." Children's Theatre
Conference Newsletter, 1 (January 1945), 1-2.
Summarizes the Children's Theatre Conference at
Northwestern University in 1944.

630 STRINGER, ARTHUR. "The Children's Theatre." Century
Illustrated Magazine, 83 (April 1912), 873.
A poem which narrates the author's feelings on
watching children leave a production at the New York
Educational Alliance.

631 "A Theatre for All Children." Literary Digest, 47 (January
11, 1913), 74-75.

632 THOMAS, CATE. "Report from the New England States." Theatre
Arts Monthly, 33 (September 1949), 55.

633 THOMAS, CHARLES. The Theatre of Youth. London: Chapman and
Hall, 1933.
Surveys children's theatre in Great Britain.

634 "Three Years of the Drama League." Nation, 98 (March 26,
1914), 322-23.
Traces the League from its inception.

635 TRANTUM, LILY ISABEL. "The Historical Development of
Children's Theatres in America." Master's thesis,
University of Washington, 1949.

636 "Unlocking the World of the Wonderful Through the Children's
Theatre." American City, 40 (January 1929), 106-07.

Children's Theatre and Creative Dramatics

HISTORY, PRE-1950

637 WALLACE, DICK. "One Hundred Thousand Children Can't Be
Wrong." Cue, 4 (August 8, 1936), 8-9, 14-15.
Discusses the WPA Children's Theatre, the Federal
Theatre Project, and a specific production of The
Emperor's New Clothes.

638 WARD, WINIFRED. "Can We Educate Emotion?" Arkansas Speech
Journal, 13 (October-November 1940), 2-4.
The answer is a qualified "yes".

639 _____. "Children's Theatre in War Time." Players Magazine,
19 (May 1943), 4-5.
Encourages children's theatre workers to continue
their work during the war.

640 _____. "Children's Theatre Plays." Drama: Northwestern
University Drama Service Guild, 18 (September 1937),
20-21.
A list of twelve plays that the author considers
outstanding is included.

641 _____. "Choosing Plays for Children." Players Magazine,
14 (July-August 1938), 7.
Discusses the author's method for selecting plays for
the Evanston Children's Theatre.

642 WELTY, SUSAN. "Children's Theatre Notes." Players Magazine,
17 (October 1940), 19.

643 _____. "In the Children's Theatres." Players Magazine,
16 (January 1940), 19.
Christmas activities at various theatres are surveyed.

644 _____. "In the Children's Theatres." Players Magazine,
16 (February 1940), 16.
Summarizes a one day meeting on Children's Theatre at
the annual AETA Convention in Chicago.

645 _____. "In the Children's Theatres." Players Magazine,
17 (February 1941), 18-19.
Approximately 3,300 children's plays were shown in
the United States in December of 1940; many are surveyed.

646 _____. "In the Children's Theatres." Players Magazine, 17
(March 1941), 18-19.
Announces the Association of the Junior Leagues of
America's intention to compile a list of theatres
producing children's plays.

CHILDREN'S THEATRE

647   WILLISON, GEORGE F. <u>Let's Make a Play</u>. New York: Harper and
        Brothers, 1940.
           Includes and analyzes twelve plays written by children,
        although the author favors informal drama over formalized
        production with a director.

648   WINSOR, FREDERICK. "Boys and the Theatre." <u>Atlantic
        Monthly</u>, 107 (March 1911), 350-54.
           Disapproves strongly of the "indiscriminate freedom"
        young boys have to attend the theatre; it corrupts their
        morals.

649   WINTHROP, PALMER. "Make-Believe for Children." <u>Drama</u>, 18
        (March 1928), 173.

650   WYATT, EUPHEMIA VAN RENSSELAAR. "Children's Audiences."
        <u>Catholic World</u>, 124 (February 1937), 699-70.

        <u>See also</u> the following entries. 122-23, 129, 201, 252, 272,
        314, 352, 368, 378-79, 381-82, 384-85, 394, 400-01, 421, 425-
        26, 431, 454, 926, 929, 955, 994, 1224, 1315, 1340, 1361,
        1459, 1507-08, 1511, 1651, 1662-63, 1674, 1685, 1687, 1739,
        1755, 2132, 2237.

DEVELOPMENT, 1950-1973

651   ADIX, VERN. "The Never Ending Search for Plays." <u>Children's
        Theatre Review</u>, 22:4 (1973), 8-9.
           Comments on children's literature that has applicabil-
        ity to children's theatre.

652   AMERICAN EDUCATIONAL THEATRE ASSOCIATION. "Operating Code
        of the Children's Theatre Conference." <u>Educational
        Theatre Journal</u>, 9 (December 1957), 351-55.
           The code which was approved by the Children's Theatre
        Conference, August, 1957.

653   BAKER, KITTY AND JEARNINE WAGNER. <u>A Place for Ideas: Our
        Theatre</u>. San Antonio: Principia Press of inity
        University, 1965.
           Gives a variety of creative dramatics and related arts
        activities, based on work done at the Dallas Theatre
        Center.

654   BARCLAY, DOROTHY. "Children's Theatre Progress." <u>New York
        Times Magazine</u>, 10 September, 1950, p. 47.

Children's Theatre and Creative Dramatics

DEVELOPMENT, 1950-1973

(BARCLAY, DOROTHY)
Various statements from practitioners of children's theatre.

655 BARNELLE, VIRGINIA. "The Theatre-Going Habits of the High School Student." Master's thesis, UCLA, 1951.
Findings, although somewhat dated, are relevant to the likes and dislikes of the pre-high school student.

656 BEHM, TOM. "Southern Children's Theatre Circuit Meets." Children's Theatre Review, 22:3 (1973), 6-9.
Concerned with touring companies available from the Southern Children's Theatre Circuit.

657 BELL, CAMPTON. "Children's Theatre Committee of AETA." Theatre Arts, 35 (January 1951), 54.

658 _____. "In My Opinion." Children's Theatre Conference Newsletter, 13 (November 1963), 3.
Concerned with the objectives and directions of the Children's Theatre Conference.

659 _____. "Theatre for Children: The Psychology of the Child Audience." World Drama, 2 (Winter 1952), 23-29.

660 BENSON, MYRA. "Report on the First International Conference and Festival of Theatre for Children." Canadian Child and Youth Drama Association News Sheet, February, 1965, pp. 5-6.

661 BIRDSALL, RUTH. "You May Want to Join the Children's Theatre Conference." Instructor, 64 (June 1955), 65, 76.

662 BOGEN, MELVIN. The Magic of Children's Theatre. Tucson, Arizona: Omen Press, 1972.

663 BOWEN, FRANCES CARY. "Educational Theatre." The Johns Hopkins Magazine, 4 (January 1953), 4.

664 _____. "The Place of Creative Dramatics." Players Magazine, 27 (January 1951), 26.
Despite the title of this article, the work is concerned primarily with the Johns Hopkins Educational Theatre and its development of programs in both formal and informal drama for children.

665 BROADMAN, MURIEL. "Children's Theatre in New York: The Off-Broadway Scene." Children's Theatre Review, 23:2 (1974), 5-6.
Surveys the children's theatre scene from 1961-73.

Children's Theatre and Creative Dramatics

CHILDREN'S THEATRE

666   BRUSH, MARTHA. "Eighth Annual Children's Theatre Meeting."
Educational Theatre Journal, 4 (December 1952), 342-49.

667   CARLSON, BERNICE W. The Right Play for You. New York:
Abingdon Press, 1960.
A book written for children to show them how to
develop a formal or informal play from stories, fables,
legends, a general theme, and so forth.

668   "Children's Theatre Conference at Tufts." Theatre Arts, 41
(November 1957), 93.

669   CHORPENNING, CHARLOTTE. "Theatre for Young Moderns." AAUW
Journal, 43 (June 1950), 210-12.
Gives criteria for good children's theatre and shows
how to start a community children's theatre.

670   CIACCO, MARY ELEANOR. "Children's Theatre Volunteers."
Players Magazine, 29 (January 1953), 90.
Comments on the involvement of the Junior League of
America in children's theatre.

671   _____. "Ninth Annual Children's Theatre Meeting." Educational Theatre Journal, 5 (December 1953), 355-63.

672   COGGIN, PHILIP A. The Uses of Drama. New York: George
Braziller, 1956.
Three chapters of this book are devoted to a discussion
of the historical development of formal and informal
drama for children.

673   COJAR, ION. "A Director's and an Author's Search for New
Means of Expression in Entertainment for Children."
ASSITEJ Quarterly Review, 1 (January-March 1967), 14-15.
The author and Aleco Popovici are concerned with a
cross-arts involvement in theatre for children.

674   COMER, VIRGINIA LEE. "The White House Conference and
Educational Theatre." Educational Theatre Journal, 3
(October 1951), 218-23.
Both formal and informal dramatics were discussed at
the conference.

675   COREY, ORLIN. "Theatre for Children - Kid Stuff or Theatre?"
Children's Theatre Review, 23:1 (1974), 14-15.
Corey's final speech as president of the CTA; reflects
on the upsurge of activity and professionalism in the
decade to 1972.

DEVELOPMENT, 1950-1973

676   COTES, PETER. A Handbook for the Amateur Theatre. London: Oldbourne Press, 1957.
        One chapter of this book is devoted to "Amateurs and Children's Theatre."

677   "CTC Awards at August Convention." Children's Theatre Review, 16 (November 1967), 7-9.
        Biographies of the winners of awards at the Twenty-Fourth Annual Meeting of the CTC are given.

678   DAVIS, DES. "An American Convention - An Australian Impression." English in Australia, 21 (July 1972) 43-49.
        Discusses the author's impression of the AETA Convention, December 1971.

679   DAVIS, JED. "From the Divisions." Educational Theatre Journal, 16 (May 1964), 198.
        Comments on the upcoming meeting of the CTC in Lawrence, Kansas.

680   _____. "From the Divisions." Educational Theatre Journal, 16 (December 1964), 393-94.
        Discusses the Twentieth Anniversary Annual Meeting of the CTC.

681   DEARBOURN, KATHRYN. "AETA Convention Meaningful." Children's Theatre Conference Newsletter, 9 (February 1959), 1-2.

682   "A Decade of Children's Theatre." Theatre Arts Magazine, 38 (November 1954), 84.
        Comments on the Tenth Anniversary Annual Meeting of the CTC.

683   DE PUGLIO, JOHN. "The Sponsor's Role." Players Magazine, 31 (May 1955), 186.

684   DIESEL, LEOTA. "Theatre USA." Theatre Arts, 43 (May 1959), 51-54.
        Lists the yearly programs of nineteen children's theatres and comments briefly on the history of the CTC.

685   DILL, MURIEL REES. "A Children's Theatre Handbook: Dramatic Instruction for the Five and Six Year Old." Master's thesis, Syracuse University, 1954.
        The handbook covers both formal and informal dramatics techniques.

CHILDREN'S THEATRE

686   DODD, DOROTHY VERNE. "Children's Theatre for the Deaf: A
        Guide to Production." Ph.D. dissertation, New York
        University, 1970.
             Dr. Dodd modifies Lowell Swortzell's eighty rules of
        playwriting [1963] to the needs of a hearing-impaired
        audience through the vehicle of a produced adaptation
        of Aurand Harris' Androcles and the Lion. The results
        were "highly supportive of the concept of pantomimic
        presentations of plays for deaf children."

687   DRAKE, SYLVIE. "Improvisational Theatre Reaching Up to the
        Kids." Children's Theatre Review, 22:2 (1973), 14-16.
             Analyzes the concepts and objectives of the Improvisa-
        tional Theatre Project [ITP], a National Endowment for
        the Arts program.

688   DUFF, ANNIS. "Life in a Looking-Glass." Horn Book, 30
        (February 1954), 50-63.
             The author describes the sustained interest of her
        children in theatre from age two on; criteria for
        eliciting good audience response are suggested.

689   DYCKE, MARJORIE L. "The AETA Convention in Washington, D.C.:
        December, 1959." Educational Theatre Journal, 12 (May
        1960), 142-48.

690   EEK, NAT. "The Adult Rights of the Child." Children's
        Theatre Review, 16 (November 1967), 1-5.
             The author shuns pampering a child audience; good
        children's theatre should appeal to adults as well as
        children.

691   _____. "Current News for ASSITEJ." Children's Theatre
        Review, 17 (February 1968), 1.
             Announces the Executive Meeting of ASSITEJ, to be
        held in Moscow.

692   _____. "Fourteen Americans Attend ASSITEJ Assembly:
        Officers Are Elected." Children's Theatre Review, 17
        (August 1968), 4, 21.

693   _____. "International Association of Theatre for Children
        and Youth - ASSITEJ." Children's Theatre Conference
        Newsletter, 15 (February 1966), 10-11.
             A definitional statement and a plea for financial
        support.

DEVELOPMENT, 1950-1973

694   _____. "The Prague ASSITEJ Conference." Children's Theatre
       Conference Newsletter, 15 (August 1966), 10-11.

695   _____. "Report from the Moscow Conference and ASSITEJ
       Executive Report," Children's Theatre Review, 17 (May
       1968), 1-4.

696   ELFENBEIN, JOSEF A. "The New York Convention." Educational
       Theatre Journal, 3 (March 1951), 60-64.
            Comments on the fact that Winifred Ward gave a history
       of children's dramatics at the AETA Convention.

697   "The Executive Committee of ASSITEJ Met in Nuremberg."
       ASSITEJ Information Bulletin, 2 (1966-67), 1-4.

698   FARRELL, JOAN ABOUCHAR. "Why Support Professional Children's
       Theatre." Children's Theatre Review, 16 (November 1967),
       14, 19-20.

699   FINLEY, WERDNA. "Children's Theatre Conference." Educational
       Theatre Journal, 12 (December 1960), 356-57.
            Describes the program at the Annual Meeting of the
       CTC in 1960.

700   FOWLER, VIRGINIA LEE. "The Application of Children's Drama
       Principles to an Educational Television Series."
       Master's thesis, Michigan State University, 1961.
            Gives statistical information based on a question-
       naire related to sixty two children's programs viewed in
       Lansing, Michigan.

701   FUNKE, LEWIS. "Show Folk Scholars." New York Times Magazine,
       28 October, 1951, pp. 20-21.
            Discusses the educational program offered by the
       Professional Children's School to child actors.

702   GAGLIANO, FRANK. "Children's Theatre Today: All It Needs is
       a First-Rate Literature." Children's Theatre Review,
       23:2 (1974), 6-7, 10-12.
            Concerned primarily with the writing and producing of
       Gagliano's The Hide-and-Seek Odyssey of Madeleine
       Gimple; the author makes many pertinent comments on the
       need for more professionalism in children's theatre, as
       well as the needs for "a sizeable dramatic literature"
       and more money.

CHILDREN'S THEATRE

703   GARD, ROBERT E.; MARSTON BALCH; PAULINE S. TEMPKIN. Theatre
        in America; Appraisal and Challenge: For the National
        Theatre Conference. Madison, Wisconsin: Denbar Educa-
        tional Research Services, 1968.
              Included is a discussion of both formal and informal
        dramatics, and their place in American theatre.

704   GARRARD, ALAN AND JOHN WILES. Leap to Life - An Experiment
        in Youth Drama. London: Chatto and Windus, 1969.

705   GEPHART, ELLEN. "The Children's Theatre Conference."
        Educational Theatre Journal, 13 (December 1961), 320-24.
              Describes the activities at the Seventeenth Annual
        Meeting of the CTC.

706   GOFF, LEWIN, Ed. "AETA Convention Report." Educational
        Theatre Journal, 19 (May 1967), 219-34.
              A thorough discussion of the substance of the
        Thirtieth Annual AETA Convention, and a discussion of
        work related to formal dramatics and creative dramatics.

707   GOLDBERG, MOSES. "An Experiment in Theatre for the 5-8 Year
        Olds." Children's Theatre Review, 19 (August 1970),
        7-11, 18.
              Shows how to apply formal theatre techniques and the
        commedia style to improvisational drama.

708   _____. "22nd Annual CTC Convention Report." Children's
        Theatre Conference Newsletter, 15 (November 1966), 17-20.
              Comments on the Twenty-Second Annual Meeting of the
        CTC.

709   GRAHAM, KENNETH L. "In My Opinion." Children's Theatre
        Conference Newsletter, 14 (August 1965), 4-5.
              Lists future objectives for the CTC.

710   GRIFFIN, ALICE. "Children's Theatre Activities." Theatre
        Arts, 39 (November 1955), 81-82.
              Summarizes the activities at the Eleventh Annual
        Meeting of the CTC.

711   _____. "Children's Theatre, USA." Theatre Arts, 38 (May
        1954), 82-86.
              Briefly notes the activities of thirty-six children's
        theatre companies.

DEVELOPMENT, 1950-1973

712   _____. "Children's Theatre, USA." Theatre Arts, 42 (May
       1958), 76-79, 92-93.
          Mentions work ongoing in thirty children's theatres.

713   HAAGA, AGNES. "Children's Theatre: Objectives and Standards."
       Players Magazine, 30 (April 1954), 161.

714   _____. "In My Opinion." Children's Theatre Conference
       Newsletter, 13 (February 1964), 1.
          Pleads for clarity of purpose and objectives for the
       CTC.

715   _____. "Twelfth Annual Children's Theatre Conference."
       Educational Theatre Journal, 8 (December 1956), 316-23.

716   _____. "The White House Conference and CTC." Children's
       Theatre Conference Newsletter, 9 (May 1960), 3-4.

717   HALL, JEANNE L. "Opportunity in Children's Theatre."
       Educational Theatre Journal, 18 (October 1966), 259-63.
          The article is primarily a defense of child actors
       performing in plays for children.

718   HENRY, MABEL CLOUGH WRIGHT. "Echoes: Children's Theatre
       Conference." Dramatics, 25 (November 1953), 26.
          Commentary on the Annual Meeting of the CTC in 1953.

719   HILL, ANN STAHLMAN AND LEILA D. PHILLIPS. "Theatre Confer-
       ence Successful." Children's Theatre Review, 17
       (November 1968), 1-8, 21.
          Describes the activities at the Twenty-Fourth Annual
       Meeting of the CTC.

720   HOBGOOD, BURNETT. "AETA Convention Report." Educational
       Theatre Journal, 19 (December 1967), 533-45.
          Included in this report is a discussion of child
       drama in England.

721   HORTON, LOUISE C. "Children's Theatre Department." Players
       Magazine, 21 (October 1954), 20-21.
          Surveys the scene in 1954.

722   _____. "Drama for Children." Dramatics, 21 (February 1950),
       18-19.
          Lists some general programs in children's theatre
       throughout the USA.

CHILDREN'S THEATRE

723 HORTON, LOUISE C. "Never Heard of It." Dramatics, 24 (March 1953), 14-15.
Encourages high school students to produce plays for children.

724 _____. "Smack in the Middle!" Dramatics, 23 (December 1951), 16-17.
Concerned with high school students performing plays for children, and universities and colleges offering related course work.

725 _____. "We Can't Give It Up." Dramatics, 24 (December 1952), 12-13.
Reference is to high school students performing plays for children.

726 "In Memoriam: Dr. Campton Bell." Children's Theatre Conference Newsletter, 13 (February 1964), 10-11.
Gives a short biography of Dr. Bell (1905-63) and includes eulogies by various practitioners of children's theatre.

727 "International Conference and Festival of Theatre for Children: London, May, 1964." Educational Theatre Journal, 16 (December 1964), 385-87.

728 International Conference on Theatre Education and Development: A Report on the Conference Sponsored by AETA. Washington, D.C., Office of Education: Department of Health, Education and Welfare, 1968.
A report on the State Department Conference, June 14-18, 1967.

729 JOHNSON, ALBERT AND BERTHA JOHNSON. Drama for Classroom and Stage. Cranberry, New Jersey: A. S. Barnes and Company, 1969.
Concerned primarily with formal dramatic techniques and children producing plays for children.

730 JOHNSON, RICHARD C. "Children's Theatre - A National Movement." Dramatics, 37 (May 1966), 24-25, 31.
Traces the early movement in children's theatre in the USA.

731 _____. "Excerpts from Printed Recommendations of the White House Conference." Children's Theatre Conference Newsletter, 10 (August 1960), 3.

DEVELOPMENT, 1950-1973

732   _____. "The White House Conference on Children and Youth."
       Educational Theatre Journal, 12 (October 1960), 218-20.
           Comments on those aspects of the conference that were
       pertinent to Children's Theatre and dramatics in general.

733   JONES, CLAIRE. "What Do Children Want in Children's Theatre?"
       Children's Theatre Review, 22:4 (1973), 10-12.
           A statistical evaluation of themes, characters, types
       of action and emotional responses that appeal to children,
       from a survey of 475 children.

734   JONES, WYATT. "The Junior League Story." Town and Country,
       110 (August 1956), 52-53, 88.
           Mentions the Junior League's involvement in children's
       theatre.

735   JOSSET, ANDRÉ AND JOHN ALLEN. "The Paris Conference on
       Youth and the Theatre." World Theatre, 2 (Winter 1952),
       4-8.
           This list of resolutions is derived from recommenda-
       tions made at the First International Theatre Institute
       Conference in Paris, 1952.

736   KASE, C. ROBERT. Children's Theatre Comes of Age. New York:
       Samuel French, 1956.
           This pamphlet gives a brief survey of children's
       theatre activities in this country from their inception.

737   KESTER, DOROTHY. "The CTC at Tufts." Educational Theatre
       Journal, 9 (December 1957), 330-35.
           Summarizes the activities of the Thirteenth Annual
       Conference of the CTC.

738   LATSHAW, GEORGE T. AJLA Children's Theatre Manual. New
       York: The Association of the Junior Leagues of America,
       Inc., 1966.
           Sets guidelines for Junior League organizations that
       are interested in producing plays for children or
       supporting their production.

739   LEE, PAGE. "Go-Dangle Tales: A Discovered Play." Southern
       Speech 16 (Winter 1972-73), 21-24.
           Defines "discovery theatre" and describes how it
       works, particularly with the Georgia State University
       Theatre players, and at the Academy Theatre for
       children in Atlanta.

CHILDREN'S THEATRE

740   LEWIS, GEORGE L. "Values from Children's Theatre Work for
      High School Students." Players Magazine, 33 (April
      1957), 159-60.
          Advocates the use of high school students to produce
      plays for children.

741   LEWIS, MARY KANE. Acting for Children: A Primer. New York:
      The John Day Company, 1969.
          Based on Miss Kane's work with eight to twelve year
      olds at the Pittsburgh Playhouse; slant is toward the
      professional and semi-professional child actor. Also
      covered are the uses of improvisation, miming and music
      in creative dramatics.

742   LOBL, MURIEL BOARDMAN. "Children's Theatre: Too Good to Be
      So Scarce." Saturday Review, 55 (September 8, 1972),
      62-66.
          Compares various children's theatre activities;
      praises the innovativeness of American Children's Theatre,
      but laments the fact that it is not as abundant or
      varied as theatre for children in England and on
      Continental Europe.

743   MASON, N. "Paper Bag Players in Hot Feet: Hunter College
      Playhouse, NYC." Dance Magazine, 45 (February 1971), 78.

744   McCARTHY, JOSEPH. "Pennsylvania Launches Traveling Players."
      Children's Theatre Review, 22:3 (1973), 5.
          Describes the activities of a touring company out of
      Penn State University, in conjunction with Pennsylvania's
      Department of Education; fifty-seven schools in central
      Pennsylvania were given performances.

745   McDAVITT, ELAINE. "The Cincinnati Convention." Educational
      Theatre Journal, 5 (March 1953), 48-56.
          Includes a report by Mouzon Law entitled "A Survey of
      College and University Courses in Children's Theatre and
      Creative Dramatics."

746   McINTYRE, BARBARA M. "Today and Children's Theatre."
      Children's Theatre Review, 18 (February 1969), 1-3, 20.
          Discusses the aesthetic and practical position of
      Children's Theatre and Creative Dramatics in terms of
      modern technology and research.

747   McSWEENY, MAXINE. Creative Children's Theatre for Home,
      School, Church, and Playground. Cranbury, New Jersey:
      A. S. Barnes and Company, 1973.

DEVELOPMENT, 1950-1973

(McSWEENEY, MAXINE)
Gives attention to both formal and informal dramatic activities for young children.

748 MOORE, STEVE. "Producing a 'Happening' for Children." Children's Theatre Review, 22:2 (1973), 20-23.
Describes an improvisational happening at a Sacramento playground, and shows the audience's reaction to it.

749 MORROW, SARA SPROTT. "A World-Wide Conference of Children's Theatre." Dramatics, 44 (October 1972), 24-26, 39.
Reports on the Fourth International Congress for Children and Youth, as well as ASSITEJ activities.

750 OBERLE, MARCELLA. "The CTC at Michigan City." Educational Theatre Journal, 11 (December 1959), 296-303.
Describes the Fifteenth Annual Meeting of the CTC.

751 "Operating Code of the Children's Theatre Conference." Educational Theatre Journal, 9 (December 1957), 351-55.

752 PETHYBRIDGE, DAVID C. Directed Drama. London: University of London Press, 1951.
Concerned with how and why Junior School students [British] create a play. The author traces the process from the conception of a theme through the formal production. Included in the book are three student-created scripts and a production analysis of each.

753 PETTET, EDWIN BURR. "The Chicago Convention." Educational Theatre Journal, 4 (March 1952), 61-66.
Mentions activities in children's theatre and creative dramatics which were discussed at the Fifteenth Annual Convention of AETA.

754 PHILBRICK, NORMAN. "The AETA Convention in Chicago: December, 1956." Educational Theatre Journal, 9 (May 1957), 124-33.

755 _____. "The AETA Convention in Chicago: December 1958." Educational Theatre Journal, 11 (March 1959), 127-34.

756 _____. "The White House Conference on Children and Youth." Educational Theatre Journal, 2 (October 1950), 258-59.

757 PHILLIPS, LEILA DOUGLAS. "A View of ASSITEJ - American Style." Southern Theatre, 16 (Winter 1972-73), 8-9.
Report on the Fourth World Congress and General Assembly of the International Association of Theatre for Children and Youth at the State University of New York in Albany, 1972. Highlights of the convention are discussed.

CHILDREN'S THEATRE

758 POPOVICH, JAMES E. "The CTC at Seattle." Educational Theatre Journal, 10 (December 1958), 325-35.
Covers the Fourteenth Annual Children's Theatre Conference Convention.

759 _____. "The Eleventh Annual Children's Theatre Conference." Educational Theatre Journal, 7 (December 1955), 338-45.

760 PRINS, RUTH BALKEMA. "Children's Theatre Workshop." Master's thesis, University of Washington, 1952.
Lists various techniques and exercises that would be useful to high school students who perform plays for children.

761 _____. "Playing Shows for Children." Dramatics, 22 (October 1950), 8, 10.
Concerned primarily with audience reaction to various themes and types of action in children's plays.

762 RADNITZ, ROBERT B. "Motion Pictures, Children, Families, Books and Responsibility." Children's Theatre Conference Newsletter, 15 (November 1966), 5-11.
Touches on theatre performances for the child audience.

763 REED, FRIEDA. "Children's Theatre - One Step Toward - The Answer." Dramatics, 36 (November 1964), 20.
Enumerates the values, to high school students, of performing plays for children.

764 _____. "Echoes: Children's Theatre Conference, August 28-30." Dramatics, 24 (November 1952), 19.
Reviews the activities of the Eight Annual Convention of the Children's Theatre Conference.

765 _____. "Echoes: Children's Theatre Conference." Dramatics, 26 (November 1954), 22.
Discusses the program at the Tenth Annual Convention of the CTC.

766 _____. "Theatre for Children." Dramatics, 26 (May 1955), 14-15.
Contains several letters, from Thespian troupes, about producing plays for children.

Children's Theatre and Creative Dramatics

DEVELOPMENT, 1950-1973

767 _____. "Theatre for Children." Dramatics, 27 (November 1955), 12-13, 22.
Gives criteria for picking a good children's play.

768 _____. "Theatre for Children." Dramatics, 27 (December 1955), 12-13.
Shows how to adapt a good children's play for television performance.

769 _____. "Theatre for Children." Dramatics, 27 (February 1956), 12-19, 25.
Contains evaluations of children's plays by various high school directors.

770 _____. "Theatre for Children." Dramatics, 27 (March 1956), 18-19.
Evaluates some new plays for children's theatre.

771 _____. "Theatre for Children." Dramatics, 28 (January 1957), 12-13.
Assesses the values of Theatre for Children (Winifred Ward), and Twenty-One Years with Children's Theatre (Charlotte Chorpenning).

772 _____. "Theatre for Children." Dramatics, 28 (April 1957), 16-17.
Concerned with musical plays for child audiences, gives particular attention to a production of The Wizard of Oz by William S. Robinson in Minot, North Dakota.

773 _____. "Theatre for Children." Dramatics, 29 (March 1958), 20-21.
Having asked "Why do you like working in Children's Theatre?", Miss Reed publishes a variety of answers by high school students.

774 _____. "Theatre for Children." Dramatics, 29 (May 1958), 22-23.
Capsulizes "Children's Theatre as Produced by High Schools", a Master's thesis by L. R. Kremer, the University of South Dakota, 1956.

775 _____. "Theatre for Children." Dramatics, 30 (February 1959), 22-23.
Lists some recommended plays for performance by high school students.

CHILDREN'S THEATRE

776 REED, FRIEDA. "Theatre for Children." Dramatics, 30 (March 1959), 22-23.
    Advocates the establishment of many more professional and semi-professional children's theatre companies, in hopes of decentralizing theatre out of the New York City area.

777 _____. "Theatre for Children." Dramatics, 31 (October 1959), 28-29.
    Material comes from Joseph Totaro, one of Miss Reed's students; he comments on his participation in children's theatre.

778 _____. "Theatre for Children." Dramatics, 31 (January 1960), 24-25.
    Evaluates the popularity of several children's theatre characters.

779 _____. "Theatre for Children." Dramatics, 32 (October 1960), 22-23.
    Reports on the first Secondary Schools Theatre Conference and a production of Helen James' Shiny Legs.

780 _____. "Theatre for Children." Dramatics, 32 (November 1960), 14-15.
    Discusses a production of A Midsummer Night's Dream by Raymond B. Olsen in Union City, New Jersey.

781 _____. "Theatre for Children." Dramatics, 32 (March 1961), 20-21.
    Miss Reed synthesizes the attitudes of major children's theatre practitioners concerning how to choose a good children's play.

782 _____. "Theatre for Children." Dramatics, 32 (May 1961), 20-21.
    Shows the applicability of the Davis and Watkins book Children's Theatre to high school groups who perform plays for children.

783 _____. "Theatre for Children." Dramatics, 33 (December 1961), 20-21.
    Gives lists of recommended plays.

784 _____. "Theatre for Children." Dramatics, 33 (May 1962), 32-33.
    Discusses the merits of Otto Forkert's recent book Children's Theatre that Captures Its Audience!

DEVELOPMENT, 1950-1973

785   . "Theatre for Children." Dramatics, 34 (December 1962), 20.
           Lists some quality children's theatre scripts and evaluates the method of selecting plays.

786   . "Theatre for Children." Dramatics, 35 (May 1964), 26-27, 34.
           Includes an essay "Choosing the Children's Play" by Claudia Catania.

787   "Region 14 Undertakes Commissioning of New Plays for Children." Children's Theatre Review, 17 (February 1968), 10-11.

788   "Regional Organizations." Children's Theatre Conference Newsletter, 3 (October 12, 1952), 3-4.
           Discusses the division of the Children's Theatre Conference into sixteen regions and gives the new directors.

789   REYNOLDS, MARYAN. "The White House Conference." Children's Theatre Conference Newsletter, 9 (May 1960), 1-2.
           Summarizes the activities of the 1960 White House Conference on Children and Youth.

790   "Roar, Lion, Roar! Theatre Where Children Take Over." Life, 71 (December 17, 1971), 155-56.

791   ROCKEFELLER, KAY. "Live Drama for Children." Child Study, 30 (Spring 1953), 18-20, 41-42.
           Comments on the value of child actors performing roles in theatre for children.

792   ROSINBUM, RALPH. "The Pursuit of Excellence." Children's Theatre Review, 17 (November 1968), 9-13.
           The author gives an extended plea for realistic plots and high-level, professional performances in plays for children.

793   SALERNI, F. LOU. "Caution: Children's Theatre May Be Dangerous." Children's Theatre Review, 22:1 (1973), 23-30.
           Discusses a successful Title I project in children's theatre in Eugene, Oregon, which was a failure from the point of view of educational administrators.

794   SANDERS, SANDRA. Creating Plays with Children. New York: Citation Press, 1970.
           Although this book consists primarily of six playlets

CHILDREN'S THEATRE

(SANDERS, SANDRA)
>for child actors, the author concludes, after discussing
the method of approaching a printed play, that the more
improvisation the better.

795 SCHAAL, DAVID G. "The East Lansing Convention." Educational
Theatre Journal, 6 (December 1954), 341-47.
>Includes a summary of Dina Rees Evans speech in which
she urges high school students to perform more quality
plays for children, and to leave adult plays to more
mature actors.

796 _____. "The New York Convention." Educational Theatre
Journal, 6 (March 1954), 61-70.
>Covers numerous aspects of formal and informal drama
for children as they were discussed at the AETA Convention.

797 SCHERTZ, MARY LOU. "The Dramatic Philosophy of Jane Addams
and Hull House Theatre Today." Master's thesis, Kent
State University, 1966.
>Includes a brief biography of Jane Addams, and
evaluates the programs in formal and informal drama at
Hull House.

798 SCHRAM, FRANCES. "Professional Theatre for the Child."
Creative Expression in Oral Language. Mabel Wright
Henry, ed. Champaign, Illinois: National Council of
Teachers of English, 1967.
>Advocates the use of professional theatre for children,
and gives a short history of the professional theatre
movement for children.

799 SCHWARTZ, DOROTHY T. "AETA Convention - 1959." Children's
Theatre Conference Newsletter, 9 (February 1960), 1-3.
>Covers topics in both formal and informal dramatics.

800 _____. "A History of the Children's Theatre Conference,
1944-55." Master's thesis, University of Alabama, 1956.

801 _____. "In My Opinion." Children's Theatre Conference
Newsletter, 14 (February 1965), 6.
>The author urges more interaction and cooperation
between child-related professions and national organizations serving the interests of the child.

802 _____. "The White House Conference and CTC." Children's
Theatre Conference Newsletter, 9 (May 1960), 2-3.

(SCHWARTZ, DOROTHY T.)
Summarizes the activities of the 1960 White House
Conference on Children and Youth.

803   SHAPIRO, STEPHEN AND RICHARD PLACE. Eds. Artists in the
Classroom. Hartford, Connecticut: Connecticut Commission
on the Arts, 1973.
Analyzes a Connecticut-based unified program of
visiting artists in theatre, art, dance, music and so
forth, and its success with children in the classrooms
that were visited.

804   SIKS, GERALDINE B. "Children's Drama in the Great Society."
Children's Theatre Conference Newsletter, 14 (August
1965), 8-9.
Objects to the dearth of good professional drama for
children, and the general lack of support for all
aspects of child related dramatics.

805   _____. "Creative Dramatics for Children." Readings in the
Language Arts. Verna D. Anderson, ed. New York:
Macmillan Company, 1964.
Gives a definition of creative dramatics and shows its
value to child development.

806   _____. "Out of Your Cage." Players Magazine, 31 (January
1955), 89-90.
Summarizes the activities of the Annual Meeting of
the CTC at East Lansing, Michigan.

807   _____. "Theatre for Youth: An International Report."
Educational Theatre Journal, 7 (December 1955), 306 14.
Covers the work in child-related dramatics in twenty-
seven countries, twelve of which also concern themselves
with creative dramatics.

808   SLADE, PETER. Children's Theatre and Theatre for Young
People. London: Educational Drama Association, 1968.
Based on a talk given at the Rea Street Centre to the
British Children's Theatre Association; traces the
history of Slade's work to 1968 and is followed by a
series of questions and answers.

809   SPENCER, SARA. "But Little Children Grow Up." Players
Magazine, 40 (May 1964), 240.
Concerned with the lack of quality children's plays
for an audience from ten to fifteen years old.

CHILDREN'S THEATRE

810 SCHWARTZ, DOROTHY T. "Children's Theatre." Encyclopedia Ameri-
     cana. New York: Americana Corporation, 1966. VI, 484-88.
     Covers theatre for and by children, as well as
     creative dramatics.

811 _____. "The Children's Theatre Conference: Annual Report of
     the Director." Educational Theatre Journal, 8 (March
     1956), 58-60.

812 _____. "Children's Theatre, Past and Present." Educational
     Theatre Journal, 7 (March 1955), 44-46.

813 _____. "CTC and the Professional Children's Theatre."
     Children's Theatre Conference Newsletter, 15 (November
     1966), 20.

814 _____. "A Decade of Children's Theatre." Theatre Arts, 38
     (November 1954), 84.

815 _____. "International Children's Theatre - ASSITEJ."
     Children's Theatre Conference Newsletter, 14 (November
     1965), 14.
     Discusses the founding of ASSITEJ and predicts its
     future needs.

816 _____. "International Children's Theatre Association."
     Children's Theatre Conference Newsletter, 14 (February
     1965), 12-13.
     Summarizes the initial activities of the International
     Children's Theatre Association, and includes dramatics in
     the overall definition of child-related drama.

817 _____. "A National Responsibility." Southern Theatre, 11:1
     (1967), 5-6, 21.
     Discusses themes and techniques that are valuable in
     a good children's play.

818 _____. "Only the Best." Children's Theatre Conference
     Newsletter, 13 (May 1964), 3.
     Describes the requirements for winning the Campton
     Bell Scholarship in Children's Theatre.

819 "Star-Shaped Roof for Outdoor Theatre." American City, 74
     (January 1959), 80.
     Illustrates the Arroyo Viejo Children's Theatre, built
     by the Oakland, California, Recreation Department.

DEVELOPMENT, 1950-1973

820   STURGILL, BEVERLY. "New Scripts Travelling Library."
       Children's Theatre Review, 17 (February 1968), 2-6, 9.
       Explains the new concept of a travelling script
       library of one-acts and full length plays for children,
       supported by the CTC.

821   SWORTZELL, LOWELL. Ed. All the World's a Stage: Modern
       Plays for Young People. New York: Delacorte Press, 1972.
       An anthology of sixteen plays for children/youths by
       authors such as Wilder, Brecht, Tagore, Menotti, and so
       forth, plus excellent critical material.

822   _____. AND NANCY SWORTZELL. "Right On, Toady! A Note on
       Relevancy in Children's Theatre." Children's Theatre
       Review, 22:2 (1973), 18-20.

823   TAYLOR, LOREN E. An Introduction to Dramatics for Children.
       Minneapolis: Burgess Publishing Company, 1965.
       Covers many facets of educational, recreational,
       creative and formal dramatics; includes a chapter on
       "Drama and Child Development."

824   Tenth Anniversary Brochure. Kansas City, Missouri: Community
       Children's Theatre, 1957.
       Documents the history and activities of the Kansas
       City Community Children's Theatre.

825   "Theatre and Youth: International Action Planned." Times
       Educational Supplement, 18 April, 1952, p. 335.
       Summarizes the activities at the International Theatre
       Institute on Theatre and Youth held in Paris in 1952.

826   "Theatre and Youth: Production by Adults." Times Educational
       Supplement, 25 April, 1952, p. 351.
       For annotation, see above.

827   "Theatre Resources for Youth, Project TRY." Children's
       Theatre Review, 16 (November 1967), 13.
       Describes the University of Delaware project and its
       continuance grant.

828   THOMPSON, ALMA. "Children's Theatre Circuit Conference
       Formed." Children's Theatre Review, 16 (November 1967),
       23-24.
       Discusses the initial activities of eight southern
       cities to organize a circuit of children's theatre
       touring companies.

Children's Theatre and Creative Dramatics

CHILDREN'S THEATRE

829 "Twentieth Anniversary of Children's Theatre Conference, August 18-22." Players Magazine, 40 (May 1964), 241.

830 WARD, WINIFRED. "Sixth Annual Children's Theatre Conference." Educational Theatre Journal, 2 (October 1950), 198-207.

831 _____. Theatre for Children. 3rd ed. Anchorage, Kentucky: Children's Theatre Press, 1958.
     A primer for people interested in all aspects of children's theatre; covers history, directing, financing, touring, performing, selecting and writing.

832 _____. "This I Remember, This I Believe." Children's Theatre Conference Newsletter, 14 (November 1964), 7-9.
     By way of acknowledging the twenty-second anniversary of the CTC, Miss Ward compliments the organization on its progress and projects its future.

833 WATKINS, MARY JANE LARSON. "Tenth Annual Children's Theatre Meeting." Educational Theatre Journal, 6 (December 1954), 348-54.

834 WEST, HELEN LOUISE CROUCH. "An Experimental Study to Determine the Need and Effectiveness of a Program of Children's Theatre for the Junior College Curriculum." Master's thesis, St. Louis University, 1952.

835 WHALEY, RUSSELL G. "The AETA Convention: August 25-27, 1965." Educational Theatre Journal, 17 (December 1965), 376-84.
     Includes a discussion of a creatively produced performance of a children's play.

836 "What is ASSITEJ?" ASSITEJ Information Bulletin, No. 1 (1966-67), 7-8.
     Gives a definitional statement about the International Association of Theatre for Children and Young People.

837 WILLIAMS, HENRY B. "The AETA Convention: December 27-29, 1964." Educational Theatre Journal, 17 (May 1965), 159-64.
     Mentions a variety of subjects related to child-related drama.

838 WILLERT, ORIEL JAMES. "Half a Century of Children's Theatre History in America." Master's thesis, University of Washington, 1953.

Children's Theatre and Creative Dramatics

DEVELOPMENT, 1950-1973

839 WILSON, MRS. KENDRICK. "Children's Theatre Conference."
Educational Theatre Journal, 15 (December 1963), 394-96.
Covers the Nineteenth Annual Meeting of the CTC at
the University of Minnesota; topics related to both
formal and informal drama are mentioned.

840 WRIGHT, LIN. "Cultural Diversity and CTA: The 1973
Convention." Children's Theatre Review, 22:4 (1973), 3.
Discusses the 1973 Annual Children's Theatre Associa-
tion Conference.

See also the following entries. 16, 43, 62, 110, 142-43, 165,
192, 243-44, 247, 253, 255, 263, 276, 285-86, 292, 297, 321,
329-30, 362, 390, 395, 398, 403, 407-08, 413-14, 416, 419,
424, 429, 432, 483, 672, 1018, 1046, 1077, 1233, 1329, 1353,
1356, 1377, 1427, 1453, 1493, 1513, 1521, 1525, 1535, 1542-
43, 1549, 1557, 1560-61, 1582-83, 1596, 1623-24, 1642, 1740,
1773, 1776, 1781, 1805, 1840, 1853, 1862, 1866, 1885, 1914,
1938, 1979, 2014, 2217.

SPECIFIC THEATRES AND DIRECTORS: PRE-1950

841 ADIX, VERN. "Utah University Has a Youth Theatre." Players
Magazine, 21 (May 1945), 24.
Surveys the second season of the Young People's
Theatre at the University of Utah.

842 ALEXANDRA, SELMA. "Need for a Children's Theatre." Drama
Magazine, 21 (May 1931), 16.
Discusses the work of Adrienne Morrison, founder of
the Children's Players of New York City.

843 BAKER, ANNE. "Let's Pretend." Woman's Journal, 13 (July
1928), 16-17, 30.
Designs for the production of Kai Khosru by the King-
Coit Children's Theatre at the Hampden Theatre in New
York City are discussed.

844 BECKET, JOHN J. "The Children's Theatre." Harper's Bazaar,
34 (January 19, 1901), 181-85.
Praises the work of the Children's Theatre at the
Carnegie Lyceum in New York City; this is the first
official children's theatre in the United States in
this century.

CHILDREN'S THEATRE

845 BELCHER, IRENE. "The Children's Playhouse of Muncie,
     Indiana." Players Magazine, 20 (January 1944), 20-21.
          Discusses a new company and the author's involvement
     with it.

846 BOLTEN, MARY. "The Children's Experimental Theatre."
     Players Magazine, 26 (December 1949), 62-63.
          Stresses the different programs of Isabel Burger's
     Children's Experimental Theatre.

847 BRAZIER, HARRIET. "Children's Theatre - A Challenge."
     National Theatre Conference Bulletin, 10 (November 1948),
     12-19.
          Shows rehearsal procedures at the Children's Theatre
     of the Cleveland Playhouse.

848 BURGER, ISABEL B. "The Children's Theatre in the Community."
     Players Magazine, 22 (May-June 1946), 10-12.
          Describes a production of O Brave New Young World
     at the Children's Experimental Theatre in Baltimore.

849 _____. "It Just Grew." Players Magazine, 21 (May 1945),
     28-29.
          More programs at the Baltimore theatre are described;
     the author also stresses the importance of creative
     dramatics to enhance a theatre program.

850 BUSH, SADIE. "A Children's Theatre." Canadian Forum, 10
     (April 1930), 264-65.

851 CABELL, ELVIRA D. "The Children's Educational Theatre: A
     Review." English Journal [College English], 1 (April
     1912), 251-55.
          More than a review of Alice Minnie Herts' book, the
     author analyses Miss Herts's techniques and policies.

852 CANDLER, MARTHA. "Consultant in Make-Believe." Woman's
     Journal, 15 (April 1930), 22-23.
          Surveys the work of Mabel Foote Hobbs, drama consultant
     for the Playground Recreation Association.

853 "The Century of the Child in the Playhouse." Current
     Opinion, 54 (February 1913), 121-23.
          Discusses the Children's Theatre of the Century
     Theatre in New York; the first production, The Racketty-
     Packetty House by Frances Hodson is illustrated.

CHILDREN'S THEATRE AND CREATIVE DRAMATICS

SPECIFIC THEATRE AND DIRECTORS, PRE-1950

854 "The Children's Civic Theatre of Chicago." Drama, 17 (October 1926), 12, 30-32.
    Analyzes the ten years of operation of the Chicago Drama League's Children's Theatre at the Civic Theatre.

855 "Children's Theatre at Cleveland." Players Magazine, 21 (May 1945), 30.
    Concerned specifically with the work of Esther Mullin from 1933 to 1945.

856 "The Children's Theatre at the University of Tulsa." Playground and Recreation, 22 (March 1929), 697-98.
    Discusses the work of Josephine Layman Story, Director of Theatre at the University of Tulsa, and her plays with child actors.

857 "A Children's Theatre for Children." Drama, 20 (November 1929), 53.
    Child actors in plays for children at the Children's Theatre of the St. Paul Players in Minnesota is discussed.

858 "Children's Theatre Group Organized to Give Training in Acting and Stage-Craft." Community Theatre Cue, 6 (October 1940), 1-2.
    Illustrates the training program for children six through seventeen at the Children's Theatre of South Bend, Indiana.

859 "Children's Theatre Is Incorporated Here to Cater to Welfare of Rising Generation." New York Times, 9 May, 1934, p. 22.
    Gives the purpose and goals of the American Children's Theatre in New York City, which had just been founded.

860 "Children's Theatre of Chicago." Drama, 17 (October 1926), 12.

861 "Children's Theatres." Drama, 21 (February 1931), 29.
    Discusses the work of Mrs. Harry E. Davis at the Children's Theatre in Columbia, South Carolina.

862 CHIPMAN, SANDS. "Story Books Come to Life in a Children's Theatre." Drama, 21 (April 1931), 27.
    Surveys the history and technical aspects of the ongoing Children's Theatre at Emerson College for the twelve years pervious to the article.

Children's Theatre and Creative Dramatics

CHILDREN'S THEATRE

863 "Cleveland's Theatre for Youth." Design, 40 (March 1939), 5-6.
   Operational procedures of the first Federal Theatre for children are discussed.

864 COIT, DOROTHY. "Introduction," Kai Khosru and Other Plays for Children as Produced by the King-Coit Children's Theatre. New York: Theatre Arts, Inc., 1934.
   Analyzes content in good children's plays, and suggests rehearsal practices with child actors.

865 COONLEY, LYDIA AVERY. "The Children's Players." Harper's Bazaar, 65 (December 1930), 126.
   A brief history of Adrienne Morrison's Children's Players at the Princess Theatre.

866 _____. "Drama for the Youngest Set." Theatre Magazine, 52 (September 1930), 40, 62.
   Discusses the first season of the Children's Players under the direction of Adrienne Morrison.

867 CRAWFORD, WINNIE MAE. "In the Children's Theatre." Players Magazine, 18 (November 1941), 19, 21.
   Surveys many children's theatres sponsored by Junior Programs, Inc.

868 _____. "In the Children's Theatre." Players Magazine, 19 (February 1943), 19.
   Tells how to start a children's theatre; suggests a combination of formal and informal drama.

869 _____. "In the Children's Theatre." Players Magazine, 19 (April 1943), 25.
   Covers technical aspects of establishing a community children's theatre. Suggests that potential organizers consider an inexpensive and beneficial program of creative dramatics.

870 CROWTHER, BOSLEY. "For Children Only." New York Times, 13 May, 1934, sec. IX, p. 1.
   Describes Clare Tree Major's 1934 season in the Children's Theatre.

871 "Cultural Entertainment for Young People." Saturday Review, 47 (November 1934), 650-51.
   Discusses touring companies out of the Junior Programs, Inc. of Maplewood, New Jersey.

Children's Theatre and Creative Dramatics

872 "The Curtain Goes Up - For Youngsters." Recreation, 41
       (February 1948), 532.
       Comments on the activities and objectives of the
       Footlight Players of Charleston, South Carolina.

873 DAGGY, MAYNARD LEE. "The Story of the 'Theatre of Youth'."
       Players Magazine, 13 (March-April 1937), 5.
       Surveys the activity of the Theatre of Youth at
       Washington State Theatre in Pullman.

874 DEVINE, GEORGE. "Young Audiences." Drama, New Series, 14
       (Autumn 1949), 13-15.
       Author describes his methods of direction at the
       Young Vic Theatre.

875 "Dramatics for Children." Playground and Recreation, 15
       (July 1921), 296.
       Discusses the second season of the Children's
       Department of the Pasadena Playhouse; children's theatres
       in Chicago and Erie, Pennsylvania are noted.

876 ELICKER, VIRGINIA WILK. "City-Wide Dramatic Program at
       Lakewood, Ohio." Players Magazine, 21 (May 1945), 24.

877 FABER, HAROLD. "New Group Prepares to Offer Suitable Play
       Program for the Young Folk." New York Times, 12
       October, 1947, sec. II, p. 3.
       Notes the founding of the Children's World Theatre
       under the protection of Monte Meacham.

878 FAGIN, N. BRYLLION. "A 'Dramatic Lady' Experiments."
       Emerson Quarterly, 22 (June 1942), 5-6.
       Discusses Isabel Burger's work in formal and informal
       drama at the Children's Educational Theatre at Johns
       Hopkins University.

879 "The First Children's Theatre [Building] in the World."
       Theatre Magazine, 37 (January 1923), 46.
       Illustrates the Heckscher Foundation Children's
       Theatre in New York City.

880 FISHER, CAROLINE AND M. C. THELTGEN. "How Two California
       Children's Theatres are Functioning in Wartime."
       American City, 58 (June 1943), 87-90.

881 FITZGERALD, BURDETTE. "Kid's Stuff." Players Magazine, 23
       (March-April 1947), 95-96.

Children's Theatre and Creative Dramatics

CHILDREN'S THEATRE

(FITZGERALD, BURDETTE)
Describes the work of high school students acting for children at the East Bay Children's Theatre in Oakland, California.

882 _____. "30,000 Children Can't Be Wrong." Players Magazine, 27 (March 1949), 136.
Describes the opening program of the Children's World Theatre in New York and their production of Jack and the Beanstalk.

883 FLANAGAN, HALLIE. Arena. New York: Duell, Sloan, and Pierce, 1940.
Recounts the brief history of the Federal Theatre Project and devotes some space to its involvement in Children's Theatre; an appendix of all plays produced for children under this program is included.

884 FORD, ALEXANDER HUME. "New England's Stage Children." New England Magazine, 33 (September 1905), 400-09.
Contains brief biographies of child actors at the Children's Theatre of Boston; included is a discussion of Franklin Sargent's Children's Theatre at Carnegie Lyecum in New York City.

885 FORD, JOHN CARTER. "The Palo Alto Summer Theatre for Children." Theatre and School, 12 (February 1934), 5-7.
Notes the work of Margaret and John Ford during a summer project at the Castilleja School in Palo Alto, California.

886 "Forty Years at Hull House." Adventurous Americans. Devere Allen, ed. New York: Farrar and Rinehart, 1932.
Discusses the environment of openness and enrichment at Hull House under the protection of Jane Addams.

887 FREITAG, BEVERLY F. "How One Children's Theatre Became Successful." School and Society, 39 (April 7, 1934), 427-30.
Notes the founding and development of the Children's Theatre of East School, Stoneham, Massachusetts.

888 GALE, ZONA. "Robin Hood in Jones Street." Outlook, 92 (June 26, 1909), 439-46.
Describes a May-pole festival, involving tenement children.

Children's Theatre and Creative Dramatics

889 GILBERTSON, ALICE. "Curtain Going Up!" Recreation, 39
      (November 1943), 432-34.
         Discusses the Playhouse for Children in Memphis,
      Tennessee, and the direction of Agnes Haaga.

890 ____. "Richmond Children's Theatre - Second Edition."
      Recreation, 37 (November 1943), 434, 474.
         Shows the re-organization of the Children's Theatre of
      Richmond, Virginia.

891 GOLDEN, BEN. "Children's Theatre on Tour." New Theatre and
      Film, 2 (October 1935), 8-9.
         The Pioneer Youth Performers of West Virginia tour
      mining towns, encouraging children to fight for free
      school books and state aid to education.

892 "Goodman Memorial Theatre." Players Magazine, 20 (November
      1943), 15-16.
         Notes the work of Charlotte Chorpenning.

893 GORDON, FRANCES E. "The Best for a Dime." Parents' Magazine,
      14 (March 1939), 20, 32, 34.
         Discusses the first programs of the North Shore
      Children's Theatre in Milwaukee.

894 HALLOCK, ANNE. "Seven Years of Drama." Playground and
      Recreation, 22 (March 1929), 692-95.
         Includes a history of the Children's Theatre at
      Margaret Fuller House in Cambridge, Massachusetts.

895 HALLOCK, ESTELLE. "Drama at Scarborough School." Progressive
      Education, 8 (January 1931), 79-80.
         Surveys dramatic activities for seventeen years in
      both formal and informal drama.

896 HARRINGTON, MILDRED. "Mrs. Major's Stock Company Plays to
      'Children Only'." American Magazine, 105 (February
      1928), 60-61.
         Presents a brief biography of Clare Tree Major and
      discusses her work at the Children's Saturday Morning
      Theatre in New York City.

897 HAUSER, BERTRAM. "Where Children Play at Giving Plays."
      Literary Digest, 86 (August 1, 1925), 25-26.
         Comments on child actors and their performances at the
      Hecksher Theatre for Children in New York City.

CHILDREN'S THEATRE

898 HEIDERSTADT, DOROTHY. "Curtain Going Up!" Wilson Library
     Bulletin, 18 (May 1944), 642-43, 675.
          Surveys a production of Cinderella by the Dramatic
     Club of the Wilson Public Library.

899 HENDERSON, ROSE. "Children's Theatre: Murals of Fairy
     Tales." International Studio, 82 (October 1925), 61-66.
          Illustrates Willy Pogany's murals at the Children's
     Theatre at the Hecksher Building; includes a brief
     biography of the artist.

900 HORTON, LOUISE C. "Drama for Children." Dramatics, 18
     (March 1947), 22-23.
          Indicates the value of Isabel Burger's work at the
     Children's Experimental Theatre in Baltimore.

901 _____. "Drama for Children." Dramatics, 18 (May 1947),
     20-21.
          Discusses the work of Dr. Frank M. Whiting at the
     Children's Theatre of the University of Minnesota and
     his production of Rip Van Winkle.

902 _____. "Drama for Children." Dramatics, 19 (February 1948),
     22-23.
          Concerned with the work of Dr. Kenneth Graham.

903 _____. "Drama for Children." Dramatics, 19 (April 1948),
     20-22.
          Includes brief notations about children's theatre in
     England, at the Trailor Theatre of Portland, Maine, and
     the forthcoming Children's Theatre Conference at the
     University of Denver.

904 HOWARD, DORIS. "Trouping the C. T. Play." Players Magazine,
     24 (February 1948), 114.
          The author, president of the East Bay Children's
     Theatre in Oakland, California, discusses technical
     aspects of touring that company.

905 "How Children Are Taught to Act: King-Coit Children's
     Theatre." Good Housekeeping, 115 (December 1942), 44-45.

906 HUMPHREY, EDITH E. "Children's Theatre Comes Home!" High
     School Thespian, 15 (March 1944), 4-5.
          Shows co-operation of the Junior League and the
     Central Junior-Senior High School of Parkersburg, West
     Virginia, to produce Jack and the Beanstalk for local
     children.

SPECIFIC THEATRES AND DIRECTORS, PRE-1950

907   HUMPHREY, GRACE. "The Portmanteau Theatre." Drama, 5
      (November 1915), 644-50.
          Discusses the philosophy of Stuart Walker.

908   "In the Children's Theatres." Players Magazine, 15
      (September-October 1938), 17, 21.
          Concerned particularly with the North Shore Children's
      Theatre of Milwaukee, although other theatres are
      mentioned.

909   "Indiana Children Create Own Theatre." Federal Theatre
      Magazine, 2 (October 1936), 21,34.
          Explores a Federal Theatre Project in Gary, Indiana.

910   JODER, ANNA BEST. "Cheyenne Got Its Children's Theatre."
      Players Magazine, 20 (November 1943), 5, 22.

911   _____. "Children's Theatre of Cheyenne." Players Magazine,
      21 (November 1944), 24-25.
          Reports on the four productions of the Children's
      Theatre of Cheyenne's first season.

912   _____. "Reports from Here and There." Players Magazine,
      22 (July-August 1946), 14-17.
          Surveys eighteen major children's theatres in the
      United States.

913   JOHNSON, RAYMOND. "Report from the South." Theatre Arts,
      33 (September 1949), 56.
          Discusses the symbiotic relationship of the Nashville
      Community Playhouse and the Nashville Children's Theatre.

914   JONES, BEATRICE ARLINE. "A Community Children's Theatre."
      Recreation, 28 (September 1934), 269, 305.
          Work at the Palo Alto Community Children's Theatre
      with Hazel Gloister Robertson is discussed.

915   JONES, SYBIL ELIZA. "A Children's Theatre." Theatre
      Magazine, 35 (May 1922), 318-19, 344.
          Author shows how to involve a community in a children's
      theatre.

916   "Juvenile Road Troupes Double Touring Area to Reach Audience
      of Two Million." Newsweek, 12 (October 3, 1938), 22-23.
          Explains the work of Clare Tree Major's Children's
      Theatre in its fifteenth season, and discusses the
      plans of the six touring companies.

CHILDREN'S THEATRE

917 KESTER, DOROTHY. "Cain Park Children's Theatre." Players
     Magazine, 20 (April 1944), 21.
          Explores Dina Rees Evans direction in the absence of
     Kenneth Graham; illustrates a production of Peter Pan,
     and comments on the number of Cain Park children who
     have gone on to do work in Children's Theatre and
     Creative Dramatics.

918 KNOW, ETHEL LOUISE. "Another Phase of Junior Drama." Drama,
     12 (October-November 1921), 50-51.
          The Grand Rapids, Iowa Junior Drama League is discussed.

919 LAFLIN, LOUIS E., JR. "The Goodman Children's Theatre."
     Drama, 19 (October 1928), 12-13, 32.
          Traces the early history and the work of Muriel Brown.

920 LAVERNE, SISTER M., O.S.F. "Illinois College Uses Large
     Cast in 'Old Woman'." Players Magazine, 19 (May 1943),
     42-43.
          Follows a three year history of the St. Francis
     Children's Theatre of Joliet, Illinois, and describes
     a production of The Old Woman Who Lived in a Shoe.

921 LAYMAN, PAULINE. "A Unique Children's Theatre." Emerson
     Quarterly, 6 (May 1928), 3-6, 8, 10.
          Traces the work of Josephine Layman Story at the
     Children's Theatre of the University of Tulsa.

922 LEE, AMY FREEMAN. Critic's Notebook. Boston: Manthorne
     and Burack, 1943.
          Gives a brief history of Clare Tree Major's Children's
     Theatre.

923 "Lights, Camera, Action!" Recreation, 39 (August 1945),
     252-56, 268.
          Highlights the filming procedures following a Palo
     Alto Children's Theatre production of Titian.

924 "Los Angeles Children's Theatre Guild." Drama Magazine, 21
     (April 1931), 30.
          Concerned with Cora Mel Patten's Children's Theatre
     programs in the Los Angeles area.

925 MACKAY, CONSTANCE D'ARCY. "The School Theatre in New York
     City." Players Magazine, 21 (May 1945), 26.
          Surveys many New York Public Schools producing plays
     with and for children.

CHILDREN'S THEATRE AND CREATIVE DRAMATICS

SPECIFIC THEATRES AND DIRECTORS, PRE-1950

926   MacKAYE, PERCY. _The Civic Theatre_. New York: Mitchell
      Kennerley, 1912.
            Chapter eight, "Imagination and the Children's
      Theatre," discusses the Children's Educational Theatre
      of New York.

927   MacKENZIE, CATHERINE. "Children's Own Theatre." _New York
      Times Magazine_, 18 January, 1947, p. 30.
            Of particular note is the fact that the Children's
      Theatre of Palo Alto, California, is the only completely
      tax-supported Children's Theatre in the United States.

928   "Magic for Moppets." _Theatre Arts_, 33 (March 1949), 59.
            Illustrates the Children's World Theatre of New York
      City's production of _Jack and the Beanstalk_.

929   MAJOR, CLARE TREE. "A Children's Theatre at Columbia."
      _Columbia University Institute of Arts and Sciences
      Institute Magazine_, 1 (May 1929), 9, 32.
            Concerned with the Saturday Morning Children's Theatre
      at McMillan Academic Theatre in New York City.

930   "Make Believe Land." _Recreation_, 39 (December 1945), 459,
      498.
            Surveys the first year of the Children's Playhouse of
      St. Louis.

931   MARYE, DONALD. "Oregon State Theatre." _Players Magazine_,
      25 (April 1949), 163-64.
            Traces the programs of several children's theatres in
      Oregon and announces the annual Oregon State Theatre
      Conference.

932   MAYNE, SHEILA. "From Never Never Land to Iran." _Arts and
      Decoration_, 24 (December 1925), 35-37.
            Reviews the King-Coit production of _Kai Khosru_ at the
      Hecksher Foundation in New York City.

933   McCABE, LIDA ROSE. "Making All the Fairy Tales Come True."
      Arts and Decoration, 18 (December 1922), 14-15, 98.
            Emphasis is on the Hecksher Foundation Children's
      Theatre in New York City; Willy Pogany's murals are
      discussed.

934   McCASLIN, NELLIE. "Children's Theatre in Indianapolis."
      Players Magazine, 21 (January 1945), 24-7.

CHILDREN'S THEATRE

935   McSWEENY, MAXINE. "Matinees by Children for Children."
      Recreation, 35 (May 1941), 91-93, 128-30.
          Traces the program of the Los Angeles Recreation
      Commission's children's matinees from their inception.

936   MEADER, DOROTHY. "Duluth Children's Theatre." School Arts,
      38 (November 1938), 85-87.

937   MEADOWCRAFT, CLARA. "At the Children's Matinee." Saint
      Nicholas, 41 (February 1914), 351-57.
          Emphasis is on the Little Theatre in New York City
      directed by Winthrop Ames, although numerous other
      theatres are cited.

938   MITCHELL, ALBERT O. "Young People's Theatre." Players
      Magazine, 25 (January 1949), 90-91.

939   MORRIS, MRS. GEORGE SPENCER. "The Educational Value of the
      Drama." Child Welfare, 8 (September 1913), 14-15.
          Concerned primarily with early Junior League involve-
      ment in children's theatre.

940   MORSE, WILLIAM NORTHROP. "The Educational Theatre." Outlook,
      89 (July 11, 1908), 572-77.
          Discusses New York State Blue Laws and how they
      contributed to the closing of the Children's Educational
      Theatre; also of note is the fact that Mark Twain was
      President of the Board of the theatre from 1908-09.

941   MOSES, J. GARFIELD. "The Children's Theatre." Charities and
      Commons, 18 (April 6, 1907), 23-24.
          An extended discussion of the policies and personnel
      of the Children's Theatre at the Educational Alliance in
      New York City.

942   "Most Democratic Theatre in the World." Harper's Weekly, 51
      (November 16, 1907), 1698-99.
          Gives some attention to the Educational Alliance's
      Children's Theatre.

943   NANCREDE, EDITH DE. "Dramatic Work at Hull House."
      Playground and Recreation, 22 (April 1928), 276-78.
          Mentions the dramatic work at Hull House under the
      tutelage of Jane Addams.

Children's Theatre and Creative Dramatics

944 NEWMEYER, SARA. "For Children It Is Not Make-Believe." New York Times Magazine, 5 December, 1948, pp. 24-26.
     The vice-president of the Children's World Theatre comments on its productions; included are quotations of children about the plays, performers, and productions of Jack in the Beanstalk and Little Red Riding Hood.

945 NICHOLS, LEWIS. "Major for Minors." New York Times, 7 March, 1948, sec. II, p. 2.
     Concerned with production policy of Clare Tree Major's Children's Theatre.

946 NICKELL, MARION F. "The Toy Theatre of Atlantic City." Theatre Magazine, 49 (June 1929), 46-47.
     Shows how a community theatre project works.

947 "Note on an East Side Fauntleroy." New York Times, 4 December, 1938, sec. X, p. 7.
     Comments on a Children's Educational Theatre production of Frances Hodgson Burnett's Little Lord Fauntleroy at the Educational Alliance; technical information is included.

948 OGDEN, JEAN. "A Theatre for Children." Recreation, 37 (February 1944), 623, 636-37.
     Summarizes the activities of the Lynchburg, Virginia, Junior League Children's Theatre.

949 OLIVER, GEORGE H. "Producing Children's Christmas Plays Successfully." New York Dramatic Mirror, 77 (December 22, 1917), 14.

950 "Our Young Thespians in Dead Earnest." Literary Digest, 85 (May 16, 1925), 26-27.
     Discusses professional child actors and a King-Coit production of Aucassin and Nicolette.

951 PALMER, WINTHROP. "Make-Believe for Children." Drama, 18 (March 1928), 173-74, 192.
     Traces the early history of the Junior League and Children's Theatre.

952 PARTRIDGE, PAULINE. "The Home of the Fairies." Sunset, 56 (April 1926), 38-39, 79.
     Gives a fifteen year history of the Children's Theatre of San Francisco; the plays of Mrs. John J. Cuddy, its director, are reviewed.

Children's Theatre and Creative Dramatics

CHILDREN'S THEATRE

953   PATTEN, CORA MEL. "How to Organize a Junior Drama League."
        Drama, 11 (October 1920), 31-32.

954   PATTEN, HAZEL R. "A Program Carried on." Recreation, 39
        (January 1946), 513-15, 558.
              Surveys work at the Seattle Junior Programs, Inc.,
        and announces the group's playwriting contest.

955   PIERCE, LUCY FRANCE. "The Children's Theatre." Green Book
        Album, 4 (July 1910), 126-28.
              Primarily concerned with the Children's Theatre of
        the Educational Alliance of New York City and its early
        founders and directors; mention is made of two children's
        theatres in England, and the work at Hull House in
        Chicago.

956   _____. "A Kindergarten for Future Playgoers." Theatre
        Magazine, 7 (June 1907), 154-56, x-xiii.
              Discusses the Children's Theatre at the Educational
        Alliance.

957   "The Play of Imagination in the Tiniest Theatre." Survey,
        34 (September 1915), 551.
              Concerned with the principles of Stuart Walker's
        Portmanteau Theatre and a production of Six Who Pass
        While the Lentils Boil.

958   POWELL, ANNE. "The Federal Children's Theatre in New York
        City." Recreation, 30 (October 1936), 344-45, 372.

959   POWELL-ARNOLD, JESSIE. "The Children's Players." Emerson
        Quarterly, 11 (November 1930), 17-18.
              Traces Adrienne Morrison's early efforts to establish
        a company of professional adult actors for children's
        theatre.

960   PYLE, MARY THURMAN. "Theatre School for Children."
        Recreation, 39 (August 1945), 230-31, 273.
              Gives a four year history of the Community Children's
        Theatre in Roanoke, Virginia.

961   "Rackety-Packety House." Outlook, 103 (January 11, 1913),
        58.
              Reviews a production of Frances Hodgson Burnett's
        Rackety-Packety House at the Children's Theatre of the
        Century Theatre in New York; comments on the Vanderbilt
        family involvement with the theatre.

Children's Theatre and Creative Dramatics

962 RAMEY, MARY GRACE. "We Give a Play in the Garden." Better
     Homes and Gardens, 9 (May 1931), 31, 86.
         Discusses a production of the Bicycle Club of Des
     Moines, Iowa, based on Longfellow's "The Masque of
     Pandors."

963 ROBERTSON, HAZEL GLOISTER. "It Belongs to Them." Recreation,
     35 (December 1941), 545-46, 582.
         Procedures and policies of the Palo Alto Community
     Children's Theatre are covered, especially how they
     select a good cross-section of plays for any given year.

964 _____. "Living Marionettes Take a Bow." Recreation, 38
     (October 1944), 357, 383.
         The Palo Alto theatre produces live marionette shows
     with child actors.

965 ROUNDS, CHARLES R. "Drama for Young and Old." School and
     Society, 38 (July 1, 1933), 16-17.
         Discusses work at the East School in Stoneham,
     Massachusetts, under Beverly Freitag, and work of the
     Community Players of Bordentown, New Jersey, under
     Nelchen T. Sievers (Miss).

966 _____. "A Theatre for Children." Education, 54 (September
     1933), 57-59.
         Initial work at the East School in Stoneham, Massachu-
     setts, is discussed.

967 SAVAGE, MRS. GEORGE. "Audiences for Tomorrow." Players
     Magazine, 22 (September-October 1945), 14, 20-21.
         Announces the first playwriting contest, sponsored by
     the Seattle Junior Programs, Inc.

968 SCHOTT, VERA WINIFRED. "The Peter Pan Players of Wichita."
     American Library Association Bulletin, 26 (October 1932),
     768-72.

969 "Season for Children's Theatre." New York Times, 17 October,
     1948, sec. II, p. 3.
         Reviews the first season of the Children's World
     Theatre and two of Charlotte Chorpenning's plays that
     were performed then; gives plans for the 1948-49 season,
     which will be the theatre's second.

CHILDREN'S THEATRE

970   SHELL, ALYCE. "A Community Children's Theatre Grows."
      Recreation, 30 (February 1936), 555-56.
        Concerned with the growth of the Palo Alto Children's
      Theatre in 1934-36 under the guidance of Hazel Gloister
      Robertson.

971   SISSON, MRS. JAMES GARDNER. "San Francisco Children's
      Theatre." Drama: Northwestern University Drama Service,
      13 January, 1938, pp. 18-19, 24.

972   SLOAN, VANDERVOORT. "Stuart Walker." Drama, 8 (February
      1918), 1-8.

973   SMITH, CATHARINE COOK. "The Child Actor in the King-Coit
      Productions." Theatre Arts Monthly, 11 (September 1927),
      720-23.

974   SMITH, LAURA A. "A Theatre to Teach Children." World's
      Work, 17 (March 1909), 11384-86.
        Traces the formal and informal dramatic work of
      Alice Minnie Herts at the Children's Educational
      Theatre; a production of The Little Princess by Frances
      Hodgson Burnett is reviewed.

975   SMITH, MARTHA LEE. "A Children's Theatre Institute."
      Curtain Rises, 1 (December 1938), 10.
        Surveys fifteen years of work of the Children's
      Theatre of the Junior League of Chicago; suggests new
      approaches in the future.

976   SPENCER, SARA. "The Character Is the Thing with Children."
      High School Thespian, 7 (May-June 1936), 10-11, 13, 16.
        Miss Spencer discusses the methods and techniques she
      has learned and developed in her career; she is presently
      [1936] working at the Children's Theatre in Charleston,
      West Virginia.

977   _____. "In the Children's Theatres." Players Magazine, 14
      (November-December 1937), 24.
        Work at Drake University, the University of Nebraska,
      in Jacksonville and Tucson is discussed; emphasis is on
      new directions.

978   _____. "In the Children's Theatres." Players Magazine, 14
      (January-February 1938), 21.
        Primarily concerned with activities at the Boston
      Junior League and The Curtain Pullers in Cleveland;
      numerous other theatres are cited.

SPECIFIC THEATRES AND DIRECTORS, PRE-1950

979 _____. "In the Children's Theatres." Players Magazine, 14
(March-April 1938), 19.
Cites seven different children's theatres in the
United States.

980 SPOOR, LOUISE DALE. "Children's Theatre at the Goodman
Closes Its Eighteenth Year." Players Magazine, 21 (May
1945), 27.

981 STORY, JOSEPHINE LAYMAN. "Unlocking the World of the
Wonderful Through the Children's Theatre." American
City, 40 (January 1929), 106-07.
Children's Theatre at the University of Tulsa is
discussed.

982 "Ten Cent Drama for San Francisco Children." Survey, 34
(April 24, 1915), 80.
Concerned with the inception of a children's theatre,
founded by the Recreation League of San Francisco.

983 "A Theatre All for Children." Literary Digest, 46 (January
11, 1913), 74-77.
Reviews the early productions of the Children's
Theatre of the Century Theatre in New York City.

984 "The 'Theatre of Youth' Players." Playground and Recreation,
22 (February 1929), 629, 653.

985 "A Theatre Workshop for Children." Recreation, 28 (October
1934), 327, 357.
A workshop production of Treasure Island with child
actors in Scarsdale, New York, is discussed.

986 THELTGEN, M. C. "Palo Alto Does It!" Recreation, 39
(October 1945), 348-49.
Gives statistics concerning the recreational program
of Palo Alto.

987 THOMAS, CATE. "Report from New England." Theatre Arts, 33
(September 1949), 55.
Comments on the Trailor Theatre of Portland, Maine.

988 "To Reorganize Children's Theatre." Charities and the
Commons, 20 (June 6, 1908), 307-08.
Announces the separation of the Children's Educational
Theatre and the Educational Alliance of New York City;
projections for the future are given.

CHILDREN'S THEATRE AND CREATIVE DRAMATICS

989 "Toward a Community Theatre: A Long-Range View." Recreation, 39 (August 1945), 235-36.
    Discusses work out of the Austin, Texas, Recreational Department.

990 TROXEL, H. E. "The Vagabond Theatre of Oakland." Emerson Quarterly, 8 (May 1928), 21.
    Gives illustrations from the Oakland Recreational Department's Theatre for Children.

991 "The University of Tulsa Fosters a Children's Theatre." Theatre Magazine, 48 (September 1928), 53.

992 VAN HERCKE, ETHYL PINE. "A Different Kind of Little Theatre." Recreation, 33 (January 1940), 549-50.
    Reviews the beginnings of the Children's Theatre Guild of Wauwatosa, Wisconsin.

993 VOGELBACK, PARTHENIA C. "Another Year of the Children's Civic Theatre." Curtain Rises, 1 (October 1938), 4.
    Traces the twenty-one years of the Children's Civic Theatre, sponsored by the Chicago Drama League.

994 WALD, LILLIAN D. The House on Henry Street. New York: Henry Holt and Company, 1915.
    Some commentary on the Neighborhood Playhouse of the Henry Street Settlement.

995 WALDRON, WEBB. "Children's Delight." Reader's Digest, 34 (January 1939), 33-36.
    Explores the beginnings of the Junior Programs, Inc. of Maplewood, New Jersey, under the direction of Dorothy McFadden.

996 WARD, WINIFRED. "The Children's Theatre in Evanston." Cameo, August, 1929, pp. 28-20.

997 _____. "Twentieth Anniversary Celebrated by the Children's Theatre of Evanston." Players Magazine, 21 (May 1945), 30, 34.

998 WELLER, CHARLES F. "A Children's Playhouse." Survey, 35 (February 19, 1916), 615.
    The work of J. Clarence Sullivan at the Children's Playhouse of Columbus, Ohio, is discussed.

SPECIFIC THEATRES AND DIRECTORS, PRE-1950

999   WELTY, SUSAN. "In the Children's Theatres." Players
       Magazine, 15 (January-February 1939), 19.
            Concerned primarily with the activities of the Junior
       Programs, Inc., of Maplewood, New Jersey; Clare Tree
       Major's touring companies are mentioned.

1000   ____. "In the Children's Theatres." Players Magazine, 15
       (March-April 1939), 21, 30.
            Comments on activity in Chattanooga, Tennessee;
       numerous other children's theatres are mentioned.

1001   ____. "In the Children's Theatres." Players Magazine, 15
       (July-August 1939), 18-19.
            Concentrates on the Municipal Young People's Theatre
       of the Girl's Trade and Technical High School in
       Milwaukee.

1002   ____. "In the Children's Theatres." Players Magazine, 17
       (October 1940), 19.
            Mentions the Jack and Jill Players of Chicago.

1003   ____. "In the Children's Theatres." Players Magazine, 17
       (January 1941), 21.
            Treats various functions of the Junior Programs, Inc.

1004   ____. "In the Children's Theatres." Players Magazine, 17
       (April 1941), 18, 28.
            Concentrates on the Children's Theatre Guild of
       Wauwatosa, Wisconsin, but includes a list of British
       plays for children.

1005   ____. "In the Children's Theatre." Players Magazine, 17
       (May 1941), 25, 36.
            A two part article that (1) comments on the Junior
       League Children's Theatre program for 1941, and (2)
       includes an annotated list of recent plays for children
       published in the United States.

1006   ____. "In the Children's Theatres." Players Magazine, 18
       (October 1941), 19.
            Mentions children's theatre work in Cleveland and New
       York; comments on articles concerned with Children's
       Theatre and Creative Dramatics in other journals.

1007   "Where Children Play at Giving Plays." Literary Digest, 86
       (August 1, 1925), 25-26.
            Traces the cross-arts programs of the Heckscher
       Theatre for Children.

CHILDREN'S THEATRE

1008   "Where Every Pupil is a Star." American Magazine, 135
       (January 1943), 108-09.
         Discusses professional training for children six
       through sixteen at the Professional Children's School in
       New York City.

1009   WHITING, FRANK M. "The Children's Audience at Minnesota."
       Players Magazine, 19 (May 1943), 38.
         Early work at the University of Minnesota is discussed.

1010   WILLSON, WINIFRED. "Where Fairy-Tales Come True." Saint
       Nicholas, 50 (April 1923), 562-69.
         Includes a discussion of the Heckscher Foundation
       Theatre and comments by its director, Gerda Wismer Hofmann.

1011   WYATT, EUPHEMIA VAN RENSALAAR. "The Drama: The Garden Wall."
       Catholic World, 161 (June 1945), 262.
         Praises the King-Coit Children's Theatre.

       See also the following entries. 125, 150, 160, 221, 310,
       314, 380, 389, 419, 425, 537, 542-44, 547, 551, 560, 565,
       573, 585-87, 613, 617, 643, 645, 1223, 1379, 1420, 1520.

SPECIFIC THEATRES AND DIRECTORS, 1950-1973

1012   ADAMS, RICHARD E. "Why and How?" Players Magazine, 30
       (January 1954), 84-85.
         Gives a six year history of the Denison [Ohio]
       Children's Theatre.

1013   "Alabama Names CT Leader Drama Consultant." Children's
       Theatre Review, 17 (February 1968), 25-26.
         Mrs. Robert I. Schwartz is appointed speech and drama
       consultant, the Alabama Department of Education.

1014   ANSON, EDITH N. "Rumpelstiltskin is Alive and Well."
       Southern Speech, 16 (Winter 1972-1973), 15.
         The work of the Florida Players, University of
       Florida, and their touring production of Rumpelstiltskin
       in Central Florida is discussed.

1015   AUSPRICH, HARRY. "A Community Project." Players Magazine,
       34 (October 1957), 10-11.
         Techniques of children's theatre and working with
       children at Iowa State College are given; reviews a
       production of Peter Pan.

Children's Theatre and Creative Dramatics

1016 BARCLAY, DOROTHY. "A Child's 'First Night' at the Theatre."
New York Times Magazine, 27 October, 1957, p. 63.
Discusses the work of Dr. Paul Kozelka at Columbia
University and how he looks at the child audience.

1017 BEHNER, ELSIE. "For and By." Players Magazine, 32
(November 1955), 41.
Discusses the work of the Jacksonville Beach, Florida,
Junior Little Theatre from 1942 to 1955.

1018 BENET, ROSEMARY. "Children's World Theatre." Saturday
Review, 33 (January 21, 1950), 47.
Summarizes the regular and touring season of the
Children's World Theatre.

1019 BLOYOM, MARIAN. "Yakima Children's Theatre Gets Its Start."
Players Magazine, 27 (April 1951), 156-57.
Discusses the initial program of a Children's Theatre
in Eastern Washington.

1020 BOBBETT, CELESTE S. "Branching Out." Players Magazine, 29
(October 1952), 16.
Shows the growth of the Children's Experimental
Theatre of Baltimore under the direction of Isabel Burger.

1021 "Bringing the Theatre to Young People." World Premier
Mondailes, No. 17 (April 1961), 2.
Work in formal and informal drama at the Phoenix
Theatre in New York City is discussed.

1022 BRINKERHOFF, MARY. "Talent Unlimited." Recreation, 43
(February 1950), 534.
Explains the program of the only children's theatre
for black children, sponsored by the Junior League of
Waco, Texas, and held at Baylor University.

1023 BROCKER, SHARON LORETTA. "Children's Theatre at Texas
Woman's University." Master's thesis, Texas Woman's
University, 1966.

1024 BUCHANAN, ROBERTA M. "Point of View." Players Magazine, 32
(December 1955), 63-64.
Discusses a production of Hansel and Gretel at the
Junior College Playmakers Theatre in St. Petersburg.

1025 "The Cain Park Creative Youtheatre." Theatre Arts, 42
(July 1958), 55.

Children's Theatre and Creative Dramatics

1026   CARROLL, DORRIT. "Taking Nonsense by the Tale." Children's
Theatre Review, 17 (February 1968), 16-18, 26.
        Cites work of the Children's Theatre of Arlington,
Virginia.

1027   CARVILLE, VIRGINIA. "The Key to Karamu House." Extension,
50 (March 1956), 20-21, 42, 45, 46.

1028   "Casa Mañana Uses Professionals to Train Children." Children's Theatre Review, 17 (February 1969), 28.
        The Casa Mañana Theatre is located in Fort Worth, Texas.

1029   "The Children's Theatre Association of Baltimore and Isabel
B. Burger." Children's Theatre Conference Newsletter, 15
(May 1966), 6-7.

1030   "Children's Theatre at the University of Kansas at Lawrence,
Kansas." Children's Theatre Conference Newsletter, 15
(February 1966), 12-25.

1031   "Chivalry in Texas." Life, 31 (July 1951), 87-88, 90, 93.
        Illustrates a production of Aucassin and Nicolette
at the Reeder School of Fort Worth, Texas.

1032   CHORPENNING, CHARLOTTE. Twenty-One Years with Children's
Theatre. Anchorage, Kentucky: Children's Theatre Press,
1954.
        The author discusses her work at the Goodman Theatre
in Chicago.

1033   The Community Children's Theatre of Kansas City. Kansas City,
Missouri: The Community Children's Theatre, Tenth Anniversary Brochure, 1957.

1034   COOK, JOAN. "Age Four (and up) on the Aisle." New York
Times Magazine, 11 October, 1969, p. 73.

1035   _____. "Truth Triumphs on a Harlem School Stage." New York
Times Magazine, 12 May, 1966, p. 77.

1036   "The Decentralized Theatre Comes to Children." Michigan
Educational Journal, 28 (January 1951), 310-11.

1037   DEPUGLIO, JOHN P. "The Sponsor's Role." Players Magazine, 31
(May 1955), 186.
        Traces the history of the Junior Entertainments, Inc.
program of Denver.

CHILDREN'S THEATRE AND CREATIVE DRAMATICS

CHILDREN'S THEATRES AND DIRECTORS, 1950-1973

1038   "Disciplined: King-Coit Children's Theatre." New Yorker, 30
        (May 22, 1954), 24.

1039   DODD, DOROTHY VERNE. "Seattle Junior Programs, Inc.: Twenty-
        Five Years of Children's Theatre." Master's thesis,
        University of Washington, 1964.

1040   DUTTON, MARGARET. "Developing a For not a By Organization."
        Players Magazine, 28 (October 1951), 20-21.
            Analyzes the history of the Children's Theatre of
        Portland, Maine.

1041   EICHSTEADT, NANCY. "Teenagers Act for Children." Recreation,
        52 (May 1959), 197-98.
            Work by the Bay Teen Players of Whitefish Bay,
        Wisconsin, is discussed.

1042   "Fairy Tale into Play." New York Times Magazine, 17 February,
        1957, p. 58.
            Discusses a performance of Jack and the Beanstalk at
        the Children's Theatre of Port Washington, Long Island.

1043   FISHER, CAROLINE E. AND HAZEL G. ROBERTSON. Children and the
        Theatre. Rev. ed. [with appendix by Edith W. Ramstad].
        Palo Alto: Stanford University Press, 1950.
            Gives a history of the Palo Alto Children's Theatre.

1044   FLYNN, RUTH STOCKARD. "A Historical Study of Dramatic
        Activities for Children at Hull House Theatre, Chicago,
        Illinois, from 1889 to 1967." Master's thesis, University
        of Denver, 1967.

1045   FORD, OPAL. "Children's Theatre Month in Lawton." Dramatics,
        38 (October 1966), 18-19, 39.
            Discusses various children's theatre activities in
        Lawton, Oklahoma.

1046   FORKERT, OTTO MAURICE. Comp. Children's Theatre That
        Captures Its Audience. Chicago: Coach House Press, 1962.
            Traces twenty years of children's theatre work at
        Goodman Theatre in Chicago, from 1938-1958; biographies
        of the three major directors are given.

1047   FREYMAN, LEONARD. "A Thriving Youth Theatre." National
        Education Association Journal, 57 (January 1968), 26-27.
            Work in formal and informal drama in the Cleveland
        area is discussed.

CHILDREN'S THEATRE

1048   GOLDEN, JOSEPH. "Draw a Magic Circle." Players Magazine, 29
        (May 1953), 176-77.
            Describes the work of a summer resident company of
        child actors at the magic Circle Theatre for Children
        at Tufts University.

1049   ____. "Off We Go." Players Magazine, 32 (May 1956), 178-
        79.
            Discusses beginning work at the Southern Tier Child-
        ren's Theatre of Elmira College, Elmira, New York.

1050   GORDON, MARY LOUISE CONTINI. "A History of Children's
        Dramatics at Cain Park from 1938 to 1958." Master's
        thesis, Kent State University, 1968.

1051   GOTS, JUDITH. "More than Make-Believe." Recreation, 47
        (September 1954), 433-34.
            Gives particular attention to the Children's Theatre
        of Syracuse University.

1052   GRIFFIN, ALICE. "Theatre Patterns in Chicago and Denver."
        Theatre Arts, 40 (November 1956), 94-95.

1053   ____. "Theatre, USA." Theatre Arts, 38 (June 1954), 82-85.
            Surveys children's theatre in this country; gives
        particular attention to a production of Huck Finn at
        Catholic University.

1054   ____. "Theatre, USA." Theatre Arts, 40 (May 1956), 62-63,
        94-95.
            Lists twenty-nine children's theatres in the USA and
        comments on the work of the late Monte Meacham at the
        Children's World Theatre.

1055   ____. "Theatre, USA." Theatre Arts, 41 (May 1957), 64-66,
        95.
            Surveys the work of twenty-three children's theatre
        organizations.

1056   GRIGGS, JOANNE LORRAINE. "Children's Theatre in Three
        American Settlement Houses in the Early Nineteen
        Hundreds." Master's thesis, University of Wisconsin,
        1963.
            Analyzes work at New York City's Educational Alliance,
        Chicago's Hull House, and the Henry Street Settlement in
        New York.

Children's Theatre and Creative Dramatics

SPECIFIC THEATRES AND DIRECTORS, 1950-1973

1057   "Growing Big." Newsweek, 64 (December 28, 1964), 55-56.
        Traces the history of the Paper Bag Players from
        1958-1964.

1058   HABERSTADT, GRACE. "Growing Pains at Charlotte." Players
        Magazine, 33 (March 1957), 134.
        Discusses the eight year history of the Children's
        Theatre of Charlotte, North Carolina, and its ongoing
        plans.

1059   HALL, JEANNE L. "Building Future Adult Theatre Audiences."
        Speech Teacher, 14 (September 1965), 237-39.
        Emphasizes children's theatre work in Hayward,
        California.

1060   HANSON, LILLY RUTH. "On Stage Teenagers." Recreation, 54
        (November 1961), 466-68.
        Productions at the Children's Theatre of the Stevenson
        Players of Oak Park, Illinois, are discussed.

1061   "Harwich Junior Theatre." Theatre Arts, 43 (August 1959), 63.
        A unique, tuition-free workshop program at the Harwich
        Junior Theatre in Massachusetts, is discussed.

1062   HAYES, RICHARD. "The King-Coit Children's Theatre."
        Commonweal, 60 (May 21, 1954), 175-76.

1063   HERGET, PATSY JOAN. "A History and Evaluation of the
        Children's Theatre of Cedar Rapids." Ph.D. dissertation,
        Iowa State University, 1957.

1064   HIERONYMUS, CLARA. "The Big News in Nashville is the
        Children's Theatre." Theatre Arts, 45 (August 1961),
        68-69, 78.

1065   HILL, ANN STAHLMAN. "Children's Theatre: A Will and a Way."
        Southern Speech, 25 (Fall 1959), 50-54.
        Describes the work of the Children's Theatre of
        Nashville, Tennessee.

1066   HOBBS, GARY. "Participatory Children's Plays: The Mirror
        Man and The Hat." Dramatics, 45 (April 1974), 11-12.
        Two productions of Brian Way plays at Drake University
        are discussed; there is also a general comment on
        participatory theatre.

CHILDREN'S THEATRE

1067   HORTON, LOUISE C. "Cooperation Plus!" Dramatics, 24 (April
        1953), 13.
            Discusses children's theatre in Painesville, Ohio,
        Sioux Falls, South Dakota, and Dearborn, Michigan.

1068   _____. "Drama for Children." Dramatics, 21 (April 1950),
        22-23.
            Stresses work at children's theatres in Baltimore,
        Chicago and Lakewood, Ohio.

1069   _____. "Drama for Children." Dramatics, 22 (November 1950),
        22-22.
            Describes the activities of the Cranbrook Summer
        School of the Theatre in Bloomfield Hills, Michigan,
        at the University of Denver and at the National Youth
        Theatre in New York City.

1070   _____. "Drama for Children." Dramatics, 22 (May 1951), 20-
        21.
            Discusses a free theatre-therapy program run by
        Robert I. Oberreich at Madison Square Garden.

1071   _____. "It's Fun!" Dramatics, 23 (April 1952), 12.
            Recounts the activity of the Children's Theatre of
        Upper Darby, Pennsylvania.

1072   _____. "They Call Her DOC." Dramatics, 23 (November 1951),
        19-20.
            The pronoun of the article's title is Dina Rees Evans.

1073   HOWELL, BEATRICE M. "The Pied Piper in Hawaii." Recreation,
        52 (November 1959), 383-84.
            Work of the Honolulu Department of Parks and Recrea-
        tion is discussed.

1074   JANIS, LENORE AND PENINNAH SCHRAM. "Producing Grown-up Plays
        for Children." Theatre Crafts, 1 (June-August 1967),
        34-40.
            Discusses a musical production of King Solomon and
        Ashmedai at the Jewish Heritage Theatre in New York City.

1075   JOHNSON, ROBERT C. "Alice for All." Players Magazine, 28
        (April 1952), 155-56.
            Illustrates a production of Eva Le Gallienne's Alice
        in Wonderland at the University of Washington's Showboat
        Theatre.

SPECIFIC THEATRES AND DIRECTORS, 1950-1973

1076   . "On the Road." Players Magazine, 26 (February 1950),
        111.
            Comments on the program of the Touring Theatre of the
        University of Washington and its production of Aladdin
        and the Wonderful Lamp.

1077   "Junior Repertory Theatre of Minneapolis." Drama, 21 (April
        1961), 29.

1078   KARTAK, THOMAS C. "Nashville Children's Theatre Experiences
        Giant Growth Through On-School Time Performances."
        Children's Theatre Review, 23:1 (1974), 5-6.
            Discusses policy changes in the 1972-73 season and
        shows how productive they were.

1079   KASE, C. ROBERT. "Delaware Children's Theatre on Tour."
        Players Magazine, 26 (April 1950), 163.
            Comments on the activities of the University of
        Delaware's Third Annual Children's Theatre Tour.

1080   KAYSER, KATHRYN E. "Children's Theatre in Colorado."
        Colorado School Journal, 4 (May 1963), 13.
            Surveys children's theatre activity across the state
        of Colorado.

1081   . "The Honolulu Story: A Community Marshals Its Forces
        for Children." Creative Expression in Oral Language.
        Mabel Wright Henry, ed. Champaign, Illinois: National
        Council of Teachers of English, 1967. Pp. 107-11.

1082   KEUSINK, POLLY. "Theatre for Pint-Sized Hamlets." American
        Home, 49 (February 1953), 24-26.
            Describes the work of Hazel Robertson at the Palo Alto
        Children's Theatre.

1083   "The King-Coit Children's Theatre." Dance Magazine, 28
        (July 1954), 38.

1084   KRAUS, JOANNA HALPERT. "Children's Theatre Baltimore Style."
        Players Magazine, 47 (April-May 1972), 204-09.
            A summary of Dr. Kraus' dissertation. See 1085.

1085   . "A History of the Children's Theatre Association
        of Baltimore, Maryland, from 1943-66." Ph.D. disserta-
        tion, Columbia University, 1972.
            "The study demonstrates that the theatre's goal of
        human development through the use of drama and the
        dynamic personality of the founder [Isabel Burger]

CHILDREN'S THEATRE

(KRAUS, JOANNA HALPERT)
influenced those who came into contact with the Children's Theatre Association.

1086   LAKE, RICHARD. "Like Adult Theatre - Only Better!" _Southern Speech_, 16 (Winter 1972-73), 19-20.
Emphasizes the work of Asolo, The State Theatre Company of Florida, its many activities and companies, and its directoral staff.

1087   LEMIRE, CLEMENT. "Debut of a Children's Theatre." _Players Magazine_, 1 (February 1966), 142-44.
Beginning work at the Newington, Connecticut, Children's Theatre is discussed.

1088   "Lexington Children's Theatre." _Southern Theatre News_, 11:1 (1967), 13, 22.
Analyzes the twenty-nine year history of the Lexington, Kentucky, Children's Theatre.

1089   "Little Mummers Render the Bard." _Life_, 55 (September 20, 1963), 120, 123.
Illustrates a performance of _The Taming of the Shrew_ in Salt Lake City.

1090   LUCAS, EDWARD R. "The Youngsters Take the Stage." _Recreation_, 53 (November 1960), 421-24.
Traces the history of the Downey, California, Children's Theatre from 1955-1960.

1091   MACHADO, MARIA CLARA. "Children's Theatre in Rio." _Americas_, 9 (February 1957), 7-10.
The author describes four productions of her own plays at the Tablado Theatre in Rio de Janeiro.

1092   MAJOR, CLARE TREE. "Child's Play." _Theatre Arts_, 36 (October 1952), 32, 84.
Miss Major discusses initial work with her own Children's Theatre company.

1093   MANLEY, BETSY ELLEN. "A History of the Nashville Children's Theatre: 1931-1967." Master's thesis, University of Georgia, 1968.

1094   MARKS, MARCIA. "The Paper Bag Players." _Dance Magazine_, 38 (June 1964), 52-55, 88-89.

Children's Theatre and Creative Dramatics

1095 _____. "Paper Bag Players: Henry Street Playhouse." Dance Magazine, 39 (December 1965), 156.

1096 _____. "The Paper Bag Players: Hunter College Playhouse." Dance Magazine, 43 (February 1969), 82-83.

1097 MASSEY, MARY ANN. "An Experimental Study of the Canyon Children's Theatre." Master's thesis, West Texas State College, 1952.
Analyzes a number of productions at the Children's Theatre of Canyon, Texas.

1098 MASTERS, LILLIAN DECKER. "Two for the Show." Dramatics, 25 (May 1954), 14-15, 32.
Describes the year's work at the Terre Haute, Indiana, Children's Theatre.

1099 MAURA ANNE, SISTER, S.S.J. "The Story of Children's Theatre in Villa Maria Academy." Children's Theatre Newsletter of the National Catholic Theatre Conference, 1 (May 1960), 2.
Comments briefly on work in children's theatre in Erie, Pennsylvania.

1100 MAXWELL, JAMES A. "Children Scare Me!" Saturday Evening Post, 230 (March 8, 1958), 24-25, 68, 71.
Gives a history of the Cincinnati Theatre for Children.

1101 McQUILLAN, MARY ANN. "A History of the Children's Theatre of Terre Haute: 1936-1948." Master's thesis, Indiana State Teachers College [State of Indiana], 1953.

1102 MEISENHOLDER, DAVID LEE. "A Study of the Children's Theatre at the University of Nebraska." Master's thesis, University of Nebraska, 1960.

1103 MEREW, ERVA LOOMIS. "Every Child on Stage." Instructor, 79 (June-July 1970), 36-39.
The author discusses a summer enrichment program in Kenosha, Wisconsin, based on creative drama techniques.

1104 METZ, SUSAN. "Silver Anniversaries Celebrated Twenty Five Years of Children's Theatre." Children's Theatre Review, 23:1 (1974), 13-14.
Gives a brief history of three theatres: Community Children's Theatre of Kansas City; Elmhurst Children's Theatre [Illinois], and the San Diego Junior Theatre.

CHILDREN'S THEATRE

1105   MEYER, JEANETTE R. "The History and Organization of the
        Racine Children's Theatre from 1933 to 1957." Master's
        [Speech] thesis, University of Wisconsin, 1958.

1106   MILLER, ANNE FOLKER. "The Richmond Project." Players
        Magazine, 27 (February 1951), 112.

1107   MISHOW, EMMA LEE. "Readers Theatre of the Young at Eastern
        Michigan University." Children's Theatre Review, 23:1
        (1974), 6.
            Explores the work of Thelma L. McDaniel, director of
        the Readers Theatre of the Young, and the organization of
        both formal and informal dramatic programs.

1108   MOHN, MARGARET E. "Children's Theatre - Minnesota Plan."
        Players Magazine, 26 (May 1950), 194-95.
            Traces a ten year history of the Young People's
        Theatre of the University of Minnesota, and discusses a
        number of its productions.

1109   "Mother Knows Best." Theatre Arts, 46 (January 1962), 9.
            Interviews Michael Kahn, Director of the Young
        People's and Children's Workshop at Circle in the
        Square, New York City.

1110   "Nashville to Get $250,000 Children's Theatre Building."
        Southern Theatre News, 3 (Spring 1959), 3.

1111   "New Nashville Children's Theatre." Southern Theatre News,
        4 (Summer 1960), 7.

1112   NICHOLS, MARTHA AND BYRON NICHOLS. "Children's Theatre:
        Washington." Players Magazine, 29 (December 1952), 60-61.
            Discusses work at the Cornish School of Allied Arts
        and its association with the Seattle Junior Programs, Inc.

1113   NICHOLSON, ANNE. "Forty-Two Years of Children's Theatre."
        Children's Theatre Conference Newsletter, 15 (August
        1966), 11-13.
            Gives a history of the Goodman Memorial Children's
        Theatre.

1114   NIGHTSWANDER, MARY. "The Davenport Park Boards Junior
        Theatre Presents 'A Home of Its Own'." Children's Theatre
        Conference Newsletter, 14 (May 1965), 10-11.

SPECIFIC THEATRES AND DIRECTORS, 1950-1973

1115 "Ninepenny Worth." Economist, 219 (June 1966), 1422.
      Discusses the need for financial aid to the Unicorn
      Theatre for Children, founded by Caryl Jenner.

1116 OBERLE, MARCELLA. "The CTC at Michigan City." Educational
      Theatre Journal, 11 (December 1959), 296-303.
          Surveys the Fifteenth Annual Conference, and work at a
      number of different children's theatres.

1117 OBERREICH, BOB. "Unique Children's Theatre." Recreation,
      45 (November 1951), 319.
          Describes work at the Madison Square Children's
      Theatre.

1118 OWEN, GENE NIELSON. "A College Serves Its Community by
      Offering Theatre for Children." Junior College Journal,
      28 (December 1957), 208-15.
          Gives a five year history of the Santa Monica City
      College's children's theatre program.

1119 _____. "Theatre for Children in Santa Monica." California
      Journal of Elementary Education, 25 (February 1957),
      137-45.

1120 "The Paper Bag Players." Children's Theatre Review, 16 (May
      1967), 12-13.

1121 "Paper Bag Players Produce a Playful Paper-Box Pageant."
      House and Garden, 134 (December 1968), 74-77.

1122 "Paper Bag Props for Holiday Fun." Parents' Magazine, 39
      (December 1964), 48-49, 80.
          Lists ideas based on the activities of the Paper Bag
      Players.

1123 PECK, SEYMOUR. "They Open in P.S.3." New York Times
      Magazine, 19 February, 1961, pp. 30-31.
          Illustrates the activities of professional theatre and
      music groups that tour the New York Public Schools.

1124 POLLETTE, JOHN. "Tryout Plays for Children's Theatre."
      Players Magazine, 28 (October 1951), 8.
          Emphasis is on a production of Geraldine Brain Sik's
      play Deep Harbor, sponsored by the Seattle Junior
      Programs, Inc.

CHILDREN'S THEATRE

1125   POLSKY, MILTON. "An Interview with Judith Martin of the
         Paper Bag Players." Children's Theatre Review, 23:1
         (1974), 1-3.
             Gives a transcript of an interview with the Paper Bag
         Players' director and founder.

1126   POTTS, NORMAN B. "Children's Theatre: Flowering in Minneapol-
         is." Players Magazine, 48 (October-November 1972), 17-23.
             Surveys major productions and practices in Children's
         Theatre in Minneapolis from 1962-72.

1127   QUINN, JANE. "A.C.T. Unlimited." Southern Speech, 16 (Winter
         1972-73), 12-13.
             Briefly traces the six seasons of the Athens, Georgia,
         Creative Theatre, under the guidance of Dr. Leighton
         Ballew, Chairman of the University of Georgia's depart-
         ment of drama and theatre.

1128   RARICK, STAN. "Trailor Theatre." Players Magazine, 35
         (December 1958), 64.
             Discusses the author's recreational drama program in
         Albuquerque, New Mexico.

1129   REED, FRIEDA. "Theatre for Children." Dramatics, 27 (May
         1956), 20-21, 26.
             A production of Percival Wilde's The Dyspeptic Ogre
         by the Thespian Troup 425 of Tucson, Arizona, is discussed.

1130   _____. "Theatre for Children." Dramatics, 28 (November
         1956), 12-13, 26.
             Describes Stan Rarick's Trailor Theatre in Albuquerque,
         New Mexico.

1131   _____. "Theatre for Children." Dramatics, 28 (May 1957),
         12-13.
             Surveys the Children's Theatre at Pontiac, Michigan,
         under the supervision of Mary Parrish.

1132   _____. "Theatre for Children." Dramatics, 29 (April 1958),
         20-21.
             Reviews the work of Odessa, Texas, High School's
         Children's Theatre programs.

1133   _____. "Theatre for Children." Dramatics, 30 (November
         1958), 20-21.
             Comments on the work of Dale Brannon at the John R.
         Rogers High School in Spokane, Washington.

Children's Theatre and Creative Dramatics

1134 _____. "Theatre for Children." Dramatics, 32 (December 1960), 14-15.
Children's theatre in Oshkosh, Wisconsin, is surveyed.

1135 _____. "Theatre for Children." Dramatics, 33 (October 1961), 22-23.
Describes the work of the Summer Children's Theatre at the Playhouse in the Park, Philadelphia, Pennsylvania.

1136 _____. "Theatre for Children." Dramatics, 34 (January 1963), 18, 28.
Comments on the Children's Theatre at the Shorewood High School in Shorewood, Wisconsin, under the direction of Walter Peck.

1137 _____. "Theatre for Children." Dramatics, 34 (February 1963), 18.
Discusses initial work in children's theatre at the Abraham Lincoln High School in Denver, under the direction of Joe Craft.

1138 _____. "Theatre for Children." Dramatics, 34 (March 1963), 20.
Assesses the work of Edwin A. Goss at the Rosemont Community Theatre in Rosemont, Minnesota.

1139 _____. "Theatre for Children." Dramatics, 34 (April 1963), 20, 26.
Describes the work of Ruth Denney at the Children's Theatre of the Lamar High School, in Houston, Texas.

1140 _____. "Theatre for Children." Dramatics, 35 (January 1964), 20-21.
Work at the North Side High School in Fort Wayne, Indiana, under James Purkhiser is discussed.

1141 _____. "Theatre for Children." Dramatics, 35 (March 1964), 26-27.
Eugenia Olson's work at the Children's Theatre of Galt, California, is discussed.

1142 _____. "Theatre for Children." Dramatics, 35 (April 1964), 20-21.
Bill Perry, of the Charles Page High School in Sand Springs, Oklahoma, discusses his Thespian Troupe.

CHILDREN'S THEATRE

1143 _____. "Theatre for Children." Dramatics, 36 (January 1965), 24-25.
Describes Arlene Diaco's work with the Thespian Troupe of Marple-Newton Community Children's Theatre in Pennsylvania.

1144 RICHARDS, STANLEY. "450,000 Miles of Children's Theatre." Players Magazine, 31 (December 1954), 66-67.
Traces Edwin Strawbridge's history as a producer of plays for children.

1145 RICKETT, OLLA GOEWEY. "Rip Returns - An Experiment with Dramatics for Children." New York State Education, 38 (April 1951), 506-08.
Describes the activities of the Children's Theatre at the State University Teachers College, Cortland, New York.

1146 "Santa Monica City College's Theatre for Children." Educational Theatre News, 5 (January 1958), 2, 4.

1147 SCHOENFELD, M. "Children's Theatre in Yonkers: Sprain Brook Library Theatre." Wilson Library Bulletin, 40 (December 1965), 352-55.

1148 SCHRAM, PENINNAH AND LENORE JANIS. "About Theatre à la Carte in New York City." Children's Theatre Conference Newsletter, 15 (August 1966), 16-19.
Traces the history of the Theatre à la Carte from 1962-66.

1149 SHADE, EDWIN. "Children's Theatre: A Community Project." Players Magazine, 28 (December 1951), 66.

1150 SHARON, MURIEL. "About the Pocket Players." Children's Theatre Conference Newsletter, 15 (February 1966), 15-18.

1151 "Short History of Wichita Children's Theatre." Children's Theatre Review, 17 (February 1968), 7-9.

1152 "Show Time for Small Fry: American Young People's Theatre." New York Times Magazine, 28 November, 1950, pp. 72-73.

1153 SLOCUMB, PAUL. "Dearborn's Fifth Season." Players Magazine, 31 (October 1954), 17-18.

SPECIFIC THEATRES AND DIRECTORS, 1950-1973

1154   SOUCEK, CAROL. "Festival Fills Campus, Hearts of Children."
        Children's Theatre Review, 23:1 (1974), 4.
                Discusses the first Children's Theatre Festival of
        the Southern California Educational Theatre Association,
        and some of its twelve productions.

1155   STAMEY, NANCY. "A Theatre Is Born." Players Magazine, 32
        (October 1955), 17.
                Discusses the beginnings of the Children's Theatre of
        Raleigh, North Carolina.

1156   SULLIVAN, DAN. "Children's Theatre in New York: Some of It
        Is Good." New York Times, 10 April, 1967, p. 41.
                Surveys fifteen children's theatre productions in
        New York City.

1157   "Tall Stories for Small Audiences." Dance Magazine, 28
        (February 1954), 57.
                Illustrates Edwin Strawbridge's production of Pecos
        Bill.

1158   "Tape Volunteers: Adventure Theatre Makes Magic." Children's
        Theatre Review, 17 (August 1968), 19-20.
                Discusses the recording of fourteen children's plays
        by the Adventure Theatre of Baltimore for the Library of
        Congress.

1159   TAYLOR, TONI. "American Classroom: Evanston, Illinois."
        Grade Teacher, 79 (September 1961), 36-41, 129-30.

1160   "Ten Years of Children's Theatre in Hawaii." ASSITEJ
        Quarterly Review, No. 2 (April June), 1967.

1161   "The Thanksgiving Award - 1966." Children's Theatre Review,
        16 (February 1967), 12-13.
                Summarizes the acceptance speech of Sara Spencer.

1162   "Theatre Resources for Youth, Project TRY." Children's
        Theatre Review, 16 (November 1967), 13.
                Analyzes the first year of operation of this project
        out of the University of New Hampshire.

1163   "Theatres for Children Only." Good Housekeeping, 149
        (October 1959), 195.
                Describes the work of the Children's Theatre Workshop
        at Ithaca, New York.

Children's Theatre and Creative Dramatics

CHILDREN'S THEATRE

1164   TUKESBURY, BEATRICE L. "Emma Sheridan Fry and Educational Dramatics." Educational Theatre Journal, 16 (December 1964), 341-48.

1165   TURNEY, EDWARD. "The Big Little World of Vincent Anthony." Southern Speech, 16 (Winter 1972-73), 16-17.
        Traces the impact of the Vagabond Marionettes and their director on Atlanta, Georgia, and the locations to which they have toured.

1166   WAGNER, JEARNINE AND KITTY BAKER. A Place for Ideas - Our Theatre. San Antonio, Texas: Principia Press of Trinity University, 1965.
        Shows a great variety of children's theatre activity in San Antonio; work in creative dramatics is also discussed.

1167   WARD, WINIFRED. "Twenty-Five Years of Children's Theatre." Players Magazine, 27 (December 1950), 60-61.
        Comments on the twenty-five years of activity at the Children's Theatre of Evanston, Illinois.

1168   "Washington Equity Theatre Adopts Chekhov Theory." Children's Theatre Review, 17 (February 1968), 23-24.
        Discusses the work of Gerald Slavet and the Garrick Players of Washington, D.C., who have taken plays by Beckett, Chekhov and Albee into the elementary schools.

1169   WEALES, GERALD. "The Jelly Bean Circuit." Reporter, 24 (May 11, 1961), 46-47.
        Covers a wide variety of different children's theatre companies in this country and analyzes the future of touring companies, as well as the financial stress they are under.

1170   WEED, HELEN. "Theatre by Children in Tacoma." Players Magazine, 26 (January 1950), 89.
        Traces five years of the history of the Tacoma Little Theatre under Betty Walton Lello.

1171   WIKSELL, JEAN STARR. "Baton Rouge: The First Four Years." Players Magazine, 27 (May 1957), 182-83.

1172   WYATT, E. V. R. "Nola and Damayanti." Catholic World, 179 (June 1954), 227-28.
        Describes a performance at the King-Coit Children's Theatre.

Children's Theatre and Creative Dramatics

1173 _____. "Theatre: A Midsummer Night's Dream." Catholic World, 187 (June 1958), 225-26.
Discusses a production of the King-Coit Company; mentions the fire that practically demolished the costumes, sets and props.

1174 XAVIER, SISTER MARY. "Children's Theatre: Iowa." Players Magazine, 29 (December 1952), 60.
Concerned with the annual children's play performed at Clarke College in Dubuque, Iowa.

1175 YEATS, NORRIS. "Children's Folk Plays in Western Oregon." Western Folklore, 10 (1951), 55-62.
Lists eleven short folk drama based on Oregon tradition; productions of the plays by child actors are discussed.

See also the following entries. 331, 445, 665, 684, 710-12, 726, 739, 741, 776-77, 780, 797, 1073, 1324, 1365, 1401, 1411, 1429, 1433, 1466, 1499, 1570, 1804.

INDIVIDUAL PLAYS AND PLAYWRITING FOR CHILDREN

1176 ADAMS, RICHARD GREENLEAF. "A Descriptive Study of Dramatic Dialogue in Six Plays for Children by the Application of Formulas for Readability." Ph.D. dissertation, University of Southern California, 1962.

1177 "An Adventure in Drama." Playground and Recreation, 23 (November 1929), 510-11.
Discusses three plays acted by children, under Wilbert R. Hemmerly, in a summer drama program in Connecticut.

1178 AIRTH, MARGIE BESS. "Percy and the Pink Witch, A Musical for Children of All Ages." Master's thesis, Baylor University, 1963.

1179 ALDRICH, DOROTHY. "An Audience Reaction Study on Reynard." Children's Theatre Review, 16 (August 1967), 22-26.
A condensation of a portion of the author's thesis; see elsewhere.

1180 ANDERSON, M. SIGNE. "The Design and Technical Direction of The Pied Piper of Hamelin." Master's thesis, University of Montana, 1967.

CHILDREN'S THEATRE

1181   ARNTAL, DORIS MARGARET. "A Prompt Book for an Arena Production of The Emperor's New Clothes." Master's thesis, University of Denver, 1961.

1182   BABB, CLARE MOSHER. "A Director's Production Book: The Magic Horn by Anne Nickolson and Charlotte Chorpenning." Master's thesis, Stanford University, 1953.

1183   BAKER, DIANNE GLASSBURN. "Director's Manual and Promptbook for 'The Trial of Mother Goose'." Master's thesis, University of South Dakota, 1965.

1184   BANNISTER, ROBERT LYLE. "Maurice Maeterlinck's The Blue Bird, a Project in Lyric Theatre." Master's thesis, University of Denver, 1947.

1185   _____. "Staging The Blue Bird." Dramatics, 19 (May 1948), 20-21.

1186   BECK, DOROTHY. "The Shoes That Were Danced to Pieces: The Adaptation and Production of a Three-Act Play for Children." Master's [Speech] thesis, Southern Illinois University, 1958.

1187   BELL, COLLINS J. "The Writing and Directing of an Original Play for Children." Master's thesis, Ohio State University, 1951.
        The title of the play is The Wonderful Cure.

1188   BERTRAM, JEAN DE SALES. "Creative Playwriting: An Original Play for Children's Theatre - Black Beard, The Prince." Master's thesis, University of Minnesota, 1951.

1189   BIRNER, WILLIAM B. Twenty Plays for Young People, A Collection of Plays for Children. Anchorage, Kentucky: The Anchorage Press, 1967.
        In the introduction to his book, the author discusses what constitutes a good children's play and how one is picked for a specific audience.

1190   BLUMBERG, FREDRIC. "Gilbert and Sullivan's The Mikado - A Production Thesis." 2 vols. Master's thesis, University of Tennessee, 1959.

1191   BOYNTON, PORTIA CECELIA. "John Newberry and His Friends." Master's thesis, Iowa State University, 1955.
        Thesis is a stage elaboration of an original radio program for the Iowa State Education Association.

INDIVIDUAL PLAYS AND PLAYWRITING FOR CHILDREN

1192   BRAIN, GERALDINE M. "Writing, Directing and Producing <u>Marco</u>
        <u>Polo</u>, A Three Act Play for Children." Master's thesis,
        Northwestern University, 1940.

1193   BRAITHWAITE, MARY R. "A Study of American Local Legends for
        Children's Theatre." Master's thesis, Michigan State
        University, 1956.

1194   BRAMWELL, RUBY PHILLIPS. "Writing the Juvenile Play."
        <u>Writer's Monthly</u>, 34 (October 1929), 219-24.

1195   BRAUN, MARILYN HELENE. "Original Scripts for Children's
        Theatre." Master's thesis, Ohio State University, 1965.
        Contains two original plays, one of which is based
        on Shakespeare's <u>The Tempest</u>.

1196   BRYAN, BETTY BROOKS. "<u>Lao, the White Eagle</u>: A Play for
        Children in Three Acts." Master's thesis, University of
        Denver, 1950.
        A play based on American Indian folklore.

1197   BURKE, BARBARA WILLOCK. "'The Gold Doubloon': A Musical
        Fantasy for Children." Master's thesis, Abilene Chris-
        tian College, 1967.

1198   BUTLER, KAROLYN KAY. "The Development and Production of an
        Original Children's Play." Master's thesis, Eastern
        Texas State University, 1967.
        The play, "In One Head and Out the Other' or, "The Z's
        and Sneezes of Zeesalot," is given with its prompt book
        and a discussion of what constitutes good children's
        drama.

1199   BYERS, JACK ADIN. "The Design and Technical Record for a
        Production of James Norris' <u>Aladdin and the Wonderful</u>
        <u>Lamp</u>." Master's thesis, San Jose State College, 1957.

1200   BYERS, RUTH. <u>Creating Theatre: From Idea Through Performance</u>
        <u>with Children and Teens</u>." San Antonio, Trinity Univer-
        sity Press, 1968.
        Shows the teacher how to initiate playwriting in the
        classroom.

1201   CALTA, LOUIS. "Aiken Will Write a Children's Play." <u>New</u>
        <u>York Times</u>, 23 April, 1966, p. 16.
        Based on Conrad Aiken's poem "The Kid" - not to be
        confused with the work of his daughter, Joan.

Children's Theatre and Creative Dramatics

CHILDREN'S THEATRE

1202   CALTA, LOUIS. "Dickens Is Only the Day's First Bout." New
York Times, 17 December, 1968, p. 58
Describes a production based on "A Christmas Carol"
performed totally by volunteer professional actors.

1203   CAMPBELL, DIXIE ANN. "An Introduction of Children's Theatre
to Ohio University Through a Production of The Emperor's
New Clothes." Master's thesis, Ohio University, 1953.

1204   CARDACI, ELIZABETH WHITE. "The Princess and the Goblin, A
Play for Children in Two Acts." Master's thesis, University of Denver, 1955.

1205   CARRAT, RAOUL. "The Princess and the Parrot." ASSITEJ
Quarterly Review, No. 3-4 (July-December 1967), 43-46.
Gives a synopsis of a French play which is included in
the same issue.

1206   CARTER, KATHLEEN L. "The Musical Peter Pan." Dramatics, 37
(January 1966), 16, 37.

1207   CHAPP, EVELYN A. "Original Plays for Children." Master's
thesis, Colorado State College, 1939.
Includes the scripts of three plays that were originally developed through creative dramatics techniques.

1208   CHASE, MARY. "Writing Tips from Small Fry." New York Times,
17 February, 1952, p. 1.
The author discusses how her script for Mrs. McThing
was improved by feed-back from neighborhood children.

1209   "Children's World Theatre: Jack and the Beanstalk." Vogue,
110 (December 1947), 170.
Concerned with the first performance of the Children's
World Theatre of New York City, in 1947.

1210   CIBULA, BETTY JANE. "Just for the Fun of It: An Original
Play for Children with an Analysis of the Writing and
Directing Problems Involved." Master's thesis, Michigan
State University, 1953.

1211   CLARIDGE, RICHARD TREPPARD. "Playwriting for the Children's
Theatre." Master's thesis, St. Louis University, 1952.
An original play, "The Love Match", based on Andersen's
"The Chimney Sweep and the Shepherdess" is included.

Children's Theatre and Creative Dramatics

INDIVIDUAL PLAYS AND PLAYWRITING FOR CHILDREN

1212   CLIFF, C. MORTON. "A Record of an Experimental Production of
        Hansel and Gretel, Including a Survey of Audience
        Reaction." Master's thesis, Bradley University, 1959.

1213   COOK, SALLY PASSMORE. "The Enchanted Marshmallows."
        Master's thesis, University of North Carolina, 1965.

1214   COOPER, ESTHER. "Writing the Juvenile Play." Writer, 61
        (February 1948), 51-52.

1215   DAHLMAN, LOIS GAIL. "An Experiment in the Composition of a
        Children's Play." Master's [Fine Arts] thesis, University
        of Ohio, 1966.

1216   DEPUGLIO, JOHN PATRICK. "The Painted Arrow" A Play for
        Children in Three Acts." Master's thesis, University of
        Denver, 1951.

1217   DETRA, ELINOR M. "Goobles and the Trouble Machine: A Play
        for Children." Master's [Education] thesis, St. Cloud
        State College, 1964.
            The score, as well as the script, of this musical is
        included.

1218   DUNNING, FLORENCE M. "A Prompt Book for a High School
        Production of The Clown Who Ran Away." Master's thesis,
        University of Denver, 1960.

1219   DYE, PATRICIA McKENNA, "How the Stars Were Made: An Original
        Children's Play and an Analysis of the Production Prob-
        lems." Master's thesis, Michigan State University, 1951.

1220   EARNSHAW, LAURA LEE. "A Study of the Antagonist in a
        Children's Theatre Play - Winnie-The Pooh." Master's
        thesis, University of Kansas, 1963.

1221   EDLAND, ELISABETH. The Children's King, and Other Plays for
        Children with Chapters on Dramatizing with Children. New
        York: Abingdon Press, 1928.
            Concerned with creating both formal and informal
        drama, and the process of evaluating the product.

1222   ELDRIDGE, GARY G. "The World of Harlequin for Children."
        Southern Theatre News, 11:1 (1967), 14-16.
            Analyzes a production of Aurand Harris' Androcles and
        the Lion.

CHILDREN'S THEATRE AND CREATIVE DRAMATICS

CHILDREN'S THEATRE

1223   EUSTIS, MORTON. "Wonderland - Broadway in Review." Theatre
        Arts Monthly, 17 (February 1933), 101-03.
                Evaluates a production of Eva Le Gallienne's adaptation
        of Alice in Wonderland.

1224   "A Fairy Tale to Be Interpreted in the Light of the Present."
        School and Society, 53 (January 1941), 77.
                Assesses Clare Tree Major's production of Maeterlinck's
        Seven Wishes.

1225   FEENEY, MARTIN AND JAMES RUSILKO. "Eighteenth Noel: A One
        Act Play." Dramatics, 43 (January 1972), 5-9.
                Gives a script of a one-act play written by a student
        and an intern teacher at Stoughton High. School, Stoughton,
        Massachusetts, and performed state-wide.

1226   GLEASON, MAY M. "A Report on the Production of the Play
        The Elves and the Shoemaker." Master's thesis, Sacra-
        mento State College, 1952.

1227   GOLDBERG, MOSES HAYM. "A Production and Script for The Wind
        in the Willows." Master's thesis, University of
        Washington, 1965.

1228   HAAGA, AGNES. "Why Not Write Your Own Play?" Recreation,
        35 (May 1941), 80-82.

1229   HALE, PAT. "High School Offers Workshop in Playwriting for
        Children's Theatre." News and Notes for Children's
        Theatre, 1 (June 1968), 1.

1230   HALL, JEANNE LUCILLE WOODRUFF. "An Analysis of the Content of
        Selected Children's Plays with Special Reference to the
        Developmental Values Inherent in the Plays." Ph.D.
        dissertation, University of Michigan, 1966.
                Analyzes twenty-five plays as to content and impact,
        and suggests criteria for evaluating children's plays in
        general.

1231   HARDWICK, MARY. "The Composition and Presentation of a
        Children's Play." Master's [Fine Arts] thesis, University
        of Ohio, 1956.
                Script and production notes for The Marshmallow
        Mushroom are given.

INDIVIDUAL PLAYS AND PLAYWRITING FOR CHILDREN

1232 HARRIOTT, SISTER MARION. "An Adaptation of The Twelve
      Dancing Princesses into Play Form." Master's thesis,
      Catholic University, 1959.

1233 HARRIS, ALBERT JAMES III. "Criteria for the Evaluation of
      Playscripts for Children's Theatre: The Magic Glen, an
      Original Children's Play." Ph.D. dissertation, Univer-
      sity of Tennessee, 1965.

1234 HARRIS, AURAND. "Writing Plays for Children." Players
      Magazine, 28 (March 1952), 142-43.

1235 HENIGER, ALICE MINNIE HERTS. "The Drama's Value for Child-
      ren." Good Housekeeping, 57 (November 1913), 636-43.
      Analyzes many contemporary [1913] productions for
      childred and criticizes some lax standards in the
      profession.

1236 HESS, JANE. "Child Audience Attitudes Toward Two Interpreta-
      tions of Long John Silver." Master's thesis, University
      of Kansas, 1967.
      Tests audience reaction to two different actors
      portraying the character of Long John Silver.

1237 HOLLOWAY, SISTER MARCELLA M., C.S.J. "Playwriting Can Be
      Fun." Players Magazine, 36 (February 1960), 102-03.
      Author analyzes her own methods of writing children's
      plays.

1238 HORTON, LOUISE C. "Drama for Children." Dramatics, 19
      (December 1947), 24-25.
      Evaluates Albert Mitchell's play Jacob Hamblin.

1239 _____. "Drama for Children." Dramatics, 22 (April 1951),
      18-19.
      Discusses a University of Denver film version of
      Little Red Riding Hood.

1240 INGHAM, LAURA ELIZABETH. "Directing Cinderella." Master's
      thesis, University of Washington, 1966.

1241 JACKSON, RICHARD EUGENE. "The Composing and Producing of
      Two Original Plays for Children: Ferdinand and the
      Dirty Knight and A Thousand and One Spells to Cast."
      Master's thesis, Kent State University, 1964.

CHILDREN'S THEATRE

1242 JAGENDORF, MORITZ ADOLF. Ed. Nine Short Plays, Written for Young People to Stage. New York: The Macmillan Company, 1928.
Introductory comments are concerned with criteria for evaluating children's plays.

1243 JONES, VIRNELLE YVONNE. "Three Original Dramatic Adaptations of Children's Stories with Prompt Books and Suggestions for Their Production." Master's [Speech] thesis, Kansas State University, 1955.
Adaptations of Beauty and the Beast, Hansel and Gretel and The Real Princess are given.

1244 JONSON, JOANNE M. "A Production Thesis of Benjamin Britten's Let's Make an Opera." Master's thesis, University of Minnesota, 1959.

1245 KARTAK, THOMAS CLIFFORD. "The Adapting of Shakespearan Comedies for Child Audiences with Acting Versions of Four Plays as Examples." Ph.D. dissertation, Northwestern University, 1971.
Discusses the methodology of adapting Shakespeare for a child audience; acting versions of A Midsummer-Night's Dream, As You Like It, The Tempest, and The Comedy of Errors are given.

1246 KEMP, CHARLES EDWIN. "The Harlequinade Repertory: A Project for a Touring Company." Master's thesis, University of Denver, 1950.
Includes costume and set designs for six harlequin one-acts, plus scripts.

1247 KENNEDY, JEAN GRANVILLE. "The Staging of an Adaptation of A Midsummer Night's Dream by William Shakespeare for a Children's Audience, and a Written Analysis of the Problems Involved in Adapting, Directing, and Staging the Play." Master's thesis, Michigan State University, 1947.

1248 KIMBROUGH, MARY BETH. "Children and Shakespeare in the Production of A Midsummer Night's Dream." Master's thesis, Baylor University, 1951.

1249 KORDUS, RICHARD S. "The Little Prince: A Stage Adaptation." Master's thesis, Wayne State University, 1966.

Children's Theatre and Creative Dramatics

INDIVIDUAL PLAYS AND PLAYWRITING FOR CHILDREN

1250   KOTTKE, THEODORE GEORGE. "The Writing and Analysis of Writing a Formal Children's Play by Using a Children's Improvisational Theatre Group Working with an Original Scenario." Ph.D. dissertation, Columbia University, 1969.
The formal play, The Rainbow Has Orange Polka Dots, was produced from tape-recorded, improvised child drama which the author analyzes and comments upon.

1251   LIEDTKE, JAMES E. "The Three Spinning Fairies: An Original Play for Children." Master's thesis, Bowling Green State University, 1955.

1252   LI, HSU. "The Spinning Maiden and the Oxherd." Master's thesis, University of Denver, 1950.
Script of the play is based on an early Chinese legend.

1253   MAHAR, ETHEL. "Joan of Arc, A Children's Play in Three Scenes." Master's thesis, University of Denver, 1949.

1254   McCONNELL, EMMA JO. "Barnaby: An Original Three Act Play for Children." Master's thesis, Smith College, 1954.

1255   McGREW, MAVIS ALBERTA. "Raggedy Ann and Andy, A Lyric Drama for Children." Master's thesis, University of Denver, 1949.

1256   McRAE, ROBERTA MARQUERETTE. "An Adaptation of The Indian Captive by Charlotte Chorpenning." Master's thesis, University of Denver, 1952.

1257   MILLIKIN, MAXINE WINSTON. "'Young Buffalo Bill', An Original Children's Play." Master's thesis, University of Denver, 1948.

1258   MONTGOMERY, ANNE E. "A Production Thesis and Prompt Book of The Princess and the Swineherd." Master's thesis, Washington State University, 1964.

1259   "Most Popular Children's Plays." Recreation, 45 (October 1951), 270.
Lists the twenty-five most popular children's plays based on information from "The Directory of 1948 Children's Theatres Operating in the United States."

CHILDREN'S THEATRE

1260   MYCUE, MARGUERITE. "The Writing and Production of The
         Picaro: An Original Play for Children." Master's thesis,
         Texas Woman's University, 1965.

1261   NEBEKER, JOLENE. "The Evolution of The Baker's Dozen; An
         Original Play for Children." Master's thesis, Michigan
         State University, 1960.

1262   NICHOLSON, MARY AGNES. "The Plain Princess by Aurand
         Harris." Master's thesis, University of Washington,
         1966.
             Analyzes the Harris play and gives production notes.

1263   ODEN, VIRGIL H. "The Secret of the Jade Goddess." Master's
         thesis, University of Denver, 1954.
             Play is based on Mayan Indian folklore.

1264   OLIN, DONALD TODD. "An Analysis and Production Book of the
         Children's Theatre Production The Magic Slipper by
         Kelly Danford and Tilden Wells." Master's thesis, Ohio
         State University, 1955.

1265   "On Stage." Dramatics, 44 (February 1973), 14-15.
             Describes a unique technical approach to Lewis
         Carroll's Alice in Wonderland, with a musical score by
         Richard Addinsell.

1266   OWEN, GENE AND HAL OWEN. "Writing Plays for College Students
         to Perform to Children." Junior College Journal, 29
         (March 1959), 414-20.
             Work in playwriting at Santa Monica City College is
         discussed.

1267   OWEN, HAL. "Writing Plays for Children." California Journal
         of Elementary Education, 25 (February 1957), 146-51.

1268   PANTENBURG, SISTER ROSALEEN, O.P. "A Critical Analysis of
         Three Plays for Children's Theatre." Master's thesis,
         Catholic University, 1956.
             The three plays are Peter Pan (Barrie), The Sleeping
         Beauty and The Emperor's New Clothes (Chorpenning).

1269   PENGEL, GEORGIA. "Albert Lea's Alice in Wonderland."
         Dramatics, 23 (April 1952), 24.
             Discusses a successful production of Alice in Wonder-
         land in Albert Lea, Minnesota.

CHILDREN'S THEATRE AND CREATIVE DRAMATICS

INDIVIDUAL PLAYS AND PLAYWRITING FOR CHILDREN

1270   POLSKY, MILTON. "Mr. Moomglmoops: Summer Drama Program."
       Parks and Recreation, 1 (April 1966), 322.
       Describes the production of The Pirates Surprise and
       Beware of the Moomglmoops, using playground equipment for
       sets.

1271   PRICE, GRACE. "Helping the Beginning Playwright." Players
       Magazine, 28 (November 1951), 38.
       Shows how young playwrights are encouraged at the
       Pittsburgh Children's Theatre; emphasis is on Madge
       Miller and Beatrice Lewis.

1272   QUINT, BEVERLY. "On Writing a Children's Play." Horn Book,
       42 (April 1966), 181-85.
       Gives specific criteria for writing children's plays.

1273   RATLIFF, JERRY MACK. "Dramatic Adaptation and Production
       Analysis of Treasure Island." Master's thesis, Baylor
       University, 1949.

1274   REED, FRIEDA. "Theatre for Children." Dramatics, 29
       (December 1957), 12-13.
       Gives Charles Lewis' attitude on students writing
       plays for children.

1275   _____. "Theatre for Children." Dramatics, 30 (April 1959),
       22-23, 28.
       Wanda Bachman evaluates an Upper Darby, Pennsylvania
       production of Pinocchio.

1276   _____. "Theatre for Children." Dramatics, 31 (April 1960),
       22-23.
       Analyzes two productions of Peter Pan, one in Ingle-
       wood, California, and one in Beaverton, Oregon.

1277   _____. "Theatre for Children." Dramatics, 31 (May 1960),
       26-27.
       Evaluates a production of Aurand Harris' Simple Simon
       at North High School in Omaha, Nebraska.

1278   _____. "Theatre for Children." Dramatics, 35 (October 1963),
       18-19.
       Comments on a production of Snow White and the Seven
       Dwarfs in Green Lake, Wisconsin.

1279   _____. "Theatre for Children." Dramatics, 35 (November
       1963), 14-15.

CHILDREN'S THEATRE

(REED, FRIEDA)
Gives a discussion of Juanita Shearer's production of
The Clown Who Ran Away at the Brazil, Indiana, High
School.

1280 RODKEY, ELOISE JEANNE. "The Production Book for The
Emperor's New Clothes." Master's [Fine Arts] thesis,
University of Oklahoma, 1940.

1281 SAWYER, ETHEL R. "Playwriting for Children." Junior League
Magazine, 26 (January 1941), 22, 59-60.
Lists criteria for plays appropriate to be toured
under Junior League auspices.

1282 SHEEHAN, WILLIAM F. "Timothy the Lion, and Other Short
Plays for Children." Master's thesis, Syracuse University, 1950.
Four short, original plays with high moral content
are given.

1283 SISSON, MRS. JAMES GARDNER. "To Playwrights - With Love."
Junior League Magazine, 22 (February 1937), 44-47.
Author analyzes her feelings about being a playwright
and about playwriting in general.

1284 SIX, SALLY N. "Adaptation of the Chinese Drama to the
American Children's Theatre." Master's thesis, University of Kansas, 1956.
A part of the thesis analyzes Madge Miller's The Land
of the Dragon; the rest of the thesis is devoted to
evaluating Chinese theatre and its applicability to
Children's Theatre.

1285 SKINKLE, DOROTHY. "The Bell That Couldn't Ring." Grade
Teacher, 87 (December 1969), 68-71.
The text for a Christmas musical that is suitable for
assemblies is given; however, the work can also be used
in a traveling production.

1286 SMITH, SUSAN CARLTON. "Lake Town in a Drop of Water: A
Dramatized Fantasy of Biological Information." Master's
[Fine Arts] thesis, University of Georgia, 1961.

1287 SNIDER, GERALD E. "Rediscovered, Revisited and Revitalized."
Dramatics, 43 (February 1972), 10-12.
The article is a report on the Shawnee Mission South
High School, Overland Park, Kansas, production of The Two
Gentlemen of Verona for a child audience.

Children's Theatre and Creative Dramatics

INDIVIDUAL PLAYS AND PLAYWRITING FOR CHILDREN

1288 SOMMERS, MARY ELIN. "The Adaptation of a Fantasy for
      Children's Theatre - Espen Cinderlad." Master's thesis,
      University of Minnesota, 1960.

1289 SONNENBERG, WALTER. "Hans and the Tulip, a Play for Children
      in Two Acts." Master's thesis, University of Denver,
      1956.

1290 STEWART, GEORGE EARL. "Niccolo and Nicollette: A Production
      Study in Children's Theatre at Abilene Christian College."
      Master's thesis, Abilene Christian College, 1967.

1291 STRAWBRIDGE, EDWIN. "The Child Audience." Players Magazine,
      21 (May 1945), 24-25.
          Discusses two projected performances of Christopher
      Columbus and The Adventures of Johnny Appleseed.

1292 SWORTZELL, LOWELL. "Five Plays: A Repertory of Children's
      Theatre to Be Performed by and for Children." 2 vols.
      Ph.D. dissertation, New York University, 1963.
          In addition to the five scripts, Dr. Swortzell
      extends Kenneth Graham's seventy-six criteria for good
      playwriting by another eighty points. A seminal work.

1293 _____. "Writing Musical Comedy for Children." Children's
      Theatre Review, 16 (August 1967), 13-15.

1294 SYMPSON, JESSIE. "Adaptation and Production of Three
      Children's Plays." Master's thesis, University of Denver,
      1950.
          Gives three original Christmas plays appropriate for
      performance in an elementary classroom, using the whole
      class.

1295 TABSCOTT, JEANNE THERESE. "The Criteria for Evaluation and
      Analysis of Five Children's Plays." Master's thesis,
      Stanford University, 1956.
          The five plays evaluated are Daniel Boone, (Leona
      Babtist), The Elves and the Shoemaker (Nora Tully and
      Charlotte Chorpenning), The Land of the Dragon (Madge
      Miller), Rumpelstiltskin (Charlotte Chorpenning), and
      Simple Simon (Aurand Harris).

1296 "Very Much Off Broadway." Theatre Arts, 36 (July 1953), 13-14.
          Productions of Spring Again (East Side Settlement
      House) and What Have You Got to Lose? (Boys Club of New
      York) are discussed.

141

CHILDREN'S THEATRE

1297   WARD, J. W., JR. "A Production Thesis of The Emperor's New
       Clothes." Master's [Speech] thesis, Kansas State
       Teachers College - Emporia, 1952.
         Describes technical aspects of a production of the
       Chorpenning play.

1298   WARD, WINIFRED. "Cinderella and the Glass Slipper as Henry
       James Might Have Written It." Touchstone, June 1919,
       pp. 208-11.

1299   _____. "House that Jack Built as Gilbert K. Chesterton
       Might Have Written It." Touchstone, September 1919,
       pp. 475-81.

1300   _____. "Sleeping Beauty as Walter Pater Might Have Written
       It." Touchstone, December 1919, pp. 118-121.

1301   _____. "Spring and the Children's Theatre." Drama: Northwest-
       ern University Drama Service Guild, 14 April, 1938, pp.
       13-16.
        Lists fourteen good plays for children; emphasis is on
       Rosemary Musil's Seven Little Rebels.

1302   WATKINS, MARY JANE LARSON. "The Writing and Production of a
       Children's Play Based upon Thackeray's The Rose and the
       Ring." Master's thesis, Michigan State University, 1955.

1303   WEISS, LAWRENCE DAVID. "A Stage Setting for Madge Miller's
       Children's Play, The Land of the Dragon." Master's
       [Fine Arts] thesis, University of Georgia, 1964.

1304   WENSTROM, DAVID DEAN. "An Experiment in Children's Drama."
       3 vols. Ph.D. dissertation, University of Utah, 1965.
        Includes scripts for eleven original plays developed
       for the Children's Theatre of Pueblo College, Pueblo,
       Colorado.

1305   _____. "Ten Tips for Writing Children's Plays." Writer's
       Digest, 48 (December 1968), 54-57.

1306   WESSEL, DOROTHY JOLEEN. "The Dancing Red Shoes: A Project in
       Children's Theatre." Master's thesis, University of
       Denver, 1948.
        Thesis includes the music for this Andersen adaptation.

INDIVIDUAL PLAYS AND PLAYWRITING FOR CHILDREN

1307   WILCOX, HUDSON FREDERICK. "Production Book: Rip Van Winkle."
       Master's thesis, University of Oklahoma, 1949.

1308   WILLIAMS, SHIRLEY CADLE. "Three Original Plays for Children."
       Ph.D. dissertation, University of Denver, 1969.
       Contains The Green Monkey, a fairy tale; Seven Months
       of Blizzard, a realistic play based on pioneer history;
       and Fiesta in Tzintzuntzan, a realistic play based on
       life in a modern Mexican village.

1309   WINTER, ADELENE. "A Study of the Techniques of Adapting a
       Fairy-Tale into a Children's Play." Master's thesis,
       Sacramento State College, 1962.
       A portion of the thesis is the author's original
       script for Rose Red and Snow-White.

1310   WOLAK, CAMILLA HOWES. "Two New Plays for Children Which
       Follow the Established Criteria of Children's Theatre."
       Master's thesis, Ohio State University, 1966.
       Criteria are derived from Davis and Watkins' Children's
       Theatre, and Chorpenning's Twenty-One Years with Child-
       ren's Theatre. The author's two plays, Rumpelstiltskin
       and Squire Gullible and the Dragon are included.

1311   WRIGHT, PHYLLIS BLANCHARD. "The Production Book for
       Cinderella of Loreland." Master [Fine Arts] thesis,
       University of Oklahoma, 1941.
       Thesis is based on the Frances Homer play.

1312   WYATT, E. V. R. "Aucassin and Nicolete." Catholic World,
       181 (July 1955), 309.
       Analyzes the King-Coit production.

1313   YOUNG, STARK. "Nola and Damayanti: King-Coit Children's
       Theatre." New Republic, 82 (May 8, 1935), 370.

       See also the following entries. 62, 111, 114, 116, 118, 135,
       143, 155, 158, 194, 200, 209, 222, 231, 297, 390, 434, 439, 451,
       507, 542, 600, 610, 612, 637, 661, 686, 702, 752, 772, 778-
       80, 843, 848, 853, 864, 882, 888, 898, 901, 906, 917, 920,
       923, 928, 932, 937, 947, 950, 957-58, 961-62, 969, 974, 985,
       997, 1006, 1014-15, 1022, 1024, 1029, 1031, 1035-36, 1046,
       1053, 1073-76, 1089, 1097, 1112, 1121, 1124, 1129, 1133,
       1145, 1148, 1157, 1167-68, 1318, 1320, 1323, 1325, 1337-38,
       1343, 1354, 1373-74, 1380-81, 1394, 1397, 1404-05, 1410,
       1416, 1418, 1442, 1444, 1456, 1499, 1741, 1793, 1948, 1977.

CHILDREN'S THEATRE

TECHNICAL ASPECTS

1314   ALLEN F. ELLWOOD. Sunbeams for Footlights: The Design and
        Construction of Playground Theatres." Recreation, 33
        (April-May 1939), 3-4, 43-44.

1315   BAILEY, E. V. "How to Organize and Operate a Children's
        Theatre." Emerson Quarterly, 6 (January 1927), 10-14.

1316   BATA, GLORIANNA. "Key to Better Play Production." Grade
        Teacher, 87 (December 1969), 74-75.
            The author advocates applying some professional
        directing techniques to school performances.

1317   BEHM, THOMAS FRANK. "A Study of the Element of Style in
        Scene Design for Children's Theatre." Master's thesis,
        University of Kansas, 1967.

1318   BEMENT, MERLIN EDWIN, JR. "The Design of the Stage Settings
        for Two Children's Theatre Touring Plays." Master's
        thesis, Michigan State University, 1956.
            Designs for Peter, Peter, Pumpkin Eater (Martha B.
        King) and The Land of the Dragon (Madge Miller) are given.

1319   BERK, BARBARA AND JEANNE BENDICK. How to Have a Show. New
        York: Franklin Watts, 1957.
            A handbook for children intending to produce plays for
        children.

1320   BOCK, FRANK GEORGE. "A Basic Set for a Trouping Children's
        Theatre." Master's thesis, University of Denver, 1951.

1321   BROCKETT, JOSEPH. "Whoosh - The Magic Crocodile." Children's
        Theatre Review, 17 (February 1968), 12-15.
            Concerned with problems in producing children's
        theatre.

1322   BRUSH, MARTHA S. "Theatres in Elementary Schools." Journal
        of the American Institute of Architects, 19 (March 1963),
        n. p.

1323   BURNETT, HAZEL MANZOR. "The Design and Execution of Costumes,
        Scenery, and Stage Lighting for an Original Two-Act
        Children's Play Entitled The Picaro." Master's thesis,
        Texas Woman's University, 1965.

TECHNICAL ASPECTS

1324 BUTTERWORTH, BETTE. "Theatre-in-the Round We Go." Recreation, 47 (June 1954), 342-43.
Concerned with the problems of staging formal plays
for children outdoors.

1325 CAVALIERI, WALTER. "The Production, Direction, and Management of a Touring Children's Play, Pippi Longstocking."
Master's [Speech] thesis, Boston University, 1954.

1326 CHILVER, PETER. Staging a School Play. New York: Harper and
Row, 1968.
Discusses techniques peculiar to the school play and
auditorium situation.

1327 _____. AND ERIC JONES. Designing a School Play. New York:
Taplinger Publishing Company, 1970.
A companion work to Staging a School Play; see above.

1328 CHORPENNING, CHARLOTTE. "Rehearsing the Children's Play."
Dramatics, 19 (December 1947), 9-10.

1329 CIACCIO, MARY ELEANOR. Prologue to Production: A Children's
Theatre Manual. New York: The Association of the Junior
League of America, Inc., 1951.

1330 CLEVENGER, JANICE ALICE. "Costume and Set Designs for a
Trouping Children's Theatre." Master's thesis, University
of Denver, 1948.

1331 COMER, VIRGINIA LEE. "Organizational Problems in Children's
Theatre." Dramatics, 20 (November 1948), 13-15.

1332 CORNELISON, GAYLE L. "The Preferences of Children for
Saturated Colors and Tints Under Simulated Dramatic
Conditions." ASSITEJ Quarterly Review, No. 1 (January-
March 1967), 16-20.
Results of this investigation show that a wide
variety of tints and hues can be used in children's
theatre productions.

1333 CRENSHAW, CLAYTON L. "A Preliminary Study of Color Association in Costume Design for Children's Theatre."
Master's thesis, University of Kansas, 1967.

1334 CROUCH, PHILENE. "Effective Organization of a University
Children's Theatre." Master's [Education] thesis, St.
Louis University, 1950.
Based on a study of the Palo Alto Children's Theatre.

CHILDREN'S THEATRE

1335   CURRIE, HELEN WORKMAN. A Psychological Approach to the
        Production of Children's Plays." Master's thesis,
        University of Michigan, 1947.
            Gives statistics on the behavioral patterns of child
        audiences.

1336   DABNEY, EDITH AND C. M. WISE. Dramatic Costume for Children.
        St. Louis: Educational Publishers, Inc., 1949.
            Concerned with costumes for child actors in plays for
        children.

1337   DAMON, DOROTHY. "A Setting." Players Magazine, 29 (April
        1953), 160-61.
            Describes a storybook set used in a production of
        The Little Lame Prince (Dorothy Drew).

1338   DAVIS, JED H. "The Art of Scenic Design and Staging for
        Children's Theatre." Ph.D. dissertation, University of
        Minnesota, 1958.
            A consideration of the technical problems of one
        hundred plays for children.

1339   _____. "The Portal - A Partial Answer." Players Magazine,
        34 (January 1958), 79-80.
            Gives specific instructions on how to construct a
        false proscenium arch.

1340   DEAN, ALEXANDER. Little Theatre Organization and Management.
        New York: Appleton and Company, 1926.
            A portion of the book is concerned with community
        children's theatres.

1341   DEWELL, HELEN A. "Children's Theatre: A Plan of Organization
        for the Small Community." Master's thesis, University of
        Denver, 1954.

1342   DUNCAN, WILLIAM IRELAND. "Directing the Children's Theatre
        Play." Handbook for Children's Theatre Directors.
        Louise C. Horton, ed. Cincinnati, Ohio: The National
        Thespian Society, 1949. Pp. 14-15.

1343   FLAUTO, JOSEPH P., JR. "Problems of Design for a Children's
        Theatre Production of The Pied Piper of Hamelin."
        Master's thesis, Bowling Green State University, 1968.

1344   "Getting Extra Mileage Out of Theatrical Posters." News and
        Notes for Children's Theatre, 1 (June 1968), 1.

146

TECHNICAL ASPECTS

1345   GRAHAM, KENNETH L. "Acting in the Children's Theatre Play."
        Dramatics, 20 (May 1949), 8-10.
            Guidelines for the director of a play with a child cast.

1346   HAAGA, AGNES. "Children's Theatre and Public Funds."
        Children's Theatre Conference Newsletter, 15 (November
        1966), 23-25.
            Discusses current [1966] federal programs capable of
        funding children's theatre projects.

1347   HELSTEIN, MELVYN B. "A Preliminary Investigation of Some
        Aspects of the Environment for Children's Theatre." Ph.D.
        dissertation, University of Minnesota, 1962.
            Discussion centers on the child audience and the
        architecture of the children's theatre.

1348   HIGGINS, JOHN. "Playground Staging." Recreation, 46 (April
        1953), 55.
            Instructions for building a small, portable stage are
        given.

1349   HILL, ANN. "Arts Funding for U.S. Children's Theatre."
        Children's Theatre Review, 18 (August 1969), 19-23, 32.
            Gives lists of state and federal funds available for
        Children's Theatre and Creative Dramatics projects [1969],
        and a brief discussion of ongoing projects.

1350   HOETKER, JAMES. Students as Audience: An Experimental Study
        of the Relationship between Classroom Study of Drama and
        Attendance at the Theatre. Research Report No. 11.
        Urbana, Illinois: National Council of Teachers of
        English, 1971.
            An extensive discussion of the differences in attitude
        between teachers and professional theatre people concern-
        ing student preparation to see plays. A valuable look at
        aesthetic, emotional and pedagogical paradoxes.

1351   HOLMES, RUTH VICKERY. Model-Theatre Craft. New York:
        Frederick A. Stokes, 1940.
            Teaches beginning stage craft and construction.

1352   HORTON, LOUISE C. Ed. Handbook for Children's Theatre
        Directors. Cincinnati, Ohio: National Thespian Society,
        1949.
            Contains six articles from Dramatics magazine, plus
        an introduction.

CHILDREN'S THEATRE

HORTON, LOUISE C.; FRIEDA E. REED; MAZIE G. WEIL. "Echoes: Children's Theatre Conference." Dramatics, 23 (November 1951), 21.
Discusses promotion procedures for children's theatre.

1354 JOHNSON, ELLIOT. "Technical Problems of Trouping the Children's Theatre Play." Players Magazine, 24 (February 1948), 114-15.

1355 JOHNSON, RICHARD C. "Casting Students for Children's Theatre." Dramatics, 37 (December 1965), 14-15, 26.

1356 _____. Producing Plays for Children. New York: Richard Rosen Press, 1971.
The thrust of this book is toward teenagers producing plays for children. Although the work is primarily concerned with formal drama and the finished product of a play's production, Johnson also devotes some space to improvisation, chamber theatre, storytelling and creative drama techniques.

1357 _____. "Rehearsing a Children's Theatre Production." Dramatics, 37 (January 1966), 24-25, 34.

1358 _____. "Selecting a Play for the Children's Theatre." Dramatics, 37 (November 1965), 14-15, 25.

1359 _____. "Starting a High School Children's Theatre." Dramatics, 37 (April 1966), 22-23, 27.

1360 _____. "A Technical Challenge." Dramatics, 37 (February 1966), 20-21, 27-28.
Illustrates some difficult technical problems in children's theatre such as special costume and make-up effects, and magic tricks.

1361 KENNEDY, JOHN S. "The Scope and Problems of Children's Theatre Production." Master's thesis, University of Oklahoma, 1947.

1362 KRAMER, E. DOROTHY. "Children's Theatre in Arena Style." Master's thesis, University of Denver, 1950.

1363 KRAUS, JOANNA HALPERT. "For Children 'Of All Ages'? Let's Be Honest in Our Advertising." News and Notes for Children's Theatre, 1 (June 1968), n. p.

TECHNICAL ASPECTS

1364   LEWIS, GEORGE L. "A Stage-Crew Handbook for Children's
Theatre Directors." Ph.D. dissertation, University of
Denver, 1954.

1365   LOBDELL, ROBERT A. "Planning a Show Wagon." Recreation, 48
(January 1955), 32-33.

1366   MacEACHRON, GRACE. "Building-Block Theatre." Theatre Crafts,
2 (January-February 1968), 12-20.
      The set is composed of blocks that mimic children's
toy building blocks.

1367   MACKAY, CONSTANCE D'ARCY. Costumes and Scenery for Amateurs.
New York: Henry Holt and Company, 1915.
      A brief section of this book is devoted to technical
aspects of children's theatre.

1368   _____. How to Produce Children's Plays. New York: Henry
Holt and Company, 1915.

1369   MacLEAN, DOROTHY GEOTIS. "A Handbook of Directing Children's
Plays." Master's thesis, Emerson College, 1966.

1370   "Making Publicity Photos Work for Ticket Sales." News and
Notes for Children's Theatre, 1 (June 1968), n. p.

1371   MARKS, PAUL. "Taking Children's Plays on the Road." Players
Magazine, 17 (October 1940), 6, 10, 28.

1372   MAWER, MURIEL; HAZEL PATTEN; MINNETTE PROCTOR. Children's
Theatre Manual: A Guide for the Organization and Opera-
tion of a Non-Profit Community Children's Theatre.
Anchorage, Kentucky: Children's Theatre Press, 1951.

1373   McRAE, JEANNE CLAIRE. "A Study of Children's Theatre: A
Study and Analysis of Organizational Problems and
Directing Techniques in a Children's Theatre with a
Handbook and Guide for Children's Theatre Directors."
Master's thesis, Baylor University, 1950.

1374   MEIKLE, JAMES. "A Dragon Mask." Players Magazine, 32 (May
1956), 186.
      Discusses mask construction for Madge Miller's
The Land of the Dragon.

CHILDREN'S THEATRE

1375   MILLER, JAMES HULL. Hub Lighting Systems for Children's
        Theatre. Chicago: Hub Electrical Company, 1960.
            This bulletin describes several systems for lighting
        small stages with a detailed description of specific
        aspects of lighting.

1376   MITCHELL, ALBERT O. "The Children's Theatre Audience."
        Handbook for Children's Theatre Directors. Louise C.
        Horton, ed. Cincinnati, Ohio: The National Thespian
        Society, 1949. Pp. 19-22.
            Shows how to handle a child audience, sometimes.

1377   MORRISON, J. S. "Building Tomorrow's Audience." American
        Education, 1 (October 1965), 24-27.

1378   MORTON, EVELYN ALICE. "A Study of the Art of Make-up for
        Children's Theatre." Master's thesis, Baylor University,
        1953.

1379   NEWTON, PETER. "The Toy Theatre: A Children's Playhouse Where
        Fairy Tales Come True." Commonweal, 28 (April 1915),
        36-41.
            Discusses technical aspects of the Toy Theatre for
        Children in New York City.

1380   OGDEN, JEAN CARTER AND JESS OGDEN. The Play Book: An Elemen-
        tary Book on Stage Technique with Nine Plays of Various
        Types and Some Suggestions for Creative Use of Plays and
        Playing. New York: Harcourt, Brace and Company, 1937.

1381   PHILIPPE, HERBERT. "Simplified Scenery for Children's Theatre."
        Players Magazine, 20 (April 1944), 20.
            Shows how female children's theatre crews cope during
        the war.

1382   POLLACK, PETER. "Children's Theatre." Theatre Arts, 38
        (August 1954), 73-74.
            Discusses children's theatre promotion, especially
        at Goodman Theatre.

1383   "Puppet Stage Folds Up for Storage." Sunset, 141 (December
        1968), 94.

1384   REED, FRIEDA. "Theatre for Children." Dramatics, 28
        (December 1956), 14-15, 23.
            Concerned with achieving special effects with make-up.

TECHNICAL ASPECTS

1385   . "Theatre for Children." Dramatics, 28 (February 1957), 16-17, 30.
Costuming high school productions is the concern of this article.

1386   . "Theatre for Children." Dramatics, 28 (March 1957), 14-15, 25.
Covers some aspects of scenery for children's theatre.

1387   . "Theatre for Children." Dramatics, 29 (January 1958), 14-15.
Discusses directing children's plays from a high school student's point of view.

1388   . "Theatre for Children." Dramatics, 29 (February 1958), 20-21.
Students discuss technical production of children's theatre.

1389   . "Theatre for Children." Dramatics, 31 (December 1959), 18-19.
Plays with all-girl casts are the subject of this article.

1390   . "Theatre for Children." Dramatics, 31 (March 1960), 22-23.
Concerned with promotion and ticket selling.

1391   . "Theatre for Children." Dramatics, 33 (March 1962), 22-23.
Deals with problems of staging children's theatre.

1392   . "Theatre for Children." Dramatics, 35 (February 1964), 22-23.
Discusses specific technical problems of staging and reproduction.

1393   . "Theatre for Children." Dramatics, 36 (February 1965), 24-25.
Comments of Maizie Weil on technical problems of children's theatre are included.

1394   REINHARDT, PAUL D. "Designing with Imagination." Children's Theatre Conference Newsletter, 15 (November 1966), 12-14.
Discusses quality in costumes for children's theatre; sketches are given for Androcles and the Lion and The Thirteen Clocks.

CHILDREN'S THEATRE

1395 "The Road Is Young." Theatre Arts, 32 (April-May 1948), 58.
A discussion of touring problems, based on the work of
the Piper Players and the Touring Players.

1396 ROYAL, PATRICIA W. "Children's Theatre Goes Traveling."
Recreation, 39 (January 1946), 535-36, 550-51.
Sponsorship of children's theatre by department
stores is considered.

1397 RUTLEDGE, PHELIA CARRACI. "The Design and Execution of
Costumes for a Production of Nora MacAlvay's Beauty and
the Beast." Master's thesis, Michigan State University,
1962.

1398 SCHRAM, FRANCES. "Observations on the Professional Theatre
for Children." Children's Theatre Review, 16 (February
1967), 13-14.
Suggests that a stronger correlation between the CTC
and professional children's theatres would be productive
for each; also covered is funding under Titles I and III.

1399 SIMON, PEGGY. "Publicity Tips for Sponsors of Professional
Touring Children's Theatre." News and Notes for
Children's Theatre, 1 (June 1968), 2.

1400 SMITH, MOYNE RICE. Plays and How to Put Them On. New York:
Henry Z. Walck, 1961.
Covers most aspects of technical production for
beginners; also includes seven plays written by children
for children, plus production notes.

1401 SMITH, ROSE MARIE. "Plans for Organizing and Managing a
Children's Theatre in Oklahoma City, Oklahoma." Master's
thesis, University of Michigan, 1952.

1402 SNOOK, BARBARA. Making Masks for School Plays. Boston:
Plays, Inc., 1972.
Discusses techniques of construction and their
application to school plays by and for children.

1403 STEELE, MIKE. "On the Road with Children's Theatre."
Children's Theatre Review, 23:1 (1974), 12-13.
Explores the touring practices and problems of the
Minneapolis Children's Theatre.

TECHNICAL ASPECTS

1404   STROH, MARY JANE. "A Developmental Approach to the Production of Children's Plays Through the Experimental Production of Little Red Riding Hood." Master's thesis, Ohio State University, 1950.

1405   SULLINGER, M. FRANCES HOLDER. "Theatre for Children: A Study and Production Book." Master's [Speech] thesis, East Texas State College, 1958.
        Technical aspects of Aurand Harris' The Plain Princess are discussed and a prompt book is included.

1406   SUTCLIFFE, MARY JEAN. "Costumes and Make-Up for Children's Theatre." California Journal of Elementary Education, 25 (February 1957), 152-57.
        Discusses how to handle many special problems, such as horses and spiders, on the set of a children's play.

1407   SWORTZELL, NANCY. "Directing Musical Comedy: With and For Children." Children's Theatre Review, 16 (August 1967), 10-13.

1408   TAYLOR, LOREN E. Formal Drama and Children's Theatre. Minneapolis: Burgess Publishing Company, 1966.
        Discusses initial work in staging and production of children's theatre.

1409   TOMPKINS, JULIA. Historical and Period Costumes for School Plays. Boston: Plays, Inc., 1974.
        Methods of costume construction for the formal school play are catalogued.

1410   "Treasure Island." Theatre Arts Magazine, 8 (April 1924), 277-78.
        Two sets by Howard Claney for the Threshold School of the Theatre, New York City, are included.

1411   "Troup 759 Sponsors Children's Theatre." Dramatics, 24 (February 1953), 21.
        Illustrates work in the Colorado Springs High School.

1412   WALTON, CECILE. The Children's Theatre Book. London: Adam and Charles Black, 1952.
        A production handbook for children concerned with dance and play programs.

Children's Theatre and Creative Dramatics

CHILDREN'S THEATRE

1413   WARD, WINIFRED. "Organizing a Children's Theatre." Drama:
Northwestern University Drama Service Guild, 14 November,
1937, pp. 16-17, 21.
Examines problems that occur when establishing a
community-centered children's theatre.

1414   _____. "Publicizing Your Children's Theatre." Players
Magazine, 18 (April 1942), 17-18.

1415   WILLIAMS, LINDA CHRISTIE. "Is Your Slip Showing?" Children's
Theatre Review, 17 (May 1968), 20-21.
Discusses economical costume design with volunteer
workers.

1416   WILSON, JAMES THOMAS, JR. "Costume Designs for Reynard the
Fox." Master's [Fine Arts] thesis, Florida State University, 1967.

1417   WILSON, MARGERY. "Children's Theatre in the Round."
Educational Theatre Journal, 2 (May 1950), 104-07.

1418   WILSON, W. HOWARD. "Settings and Lighting for Children's
Theatre." California Journal of Elementary Education,
25 (February 1957), 158-59.

1419   WOODY, REGINA. "Our Best Cellar Theatre." Parents' Magazine,
11 (February 1936), 30, 60-61.
Discusses the technical aspect of constructing a
neighborhood theatre.

1420   WRIGHT, LAURA F. "Organization and Administration of
Children's Theatres in the Upper Mid-West." Master's
thesis, Marquette University, 1947.

1421   YOUNG, MARGARET MARY. "The Child in the Theatre." Players
Magazine, 8 (June 1932), 3-4, 21.
Discusses child actors and child technical crews at
the Children's Theatre of the University of Iowa.

See also the following entries. 143, 155, 158, 183, 206,
270, 405-07, 414, 484, 539, 593, 599, 618, 683, 736-37, 831,
847, 858, 869-71, 976, 992, 1046, 1064, 1081, 1092, 1109, 1122,
1150, 1179-88, 1190, 1192, 1196, 1210, 1212, 1216, 1218-19,
1226-27, 1231, 1240-41, 1243, 1246-49, 1255-58, 1262, 1265,
1273, 1280, 1284-85, 1289-90, 1306-07, 1311, 1434, 1499,
1507, 1543, 1546-47, 1932.

Children's Theatre and Creative Dramatics

IN EDUCATION AND THE SCHOOLS

1422   ALLEN, JOHN. "Teachers and Theatre People." World Theatre,
        2:3 (1952), 7-8.
            Concerned with both formal drama and creative dramatics,
        and the lack of understanding between educators and
        theatre people; there is also a discussion of the first
        ITI meeting on Theatre for Children and Youth, held in
        Paris, 1952.

1423   BAKER, GOERGE P. "What the Theatre Can Do for the School."
        Ladies' Home Journal, 30 (January 1913), 26.

1424   CASILI, M. RENGO. "Theatre for Children, Factors in the
        Development of the Individual." ASSITEJ Quarterly
        Review, 2 (January-March 1968), 10.
            Summarizes the author's more extended statement, in
        French (pp. 5-10), in the same issue.

1425   COHEN, HELEN LOUISE. "Education in the Theatre Arts."
        Theatre Arts Magazine, 7 (October 1924), 388-92.
            Work of Clare Tree Major, in conjunction with the
        New York Association of Teachers of English, at the
        Threshold Playhouse in New York City is discussed.

1426   COLLINS, LILLIAN FOSTER. "The Little Theatre in School."
        Drama, 20 (November 1929), 52.
            Shows how to organize a little theatre, as an out-
        growth of an English program.

1427   DAVENPORT, JUDITH K. "An Evaluation of Theatre Resources for
        Youth: Project TRY." (June 20, 1967). Typescript
        available from the University of New Hampshire or on
        ERIC fiche #ED013829.
            A project concerned with touring companies, creative
        dramatics and play direction, training programs, and
        their impact on the sensitivity awareness of elementary
        school children in the state of New Hampshire.

1428   DICKSON, BELLE L. "Use Your Auditorium." School Executive,
        61 (January 1942), 20-21, 58.
            Shows how to plan weekly creative activities for
        school assemblies.

1429   DINGES, SUSAN. "Teens on Tour." Children's Theatre Review,
        23:1 (1974), 8-9.
            Discusses the formal dramatic activities of high
        school-aged students who have a thorough basis in
        creative dramatics from work in the Creative Dramatics
        Workshop for Children at the University of Missouri-Kansas
        City.

155

CHILDREN'S THEATRE

1430   FINCKE, MILDRED GIGNOUX. "Learning via Dramatics." Parents'
       Magazine, 15 (February 1940), 20-21, 75-76.
           Explores both the use of creative dramatics and formal
       drama as an educational tool.

1431   FLEMING, MARTHA. "The Making of a Play." Elementary School
       Teacher, 8 (September 1907), 15-23.
           Emphasis is on educational dramatics (creative drama)
       in a sixth grade history class.

1432   FLETCHER, JUANITA. "Theatre Teaching in the Elementary
       School." Educational Theatre Journal, 19 (Special Issue:
       June 1967), 288-90.
           Advocates informal drama, puppetry and rhythmic
       activities in the elementary school.

1433   FORNCROOK, MRS. RUTH. "Parent-Teacher Association Co-operate
       in a Children's Theatre Project." California Journal of
       Elementary Education, 25 (February 1957), 161-63.
           Concerned with a project associated with the Santa
       Monica City College Children's Theatre and the Santa
       Monica Council of Parents and Teachers.

1434   FRY, MRS. EMMA VIOLA SHERIDAN. Educational Dramatics. Rev.
       and enlgd. ed. New York: L. A. Noble, 1917.
           As the originator of "educational dramatics", the
       author defines the concept and discusses its methodology.

1435   GAIR, SONDRA B. "Theatre: A Total Art Experience for
       Children." Art Education, 23 (November 1970), 28-30.
           Deals with elementary school curriculum enrichment
       through formal drama.

1436   GOODREDS, VINCENT S. "Education in Dramatics or Drama in
       Education." Education, 54 (May 1934), 564.

1437   HAUN, RUTH H. "A Child in the Play." Speech Teacher, 5
       (September 1956), 223-25.

1438   HENRY, MABEL WRIGHT. "Why Children's Theatre?" Creative
       Expression in Oral Language. Mabel Wright Henry, ed.
       Champaign, Illinois: National Council of Teachers of
       English, 1967.
           Strongly considers the use of Children's Theatre
       productions to enrich culturally deprived children.

IN EDUCATION AND THE SCHOOLS

1439   HIGGINS, ELIZABETH JUNE. "The Play That Grew About Rumpelstiltskin." Instructor, 70 (November 1960), 31, 50.
Creative dramatics work with second graders yields a
formal production.

1440   HOCHHAUSER, JACK. "Our Theatre in the Round." Instructor,
66 (November 1956), 75, 98, 100.
Discusses a gymnasium play that originated from a
creative dramatics exercise.

1441   HOLT, ALICE M. DONOHO. "The Process of Adapting Children's
Literature into Short Plays for Use in the Early Junior
High Years." Master's thesis, Texas Woman's University,
1959.

1442   HORTON, LOUISE C. "Children's Theatre in Your School."
American City, 36 (June 1951), 9-11.
Discusses basic techniques for establishing a
children's theatre, with child actors, in a school;
a brief bibliography is included.

1443   _____. "Drama for Children." Dramatics, 18 (December 1946),
20-21.
Shows how to interest high school students in
performing plays for children.

1444   HUBBARD, EVELYN. "Children's Theatre in the Classroom."
Players Magazine, 24 (November 1947), 42-43.
Treats the Junior High School Children's Theatre in
Waco, Texas; a production of The Ghost of Mr. Penny is
also discussed.

1445   _____. "Children's Theatre Is More Fun." Texas Outlook, 32
(December 1948), 21-22.
Discusses the necessity of interesting high school
students in performances for children; a list of suitable
plays is included.

1446   HUME, SAMUEL J. AND LOIS M. FOSTER. Theatre and School.
New York: Samuel French, 1937.
Strongly favors informal drama over formal drama for
children because of its greater sincerity and educational
value.

1447   HUMISTON, BEATRICE. "The Theatre as an Educational Institu-
tion." Quarterly Journal of Speech Education, 5 (March
1919), 120-27.

CHILDREN'S THEATRE

1448 JOHNSON, RICHARD C. "Meeting the Children's Theatre Audience."
      Dramatics, 37 (March 1966), 22-23, 26.
          Shows ways to allow a child audience to make contact
      with performers.

1449 _____. "Why Children's Theatre in High School?" Dramatics,
      37 (October 1965), 18-19, 36-37

1450 KEENER, BEVERLY, M. "Introducing Children to the World of
      Theatre." Elementary English, 43 (December 1966), 892-93.
          Describes a New Haven project with children of low-
      income families and the effect of a theatre experience
      on these children.

1451 KENNER, FREDA. "Children's Theatre in High School." Players
      Magazine, 34 (May 1958), 178-79.
          Explains the value of good high school drama for
      children and gives examples from the productions of the
      Messick High School in Memphis, Tennessee.

1452 KERR, JOHN. "Drama with and for Children: A Review."
      Educational Theatre Journal, 13 (May 1961), 141-42.
          More than a review of Winifred Ward's book, it is a
      testament to her work in child-related drama.

1453 KREMER, LESTER R. "Trends in High School Children's Theatre."
      Dramatics, 29 (May 1958), 22-23.

1454 LAKE, GOLDIE. "The Ready-Made Play." Instructor, 70
      (November 1960), 31, 50, 63.
          Analyzes shifting attitudes in education toward formal
      and informal drama.

1455 LAYNE, WILLIAM JOSEPH. "The Effect of Curricular Dramatics
      on Children's Acting Skill." Ph.D. dissertation, North-
      western University, 1970.
          Discusses work with seventh grade students in
      Wilmette, Illinois, who participated in curricular creative
      dramatics. Study shows that they "excel significantly in
      acting behaviors over seventh grade students who have
      not had such opportunity. It was not determined whether
      sex was a factor...."

CHILDREN'S THEATRE AND CREATIVE DRAMATICS

IN EDUCATION AND THE SCHOOLS

1456   LEECH, ROBERT MILTON. "Education Through Theatre for Children." Ph.D. dissertation, University of Tennessee, 1962.
Concerned with children's literature for plays, the general history of children's theatre, children's theatre in Southwestern United States, and at Texas Western College; the original script of the author's play, Commanche Eagle, is included.

1457   LEWIS, GEORGE L. "Children's Theatre and Teacher Training." Players Magazine, 27 (October 1950), 11.
Discusses combination programs between the Brigham Young University Children's Theatre and the University's College of Education.

1458   MACKAY, CONSTANCE D'ARCY. "Drama in Which Young People Can Participate: The School and the Community Celebration." Drama, 16 (October 1925), 32-33.
The author discusses the differences between professional Children's Theatre and drama in the schools.

1459   MASTERS, LILLIAN DECKER. "Creative Dramatics and Children's Theatre." Teachers College Journal, 12 (November 1940), 31, 36.
Evaluates and delineates the differences between creative dramatics and formal children's theatre.

1460   McCONAUGHY, JAMES LUKENS. The School Drama. New York: Bureau of Publications, Columbia University Teachers College, 1913.
An early survey of the theatre scene in education.

1461   MEEK, BERYL. "The Establishment of a Children's Theatre in a Teacher Training Institute." Ph.D. dissertation, New York University, 1942.

1462   MORE, GRACE VAN DYKE. "When Children Perform in Public." National Education Association Journal, 20 (January 1931), 13-14.
Shows elementary school teachers how to work with children in formal productions.

1463   MURRAY, JOSEPHINE AND EFFIE G. BATHURST. Creative Ways for Children's Plays. New York: Silver Burdett Company, 1938.
Surveys the contemporary scene [1938] in educational drama.

Children's Theatre and Creative Dramatics

CHILDREN'S THEATRE

1464 NEIDERMEYER, FRED C. AND LINDA OLIVER. "The Development of
Young Children's Dramatic and Public Speaking Skills."
Elementary School Journal, 73 (November 1972), 95-100.
Discusses the results of a two-year study with
kindergarten and first-grade students and the effects of
this experimental program on their ability to act and
speak.

1465 OMMANNEY, KATHERINE ANNE AND PIERCE C. OMMANNEY. The Stage
and the School. New York: Harper and Brothers, 1950.
Chapter VIII, "Pantomime," is of particular value.

1466 OSBORNE, ROSALIE HOFF. "Let's Be Somebody: Old Tales
Dramatized for Children." Master's thesis, Sul Ross
State College, 1951.
Contains twelve brief plays suitable for performance
by fourth grade children.

1467 PLESCIA, GILLIAN L. "Theatre in the Schools." Children's
Theatre Review, 23:2 (1974), 12-14.
Shows the integration of formal and informal drama
into the school system, and its effect on pedogogical
procedures.

1468 PUTNAM, SARAH A. "Working at Play and Playing at Work."
Progressive Education, 8 (January 1931), 71-72.
Traces the dramatic activities of children in
schools from age four through seventeen.

1469 REED, FRIEDA. "Children's Theatre for High School Students."
Dramatics, 21 (April 1950), 8-9.
Discusses the benefits, to high school students,
derived from performing plays for children.

1470 _____. "Theatre for Children." Dramatics, 26 (December
1954), 10-11.
Urges high school drama students to do more plays for
children.

1471 _____. "Theatre for Children." Dramatics, 26 (January 1955),
14-15.
Condenses reports by high school directors of
children's theatre.

Children's Theatre and Creative Dramatics

IN EDUCATION AND THE SCHOOLS

1472 _____. "Theatre for Children." Dramatics, 26 (March 1955), 12-13, 24.
Discusses the technical problems and successes of three high school touring comapnies for children.

1473 _____. "Theatre for Children." Dramatics, 27 (October 1955), 18-19.
Reviews children's theatre in several high schools.

1474 _____. "Theatre for Children." Dramatics, 27 (April 1956), 14-15, 27.
Discusses initial children's theatre productions at two high schools.

1475 _____. "Theatre for Children." Dramatics, 28 (October 1956), 16-17.
Lists several plays suitable for high school students performing to child audiences.

1476 _____. "Theatre for Children." Dramatics, 29 (November 1957), 12-13, 23.
Again pleads that high school students produce plays for children; the Children's Theatre Conference at Tufts is mentioned.

1477 _____. "Theatre for Children." Dramatics, 32 (January 1961), 20-21.
Gives high school student's opinions about working for child audiences.

1478 _____. "Theatre for Children." Dramatics, 32 (February 1961), 20-21.
Advocates that children's theatre is the richest aspect of high school dramatics.

1479 _____. "Theatre for Children." Dramatics, 33 (November 1961), 22-23.
Tells high school drama students to do plays for children.

1480 _____. "Theatre for Children." Dramatics, 33 (January 1962), 16-17.
Discusses the educational value, for high school students, of working in productions for children.

1481 _____. "Theatre for Children." Dramatics, 33 (April 1962), 18-19.

CHILDREN'S THEATRE AND CREATIVE DRAMATICS

CHILDREN'S THEATRE

(REED, FRIEDA)
Describes opportunities in the field of children's theatre for students who have graduated from high school.

1482 _____. "Theatre for Children." Dramatics, 34 (November 1962), 14.
Once again Miss Reed urges high school students to work in plays for children.

1483 _____. "Theatre for Children." Dramatics, 34 (May 1963), 22, 26.
Contains interviews with two of Miss Reed's students at Upper Darby High School in Pennsylvania.

1484 _____. "Theatre for Children." Dramatics, 35 (December 1963), 22, 25.
Gives reasons for high school students to produce plays for children.

1485 _____. "Theatre for Children." Dramatics, 36 (October 1964), 26-27.
Discusses theatre workshops for students in grades five through eight.

1486 _____. Theatre for Children." Dramatics, 36 (May 1965), 24-25.
Shows Thespian groups, who have not produced plays for children, how to get started.

1487 REELY, ANN. "Children's Theatre, An Activity for Secondary-School Pupils." Bulletin of the National Association of Secondary-School Principals, 33 (December 1949), 127-29.
Children's theatre programs in high schools in Denver, Seattle and Minneapolis are discussed.

1488 ROBERTS, VERA MOWRY. "Theatre Education in the United States." Educational Theatre Journal, 20 (April 1968), 308-10.
Delineates various types of educational theatre in the United States, and makes a distinction between creative dramatics and children's theatre.

1489 SCHAUS, LUCIBEL. "Original Dramatic Adaptations Supplementary to the Scott, Foresman Series in First Grade." Master's [Education] thesis, Boston University, 1955.

Children's Theatre and Creative Dramatics

IN EDUCATION AND THE SCHOOLS

1490 SHIPOW, EMANUEL. "A Comparative Study of the Integration of
Theatre and Drama into Education: Moscow, London and
Los Angeles." Ph.D. dissertation, University of California - Los Angeles, 1970.
A comparative study intended to support the cultural
exchange of feasible and economical drama-related programs
and information.

1491 SIMMONS, SISTER MARY BENEDICT. "An Analysis of the Educational Advantages of Formal Dramatics for the Elementary
School Child." Master's thesis, Catholic University,
1962.

1492 SINTIMBRANU, MIRCEA. "Art and Teaching in the Field of
Theatre for Children." ASSITEJ Quarterly Review, 2
(January-March 1968), 2.
A concise statement about the longer article, in
French, in the same issue (pp. 23-24).

1493 SMITH, HARVEY K. "Common Hazards of the School and College
Theatre." Educational Theatre Journal, 2 (March 1950),
32-36.

1494 SQUIRE, TOM. "Children of the Theatre." Theatre Arts
Magazine, 21 (November 1937), 888-93.
Discusses the work of Jean Greer Robinson at the
Professional Children's School in New York City.

1495 STILLING, VERA. "Bringing Children's Theatre Inside Schools
Offers Rich Rewards." News and Notes for Children's
Theatre, 1 (June 1968), n. p.

1496 STRAUSS, IVARD N. "Dramatics as a Dynamic Force in Education." Education, 56 (October 1935), 75-81.

1497 SWEET, FAYE. "Some Practical Suggestions for Drama in
Rural Schools." Elementary English Review, 5 (June 1929),
177-78.

1498 "The Theatre As An Educational Agent." Current Literature,
45 (October 1908), 441-44.
Discusses the impact of the Children's Educational
Theatre in New York City.

1499 "Theatre-At-the Schools." New Yorker, 37 (May 20, 1961),
35-36.
Technical aspects of the Phoenix Theatre's touring
company and its production of The Taming of the Shrew are
discussed.

CHILDREN'S THEATRE

1500   VIERECK, PHILLIP. "A Play Can Teach." Instructor, 65
        (March 1956), 45, 47.

1501   WARD, WINIFRED. "Why a Children's Theatre?" Southern Speech
        Bulletin, 6 (March 1941), 79-83.
            Emphasis is on formal drama for children and its
        value to them, although creative dramatics, especially in
        Evanston, is discussed.

1502   WISE, CLAUDE MERTON. Dramatics for School and Community.
        Cincinnati: Kidd Company Publishers, 1923.
            Discusses the effects of formal drama in the schools;
        numerous bibliographies are included.

1503   WOODS, MARGARET S. "Dramatic Arts within the Reach of Every
        Child in the Nation." Washington Parent Teacher, 9
        (November 1957), 19.

1504   WRIGHT, LAURA. "The Forgotten Audience." Dramatics, 24
        (October 1952), 26-27.
            Suggests the value of high school students performing
        to child audiences.

1505   YODER, SARAH. "Not on Every Bush." Instructor, 82 (March
        1973), 81, 84.
            Comments on the values of formal and informal perfor-
        mance by children for children.

        See also the following entries. 1, 112, 118, 124, 135, 139-
        40, 149, 153-54, 160, 179, 186, 188, 192, 201, 208, 221, 519,
        555, 578, 611, 655, 663, 729, 736, 826, 895, 997, 1043, 1047,
        1135, 1137, 1145, 1168, 1218, 1225, 1229, 1237, 1244, 1266,
        1274, 1277-79, 1286-87, 1294, 1322, 1326-27, 1334, 1350,
        1357-59, 1371, 1387-90, 1392, 1411, 1501, 1684, 1709, 1718,
        1789, 1862-63, 1866, 1879, 1942, 2010, 2162, 2213, 2217.

HISTORY: PRE-1950

1506   BLANK, EARL W. "Let Them Act it Out." Parent's Magazine,
        22, (March 1947), 30-31, 94-95.
            A definition of creative dramatics is given and the
        author shows how mothers can use it in their own
        nieghborhoods.

1507   BROWN, CORINNE. Creative Drama in the Lower School. New
        York: D. Appleton and Company, 1929.
            All types of dramatic activities, formal and informal,
        are explored and loosely applied to the elementary school
        situation.

1508   BURGER, ISABEL B. "Children's Theatre: Creative Dramatics."
        Players Magazine, 24 (January 1948), 88-90.
            Emphasis is on the improvisational values of creative
        dramatics as a technique for preparing children's plays
        for an audience

1509   _____. "The Creative Dramatics Project in the Trailer Park,
        Part I." Players Magazine, 20 (April 1944), 6-7, 26-27.
            Shows USO personnel how to conduct creative dramatics
        sessions.

1510   _____. "The Creative Dramatics Project in the Trailer Park,
        Part II." Players Magazine, 20 (May 1944), 6-7, 25-27.
            Shows USO personnel how to prepare children for a
        public demonstration of creative dramatics.

1511   _____. "An Education Experiment in Creative Dramatics."
        Players Magazine, 19 (May 1943), 32-34, 38.
            Work at Johns Hopkins University's Children's Experi-
        mental Theatre is discussed.

1512   CAMPBELL, ELISE HATT AND LEONA GEIGER. "Dramatics in Three
        Age Groups." Progressive Education, 12 (October 1935),
        403-08.
            Work with five through fourteen year olds at the
        Merrill-Palmer School in Detroit is described.

CREATIVE DRAMATICS

1513 CHORPENNING, CHARLOTTE. "Putting on a Community Play."
      Quarterly Journal of Speech, 5 (January 1919), 31-44.
          Many facets of the author's early work with children
      are explored.

1514 COOK, H. CALDWELL. The Play Way. London: Heinemann, 1919.
          An early exploration of educational drama and related
      activities in Great Britain.

1515 CRISTE, RITA. "Creative Dramatics Demonstration." Education-
      al Theatre Journal, 1 (December 1949), 105-06.
          A report on a Children's Theatre Conference demonstra-
      tion and its results.

1516 DALZELL, CLOYDE DUVAL. "New Settings for Old Stories."
      Quarterly Journal of Speech, 18 (June 1932), 422-32.
          Emphasis is on creative dramatics, but film, radio,
      ballet, opera and other related subjects are covered.

1517 DeMAY, AMY J. "We Made Our Own Plays." Elementary English
      Review, 21 (April 1944), 151-52, 158.
          Author reminisces about her childhood, and elaborates
      on the improvisational abilities of children in general.

1518 DIXON, C. MADELINE. High, Wide and Deep. New York: The John
      Day Company, 1938.
          Explores the physical and social needs of the young
      child; some discussion of the value of creative dramatics
      as an instrument of maturation.

1519 "Drama from the Ground Up." Recreation, 39 (August 1945),
      233-34, 278.
          Distinguishes between creative dramatics per se, and
      other, more formal, aspects of creative drama.

1520 EVANS, ELIZABETH. "Creative Dramatics: Children Love It."
      Players Magazine, 25 (February 1949), 112-13.
          A brief history of the use of creative dramatics in
      Seattle, Washington.

1521 FITZGERALD, BURDETTE. "Children's Theatre Conference."
      Players Magazine, 24 (December 1947), 64.
          Concerned primarily with creative dramatics work done
      at the Third Annual Meeting at the University of Indiana.

1522 FORBUSH, WILLIAM BYRON. Dramatics in the Home. 3rd ed.
      New York: Abingdon Press, 1914.
          Discusses dramatic play and pantomime in the home and
      church school.

Children's Theatre and Creative Dramatics

1523 GARDNER, EMELYN E. AND ELOISE RAMSEY. A Handbook of Children's Literature: Methods and Materials. Chicago:
Scott, Foresman and Company, 1927.
Offers the opinion that not all children's literature
is appropriate to informal drama, and evaluates the
types of literature that are.

1524 GWIN, E. H. Story Hour Becomes an Asset." Wilson Library
Bulletin, 18 (May 1944), 648-49.
Covers story dramatization in the library.

1525 HORTON, LOUISE. "Children's Theatre Conference." Players
Magazine, 21 (October 1944), 20-21.
Reports on the initial meeting of the Children's Theatre
Conference; both creative dramatics and children's theatre
subjects are covered.

1526 JACKSON, RUTH E. "The Dramatic Instinct." Master's thesis,
Ohio Wesleyan University, 1913.
Concerned with the dramatic instinct in children and
adults; gives some attention to story dramatization and
informal dramatics.

1527 MARKEY, FRANCES V. Imaginative Behavior of Preschool
Children. New York: Bureau of Publication, Columbia
University Teachers College, 1935.
A methodological approach to the quantification of
children's imaginative and dramatic play.

1528 RICHARDSON, NORMAN E. Ed. The Dramatic Instinct in
Children. 4th ed. New York: Abingdon Press, 1914.
Recommends informal drama in the home and school for
its moral and inspirational value.

1529 RUSSELL, ELIZABETH FATHERSON. "Dramatic Activities and
Preferences of Children from Two Socio-Economic Back-
grounds." Ph.D. dissertation, Columbia University
Teachers College, 1941.
Numerous dramatic exercises with children of high and
low economic backgrounds are discussed.

1530 SAWYER, RUTH. The Way of the Storyteller. New York: The
Viking Press, 1945.

A comprehensive introduction to the art of the story-
teller; by implication, the book discusses techniques of
introducing a story into a creative dramatics situation.

Children's Theatre and Creative Dramatics

CREATIVE DRAMATICS

See also the following entries. 119, 122-23, 129, 147, 151, 158, 201, 268, 270, 312, 325-27, 336, 353, 358-59, 368, 372, 377, 385, 388-89, 394, 400-01, 410, 415, 420, 431, 548, 559-60, 583, 587, 590, 593, 595, 597, 618, 638, 647, 869, 897, 900, 904, 911, 974, 1206, 1420, 1422, 1428, 1430, 1434, 1447, 1459, 1463, 1502, 1519, 1651, 1662, 1675-76, 1679, 1715, 1717-18, 1732, 1755-56, 2237.

DEVELOPMENT: 1950-1973

1531 ALDRICH, DOROTHY. "Children of the City Streets." Children's Theatre Conference Newsletter, 15 (November 1966), 14-16. Describes a Pittsburgh project with black, inner-city children; results were improved self-image for the child and a modification of the authority-antipathy syndrome.

1532 "Arts and Humanities Programs in Action." Instructor, 79 (May 1960), 46-52. Cites two cities, Philadelphia and University City, Missouri, that have ongoing projects in creative dramatics.

1533 BELL, CAMPTON. "Winifred on the Wing." Children's Theatre Conference Newsletter, 2 (November 1951), 3. Covers a broad range of Miss Ward's activities.

1534 _____. "Winifred Ward." Children's Theatre Conference Newsletter, 2 (May 1951), 4. Comments on Miss Ward's retirement from Northwestern University, and surveys her career in creative dramatics and children's theatre.

1535 BIRDSALL, RUTH. "About Dramatizing Stories." Instructor, 62 (May 1953), 78-79. Amplifies on the ideas established in Winifred Ward's book Stories to Dramatize.

1536 BIROC, JOHN. "Creative Dramatics and the Adolescent." Children's Theatre Review, 22:1 (1973), 14-23. Gives a thorough evaluation of the state of creative dramatics in 1973; discusses objectives and techniques, and comments on the extent of educational material available.

1537 BLACKIE, PAMELA; BESS BULLOUGH; DORIS NASH. Drama. New York: Citation Press, 1972. Of particular importance are the essays "Basic and Expressive Movement - A World of Action, Thought and Feeling" (Bullough), and "Drama in the Infant School" (Nash).

DEVELOPMENT: 1950-1973

1538   BLAND, JANE C. Art of the Young Child: Understanding and
        Encouraging Creative Growth in Children Three to Five.
        Rev. ed. New York: Museum of Modern Art, 1968.
            Covers a multi-level, mixed-media approach to stimula-
        ting young children.

1539   BODWIN, SHIRLEY. "How We Banish Fears at Our House."
        Parents' Magazine, 29 (August 1954), 34-36, 100-03.
            The "how" is a creative dramatics approach to
        understanding uncomfortable situations and emotions.

1540   BRADLEY, DAVID. "Why Teach Drama?" Opinion: The Journal of
        the South Australian English Teachers' Association, 12
        (August 1968), 19-27.
            The author advocates the integration of improvisation
        and creative drama into a literary study of drama.

1541   BRADY, BEA. "The Play's Not the Thing." Grade Teacher, 85
        (March 1968), 82-83.
            The actors and the actions are the thing according
        to this discussion of informal dramatics techniques.

1542   BRENES, ELEANOR H. "Make Your Own Play." Grade Teacher, 74
        (March 1957), 38, 86, 89.
            Shows how a teacher and students co-operatively can
        create a play; has general application to all creative
        dramatics situations.

1543   BURGER, ISABEL B. Creative Play Acting: Learning Through
        Drama. 2nd ed. New York: The Ronald Press, 1966.
            Focuses on creative dramatics and pantomime; numerous
        examples are given.

1544   CALABRIA, FRANCES R. "The WHY of Creative Dramatics."
        Instructor, 77 (August-September 1967), 182, 186.
            A brief definition of creative dramatics and what it
        can accomplish for the primary child are given.

1545   "Children's Theatre Founder 'Retires': Isable B. Burger."
        Children's Theatre Review, 17 (August 1968), 12.
            Recounts Isabel Burger's work in creative dramatics
        after she retired as Director of the Children's Theatre
        Association of Baltimore.

1546   "Creativity in Impersonation." Instructor, 71 (May 1962), 3,
        89.
            Calls for purity in role-playing; the author would
        eliminate all the mechanical trappings of children's
        theatre except creativity.

CREATIVE DRAMATICS

1547   CROSSCUP, RICHARD. Children and Dramatics. New York: Charles
        Scribners, Sons, 1966.
            Concerned primarily with creative dramatics and its
        related arts, for the child eight-years-old and up.

1548   DENNIS, BARBARA. "Christmas is a Seasonal Happening."
        Children's Theatre Review, 18 (May 1969), 18-20.
            The author discusses a child's-eye view of Christmas
        as demonstrated through a creative dramatics workshop;
        includes a tongue-in-cheek evaluation of the audience's
        [parents'] reaction.

1549   DINGES, SUSAN S. "Experiment at KCU." Players Magazine, 36
        (May 1960), 185-86.
            Traces an eight-year history of the development of
        creative dramatics programs at the University of Kansas
        City, Missouri.

1550   DOOLITTLE, JOYCE. "Fifty Stories for Creative Dramatics."
        Master's thesis, Indiana University [State of Indiana],
        1955.

1551   Du BOIS, ELOISE BARCLAY. "Values and Techniques of Creative
        Dramatics." Childhood Education, 47 (April 1971), 368-70.
            A companion piece to "Expanding the Child's World
        Through Drama and Movement" by Eloise Hayes, in the same
        issue.

1552   FAVAT, F. ANDRE. "Child and Tale: An Hypothesis on the
        Origins of Interest." Ph.D. dissertation, Harvard
        University, 1971.
            Although this dissertation is not directly related to
        creative dramatics, Dr. Favat's exploration of the child's
        interest in and need for fantasy and reality at different
        levels in his cognisance is pertinent to the choice of
        materials for children's theatre and creative dramatics,
        as well as participatory drama.

1553   FERIK, M. I. "Crescendo: Creative Dramatics in Philadelphia;
        Free Library Program." Wilson Library Bulletin, 43
        (October 1958), 160-64.

1554   FIELD, CAROLYN W. "Creative Dramatics in Philadelphia."
        Wilson Library Bulletin, 40 (December 1955), 344, 349-51.
            Recommends the use of creative dramatics in library
        situations.

DEVELOPMENT: 1950-1973

1555 FITZGERALD, BURDETTE S. World Tales for Creative Dramatics
and Storytelling. Englewood Cliffs, New Jersey: Prentice-
Hall, 1962.
More than a hundred stories are included; the appendix,
which catalogues stories by age groups, is particularly
valuable.

1556 "Five-Year Report of the Creative Dramatics Community Program." Seattle, Washington: The Seattle, Washington, PTA
Council, 1953.

1557 GAMBLE, TERI KWAL AND MICHAEL WESLEY GAMBLE. "The Theatre of
Creative Involvement: An Introduction to Drama for
Children." Speech Teacher, 22 (January 1973), 41-43.
Traces the impact of dramatic activities and story-
telling on the creative awareness and development of
young children.

1558 GARRETT, CHARLOTTE. "Her Majesty's Hour." Instructor, 65
(April 1956), 43, 61.
Describes a creatively enacted May Day Celebration.

1559 GOULD, ROCHELLE BARBARA. "Criteria for the Selection of
Poetry for Creative Dramatics." Master's thesis,
University of Wisconsin, 1963.

1560 HAAGA, AGNES. "Creative Dramatics: An Excellent Try-Out
Method." Dramatics, 16 (March 1955), 6-7.

1561 _____. "The White Conference and CTC." Children's Theatre
Conference Newsletter, 9 (May 1960), 3-4.
Although this article includes commentary on both formal and informal dramatics, emphasis is laid on creative
dramatics and its place in the educational system.

1562 _____. AND PATRICIA A. RANDLES. Supplementary Materials for
Use in Creative Dramatics with Younger Children. Seattle,
Washington: University of Washington Press, 1952.

1563 HALE, PAT. Ed. Participation Theatre for Young Audiences.
New York: New Plays for Children, 1972.
The handbook includes a definition of participatory
theatre as it is practiced in the USA, with comments by
various practitioners; the second part is concerned with
technical aspects of participatory theatre.

1564 HANSEN, SHIRLEY. "The Joy of Creating Your Own Play."
Grade Teacher, 82 (December 1964), 10-11, 92-94.
Lists five basic steps for creative dramatics and
applies them to the process of creating a play.

CREATIVE DRAMATICS

1565   HARTLEY, RUTH E; LAWRENCE K. FRANK; ROBERT M. GOLDENSON.
        Understanding Children's Play. 2nd ed. New York:
        Columbia University Press, 1964.
            Two chapters are devoted to a discussion of the place
        of dramatic play in the growth of the young child.

1566   HAYWOOD, MARY ELIZABETH. "Creative Dramatics: (How I Do It)."
        Instructor, 64 (October 1954), 35.
            Explores the process of directing creative dramatics
        for the beginning teacher or leader.

1567   HILL, WILHEMINA; HELEN K. MACINTOSH; ARNE RANDALL. How
        Children Can Be Creative. Washington, D.C.:Government
        Printing Office, 1954.
            Several pages of this brief bulletin deal particularly
        with dramatic expression.

1568   HIRSH, KENNETH WILLIAM. "Children's Discrimination Between
        and Reaction to Actuality and Make-Believe in Violent
        Television/Film Messages." Ph.D. dissertation, University
        of Oregon, 1969.
            While this dissertation is concerned primarily with the
        reaction of 6, 7, 9, and 13 year olds to mass media
        violence, the hypothesis dealing with a child's reality
        concept formation can be applied to the way he acts out
        violence and reacts to it.

1569   HODGSON, JOHN AND ERNEST RICHARDS. Improvisation: Discovery
        and Creativity in Drama. New York: Barnes and Noble,
        1967.

1570   HORTON, LOUISE C. "Drama for Children." Dramatics, 22
        (December 1950), 20-22.
            Expands on and evaluates the ideas established in
        Isable Burger's book Creative Play Acting.

1571   HOWARD, VERNON. Ed. Complete Book of Children's Theatre.
        Garden City, New York: Doubleday and Company, 1969.
            A somewhat weak recital of games, jokes, riddles, and
        so forth, loosely related to child drama.

1572   HUGHES, ANNA MAY. "Participatory Children's Theatre."
        Dramatics, 44 (March 1973), 17-19.
            A discussion of the Brian Way methodology.

172

DEVELOPMENT: 1950-1973

1573   HUTSELL, WALTER EUGENE. "Personality Factors of Dramatic
       Creativity." Master's thesis, University of Arkansas,
       1961.

1574   HYMES, JAMES L. "Stimulating Good Dramatic Play." Grade
       Teacher, 81 (June 1964), 24, 92-98.
           Concerned with the dramatic activities of five-year
       olds.

1575   "Institute for Creative Dramatics Teachers Set." Children's
       Theatre Review, 17 (May 1968), 12, 19.
           Announces a six-week advanced course in creative
       dramatics at the University of Minnesota, and its
       objectives.

1576   IRWIN, ELEANOR CHIMA. "The Effect of a Program of Creative
       Dramatics Upon Personality as Measured by the California
       Test of Personality, Sociograms, Teacher Ratings and
       Grades." Ph.D. dissertation, University of Pittsburgh,
       1963.
           The results were positive.

1577   JOHNSON, RICHARD C. "Excerpts from Printed Recommendations
       of the White House Conference." Children's Theatre
       Conference Newsletter, 10 (August 1960), 3.

1578   KARIOTH, EMIL JOSEPH. "Creative Dramatics as an Aid in
       Developing Creative Thinking Abilities." Ph.D. disserta-
       tion, University of Minnesota, 1966.
           The results of this experiment with fourth grade
       children suggest that creative dramatics does not
       appreciably affect "the culturally disadvantaged child's
       attitude toward problem-solving and self-concept."

1579   _____. "Creative Dramatics as an Aid in Developing Creative
       Thinking Abilities." Speech Teacher, 19 (November 1970),
       301-09.
           For annotation, see above.

1580   KASE, CHARLES ROBERT. Ed. Stories for Creative Acting:
       Stories Recommended and Used Successfully by Leading
       Creative Dramatics Directors and Teachers. New York:
       Samuel French, 1961.

1581   KELLY, ELIZABETH Y. The Magic If: Stanislavski for Children.
       Baltimore: National Educational Press, 1973.
           The method discussed leads children to ask the question
       "What would I do if ..." and then answer it dramatically.

173

CREATIVE DRAMATICS

1582 KERMAN, GERTRUDE L. Plays and Creative Ways with Children. Irvington-on-Hudson, New York: Harvey House, 1961.
The first part of this book is devoted to an exploration of creative dramatics techniques with young children; the second part includes one-act plays suitable for performance.

1583 KESTER, DOROTHY. "The CTC at Tufts." Educational Theatre Journal, 9 (December 1957), 330-35.
The majority of this conference is related to creative dramatics.

1584 KINGSLEY, WILLIAM HARSTEAD. "Happy Endings, Poetic Justice, and the Depth and Strength of Characterization in American Children's Drama: A Critical Analysis." Ph.D. dissertation, University of Pittsburgh, 1964.
Gives arguments for and against happy endings in children's plays.

1585 LACKEY, ORLEAN. "Children's Theatre: Dramatic Renaissance in Alabama." Players Magazine, 35 (January 1959), 81.
Recounts the work of Mrs. Robert Schwartz in the Birmingham area and the financial support she receives from Loveman's Department Store.

1586 LAWTON, CHARLOTTE STEINKAMP. "A Study in the Preparation and Use of Video Tapes of Sessions in Creative Dramatics." Master's thesis, University of Northern Iowa, 1968.

1587 LEASE, RUTH AND GERALDINE B. SIKS. Creative Dramatics in Home, School and Community. New York: Harper and Brothers, 1952.
The book, proper, is concerned with the various techniques of creative dramatics; the three appendices - materials for dramatization, dramatic play and pantomime, and a bibliography - are particularly valuable.

1588 LORCH, THOMAS M. "Sensitivity Training and the Teaching of Humanities." Unpublished typescript, available on ERIC fiche #ED041910.
The author devotes much space to improvisation and informal drama.

1589 "Loveman's Department Store and Creative Dramatics." Children's Theatre Review, 16 (August 1967), 27-28.
Concerned with the financial assistance from a department store in Alabama which supports creative dramatics and a drama consultant for statewide teachers.

Children's Theatre and Creative Dramatics

1590   McINTYRE, BARBARA AND RUTH HELVENSTON. "An Experimental
        Workshop - Creative Activities for Children." For the
        Children's Civic Theatre Society, Inc., August, 1954.
        [typescript]

1591   MILLER, VERA V. "Creativity and Intelligence in the Arts."
        Education, 82 (April 1962), 488-95.
            Among other things, this article surveys the relation-
        ship between intelligence and the dramatic arts; it
        hypothesizes that improvisational talents are less
        dependent on intelligence than music or writing.

1592   MORTENSEN, LOUISE HOVDE. "Creative Drama Place Exercises."
        Elementary English, 31 (March 1954), 163.
            Describes Portia Boynton's Creative Workshop at Drake
        University.

1593   MOSS, ALLYN "Tigers in the Classroom." Mademoiselle, 42
        (January 1956), 118-19, 132-33.
            Comments briefly on the work of Ann Shaw in Evanston,
        Diane Samuelson in Seattle, and Rutheen Rubin in Rockway,
        New York.

1594   MUSSELMAN, VIRGINIA. Informal Dramatics. New York: National
        Recreation Association, 1952.
            Covers a wide range of dramatic activities, including
        pantomime, improvisation, skits, and so forth.

1595   NORTON, SANDRA K. "Creative Dramatics: Methods, Techniques,
        and Future Directions." Children's Theatre Review,
        22:1 (1973), 5-8.
            Advocates that curricula be devised "which encourage
        our students to take and take and take and experience and
        experience creative dramatics throughout their teacher
        training."

1596   OBERLE, MARCELLA. "The CTC at Michigan City." Educational
        Theatre Journal, 11 (December 1959), 296-303.
            Covers the Fifteenth Annual Convention of the
        Children's Theatre Conference.

1597   OSBORNE, ROSALIE HOFF. "Old Tales Dramatized for Children."
        Master's thesis, Sul Ross State College, Texas, 1951.

1598   PICKARD, P. M. I Could a Tale Unfold. New York: The Humani-
        ties Press, 1961.
            The author analyzes the function of fear and horror in
        children's literature; has application to story telling
        and informal dramatization.

CREATIVE DRAMATICS

1599   PIQUETTE, JULIA C.   "A Survey of the Contemporary Outlook
       Relative to the Teaching of Creative Dramatics as
       Evidenced in Selected Writings in the Field, 1929-1959."
       Ph.D. dissertation, Northwestern University, 1963.

1600   PIRTLE, ANN B.   "The Potential of Creative Dramatics."
       Instructor, 71 (March 1962), 6, 103.
            States that creative dramatics helps a child to cope
       with a changing and somewhat unpredictable world.

1601   PITCHER, EVELYN G. AND ERNEST PRELINGER.   Children Telling
       Stories.   New York: International Universities Press,
       1963.
            An in-depth discussion of how children, two to five
       years old, create and tell stories; included is a
       discussion of frequently recurring themes.

1602   POLSKY, MILTON.   "The Arts: Acting's in the Bag."   Teacher,
       90 (December 1972), 57-58.
            Step-by-step procedure for opening up improvisation,
       using the paperbag prop technique.

1603   _____.   "Children Become Quick-Change Artists."   Teacher, 90
       (May/June 1973), 64-65.
            Polsky discusses several theatre games that activate
       the child's imagination.

1604   _____.   "Say It with Shadows."   Dramatics, 45 (May 1974),
       18-21.
            Describes a combination informal-formal drama
       procedure: with people, puppets, anything.   Directs some
       attention to shadow role-playing as a simple method to
       forestall inhibitions.

1605   _____.   "Sono-Mime: A New Theatre Game."   Dramatics, 44 (May
       1973), 18-19, 31.
            "Sono-mime can be simply defined as follows: Two
       players act out a situation in pantomime while two other
       players on the sidelines vocalize their dialogue and/or
       sounds."   Article discusses procedures, development,
       staging, evaluation and uses.

1606   _____.   "To the Moon: Learning with Creative Dramatics."
       Instructor, 79 (January 1970), 69-70.
            Concerned with creative dramatics as applied to space
       travel.

CHILDREN'S THEATRE AND CREATIVE DRAMATICS

DEVELOPMENT: 1950-1973

1607 _____. "Twist and Turns: A Theatre Game." Dramatics, 45
      (January 1974), 16-17.
            An interesting variation on some Spolin improvisation-
      al techniques, generally applicable to most creative
      drama situations, plus some "pointers for participants."

1608 POPOVICH, JAMES. "Essential Considerations in the Teaching
      of Creative Dramatics." Speech Teacher, 8 (November
      1959), 283-87.
            Traces a twenty-five year history of the teaching of
      creative dramatics in colleges and universities.

1609 RANDALL, GEOFF. "Creative Drama: Origins and Use." Opinion:
      The Journal of the South Australian English Teachers
      Association, 11 (December 1967), 35-39.
            Makes an association between primitive self-expression
      and creative drama; concludes with suggestions for initial
      work in creative dramatics.

1610 RANDOLPH, BARBARA. "Fifth-Century B.C. Greek Theatre as a
      Basis for Teaching Creative Dramatics for Children."
      Master's thesis, Baylor University, 1966.

1611 RINGNALDA, MARGARET B. "Plays for Living and Learning."
      Players Magazine, 33 (November 1956), 32-33.
            Describes creative dramatics activity and puppetry in
      Salem, Oregon.

1612 ROYAL, CLAUDIA. Storytelling. Nashville, Tennessee:
      Broadman Press, 1955.
            Gives a partial consideration of improvisation and
      storytelling.

1613 SAMUELSON, D. "Why Not Take a Summer Course in Creative
      Dramatics?" Instructor, 65 (June 1956), 65, 75.
            Discusses the teacher's need for a multi-level
      approach to the creative and creating child.

1614 SCHWARTZ, SHEILA. "New Methods in Creative Dramatics."
      Elementary English, 36 (November 1959), 484-87.
            Describes the creative arts program at the Children's
      Center for Creative Arts at Adelphi College.

1615 SHANE, PHYLLIS J. "Dramatization." American Childhood, 35
      (May 1950), 19-20.
            Discusses the values of creative dramatics and panto-
      mime to the reticent child and the slow learner.

CREATIVE DRAMATICS

1616 SHARPHAM, JOHN RAYMOND. A Descrptive Study of Creative
Drama at the Secondary Level in England." Ph.D.
dissertation, University of Colorado, 1972.
Shows that creative drama in England, especially on
the secondary level, is much more extensive than in the
USA, although not radically different in approach.

1617 SHAW, A. M. "Taxonomical Study of the Nature and Behavioral
Objectives of Creative Dramatics." Educational Theatre
Journal, 22 (December 1970), 361-72.

1618 SHEDLOCK, MARIE. The Art of the Story-Teller. New York:
Dover Publishers, 1952.
Discusses the techniques that must be mastered before
story telling (in schools, libraries or creative dramatics
situations) can become an art.

1619 SIKS, GERALDINE B. Children's Literature for Dramatization:
An Anthology. New York: Harper and Row, 1964.
A collection of poetry and stories for elementary and
middle school students to use in creative dramatics.

1620 _____. Creative Dramatics: An Art for Children. Harper and
Brothers, 1958.
A primer for course work, on the college or university
level.

1621 SLADE, PETER. Child Drama. London: University of London
Press, 1954.
Stresses the values of creative dramatics, as opposed
to the more formalized children's theatre; an excellent
source book on the basic philosophy of child drama in
England.

1622 _____. Dramatherapy as an Aid to Becoming a Person. East
Dulwich, England: Greaves, 1959.
Concerned primarily with the function of psychodrama
and role-playing as they apply to the child.

1623 _____. Experience of Spontaneity. New York: Fernhill House,
1968.
Delves into the uses of improvisation and child drama.

1624 _____. Introduction to Child Drama. Mystic, Connecticut:
Verry, Lawrence, 1958.
Summarizes the work published earlier in Child Drama;
the book concludes with a series of questions and answers
related to creative dramatics, mime and improvisation.

CHILDREN'S THEATRE AND CREATIVE DRAMATICS

DEVELOPMENT: 1950-1973

1625 SPOLIN, VIOLA. Improvisation for the Theatre: A Handbook of
Teaching and Directing Techniques. Evanston, Illinois:
Northwestern University Press, 1963.
Derived from the author's experiences as Director of
the Young Actor's Company in Los Angeles; the improvisational techniques and theatre games are of particular
value to the creative dramatics leader.

1626 TAYLOR, LOREN. Informal Dramatics for Young Children.
Minneapolis: Burgess Publishing Company, 1965.
The first part of this book evaluates dramatic play
in terms of children, leaders and material available;
the second and third parts cover mime, story plays,
action songs, and rhythmic activities.

1627 TAYLOR, MARGARET PALMER FISK. Time for Discovery. Philadelphia: United Church Press, 1964.
Concerned with the dimensions of dramatic movement;
shows its application to general and religious situations.

1628 "Theatres Find Improvisational Plays Successful Ventures."
Children's Theatre Review, 18 (May 1969), 14, 18.
The author discusses creative dramatics and role-
playing techniques as explored by the Eastside Theatre
of St. Paul, Minnesota, and at Washington, D.C.'s Arena
Stage.

1629 TUCKER, JOANNE KLINEMAN. "Movement in Creative Dramatics."
Children's Theatre Conference Newsletter, 15 (May 1966),
9-12.
Stresses the conscious use of movement and rhythmic
activities in creative dramatics.

1630 TURNER, IAN. Ed. Cinderella Dressed in Yella: The First
Attempt at a Definitive Study of Australian Children's
Play Rhymes. New York: Taplinger, 1972.
Material in this source book has the potential to be
expanded into creative dramatics activities.

1631 TYAS, BILLI. Child Drama in Action. New York: Drama Book
Specialists, 1971.
A handbook describing and elaborating on twenty-two
creative dramatics each based on a particular theme,
i. e. "improvising listening ability, awareness of
climax, de-climax," and so forth; also includes lesson
plans.

179

CREATIVE DRAMATICS

1632   VAN TASSEL, KATRINA AND MILLIE GREIMANN. Creative Dramatiza-
        tion. New York: Macmillan, 1973.
            A comprehensive approach to creative dramatics,
        movement and rhythmic activities with very young
        children.

1633   WALKER, PAMELA PRINCE. Seven Steps to Creative Children's
        Dramatics. New York: Hill and Wang, 1957.
            The final goal of the work discussed in this book is
        play production, via creative dramatics.

1634   WARD, WINIFRED. "Creative Dramatics." Recreation, 47
        (November 1954), 547-48.
            Gives a step-by-step definition of creative dramatics.

1635   _____. "How to Dramatize a Story." American Junior Red
        Cross News, (January 1951), 14-15.
            Discusses creative dramatics without a leader.

1636   _____. "How to Play a Story." Asia Calling, 5 (April 1951),
        8-9.
            A reprint of the above.

1637   _____. "Like Johnnie Appleseed." Cameo, 19 (February 1952),
        20.
            Discusses the author's activities since she retired.

1638   _____. Stories to Dramatize. Anchorage, Kentucky: Children's
        Theatre Press, 1952.
            An anthology of graded stories to be used in creative
        dramatics.

1639   WATKINS, MARY JANE LARSON. "Tenth Annual Children's Theatre
        Meeting." Educational Theatre Journal, 6 (December 1954),
        348-54.
            Discusses Winifred Ward's demonstrations of creative
        dramatics.

1640   WAY, BRIAN. Development Through Drama. New York: Humanities
        Press, 1967.
            Shows the development of awareness and its relation-
        ship to creative drama, improvisation, rhythm and
        characterization, for the beginning and advanced student.

1641   WEIS, LOIS DEVOE. "Creative Dramatics: A Comparative Study."
        Master's thesis, Ohio State University, 1966.

DEVELOPMENT: 1950-1973

(WEIS, LOIS DEVOE)
Compares and contrasts a year's work in creative dramatics in a classroom situation, and as it was developed at a community junior college.

1642 WHITNEY, DON. "Instant Replay in Children's Theatre." Dramatics, 43 (January 1972), 36.
A commentary on Thespian Troup 934 of Tillamook, Oregon's performance of The Clown and His Circus, and on an instant replay of the work by the audience through improvisation.

1643 "Winifred Ward Receives Honorary Degree for Michigan." Children's Theatre Review, 19 (November 1970), 1, 24.

1644 WRIGHT, MARY ELIN SOMMERS. "The Effects of Creative Drama on Person Perception." Ph.D. dissertation, University of Minnesota, 1972.
Studies creative dramatics with boys and girls ten to eleven years old. "A hypothesis growing from this study is that girls learn daily in our society to be sensitive to the thoughts and feelings of others but boys apparently receive less experience in this area. Creative drama is a demonstrated means for helping boys develop role-playing skills."

1645 YORK, ELEANOR. "Notes on the 23rd Annual Meeting." Children's Theatre Conference Newsletter, 9 (February 1960), 2-3.
Gives specific recommendations for teaching creative dramatics in teacher's colleges, based on suggestions made by Campton Bell.

See also the following entries. 16, 43, 67, 110, 112-13, 127, 133, 142, 191, 246, 253, 257, 280, 286, 288, 293, 300, 322, 328, 335, 347, 355-56, 363-64, 366, 369, 374, 387, 392, 395, 398-99, 403, 407-08, 411, 416, 424, 428, 430, 432, 504, 530, 653-54, 661, 664, 666-67, 672-74, 685, 703-05, 707, 713, 717, 732, 737, 747, 758, 790, 794, 808, 810, 830, 838, 1012-13, 1019-21, 1040, 1042-44, 1047-48, 1050-51, 1063, 1070, 1081, 1092, 1155, 1159, 1162, 1164, 1166, 1170, 1174, 1200, 1207, 1215, 1221, 1250, 1321, 1324, 1341, 1346, 1349, 1364, 1373, 1439-40, 1454-55, 1462, 1500-01, 1505, 1794, 1803, 1809, 1819, 1856, 1931, 2031, 2038, 2194.

CREATIVE DRAMATICS

IN EDUCATION AND THE SCHOOLS, GENERAL: PRE-1950

1646 ALDER, LOUISE M. AND CAROLINE W. BARBOUR. "Suggestive Curriculum Material for the Four and Five Year Old Kindergartens, Part II." Childhood Education, 6 (December 1929), 165-72.
Advocates "spontaneous" dramatics in the classroom, and gives some creative dramatics techniques.

1647 ALLEN, MABLE CLARE. "Creative Dramatics as a Factor in Elementary Education." Master's thesis, Northwestern University, 1929.
Gives a history of creative dramatics in education.

1648 ANDERSON, LEONORA AND FLORENCE McKINLEY. An Outline of Physical Education for the First and Second Grades. New York: A. S. Barnes and Company, 1930.
Of primary interest in this book are Parts I, II, and IV, which cover dramatic play with and without music; planned programs are given.

1649 BERMAN, SADYE A. "Primary Pupils Create Plays." Instructor, 55 (September 1946), 20, 88.
Creative dramatics leads to a written and performed play.

1650 BICE, MARGARET GARRET. "Let's Play It." Childhood Education, 8 (May 1932), 463-467.

1651 BOAS, GUY AND HOWARD HAYDEN. Eds. School Drama, Its Practice and Theory. London: Methuen, 1938.
Concerned with drama in the classroom, dramatic play of young children, and the uses of mime, movement and ballads.

1652 BROWN, CORINNE. "Dramatics - A Creative Expression." Childhood Education, 4 (September 1927), 21-25.
Covers a wide spectrum of drama-related subjects in the classroom.

1653 BROWN, EVA. "Charm of Dramatization for Primary Pupils." Normal Instructor and Primary Plans, 34 (November 1924), 60-99.
Discusses the social and emotional, as well as creative, benefits of informal drama through the vehicle of a spontaneous presentation of "Hiawatha".

Children's Theatre and Creative Dramatics

1654   BURGER, ISABEL B. "Creative Dramatics at School 122."
       Players Magazine, 25 (May 1949), 186.
           Concerned primarily with teacher training and its
       effects on a creative dramatics demonstration at School
       122.

1655   CAMPBELL, HELEN M. "Informality in Dramatics." Educational
       Methods, 8 (October 1933), 35-41.
           Gives many examples of the uses of creative dramatics
       in the classroom.

1656   CHAPEL, HAZEL HESTER. "The Function of Dramatization in the
       Elementary School." Master's thesis, North Texas State
       Teacher's College, 1945.
           Weighs the merits of formal and informal drama against
       each other and concludes that both have their values in
       the school situation.

1657   COLE, NATALIE. The Arts in the Classroom. New York: The
       John Day Company, 1940.
           Discusses creative work with the "average" child;
       emphasis is on rhythmic movement, dance and the graphic
       arts.

1658   COOK, HENRY CALDWELL. The Play Way: An Essay in Educational
       Method. 2nd ed. New York: Frederick A. Stokes Company,
       1917.
           Concerned with the child's dramatic responses to
       reading material; one section of the book is devoted to
       dramatic enactment of literature.

1659   CRAIG, ANNE T. "The Development of a Dramatic Element in
       Education." Pedagogical Seminary, 15 (March 1903), 75
       81.
           Recommends that written material be kept to a mimimum
       to aid creative drama.

1660   CURRAN, PAULINE L. "A First Grade Adventure with Trains."
       Progressive Education, 10 (January 1933), 41-45.
           After visiting a rail yard, children create a play;
       the author finds that their creative awareness is much
       improved after this venture.

1661   CURTIS, HENRY S. "The Drama in Education." School and
       Society, 29 (June 1929), 793-97.
           States that dramatic activity should not carry a
       pejorative moral implication because drama is a natural
       expression in children.

CREATIVE DRAMATICS

1662   D'AMICO, VICTOR E. "Theatre Art as Education." Progressive
       Education, 13 (May 1936), 356-63.
           Covers curriculum approaches in elementary and
       secondary education.

1663   ____. "Theatre as a Teaching Tool." Theatre Arts Magazine,
       28 (July 1944), 406-09.
           Suggests ways to use drama at all levels of education,
       from primary grades through college.

1664   DeMAY, AMY J. "A Fifth Grade Dramatization of the Pied Piper."
       Elementary English Review, 13 (October 1936), 220-22.
           Feels that even the most spontaneous creative drama
       must be started and contained by the teacher.

1665   DeVORE, EMILY. "Story-Playing in School." California Journal
       of Elementary Education, 14 (February 1946), 153-62.
           Discusses the benefits of informally dramatizing
       literature.

1666   DEWEY, JOHN. The School and Society. Rev. ed. Chicago:
       University of Chicago Press, 1915.
           A seminal work; gives justification for and impetus
       to much early work in Children's Theatre and Creative
       Dramatics.

1667   ____. AND EVELYN DEWEY. School of Tomorrow. New York:
       E. P. Dutton and Company, 1915.
           Evaluates the benefits and problems of integrating
       dramatics into the school system.

1668   DIXON, C. MADELEINE. Children Are Like That. New York: The
       John Day Company, 1930.
           Evaluates the needs of pre-school children; devotes
       one chapter to dramatic play.

1669   DURLAND, FRANCES CALDWELL. "The Child and Dramatics."
       Elementary School Journal, 38 (June 1938), 759-66.
           Author discusses the value of creative dramatics,
       using her own experiences as evidence.

1670   EDMONDS, MARY D. "Let's Help You Find It: Plays for Class-
       room Use." Progressive Education, 21 (February 1944),
       61, 95-97.
           A bibliography of formal plays for child actors plus
       an introduction.

IN EDUCATION AND THE SCHOOLS, GENERAL: PRE-1950

1671   ELMER, MARION SHORT. "A 'Scriptless' Play Prepared in
       School." Instructor, 55 (November 1945), 24-25, 60.
       Based on a Thanksgiving exercise.

1672   ERICKSON, HELEN. "Creative Expression in the Sunset Hill
       School." Progressive Education, 1 (July-August-September
       1924), 84-87.
       Explores work in history with third and sixth graders.

1673   _____. Nurturing Sincerity in Dramatics." Progressive
       Education, 8 (January 1931), 3-5.

1674   EVANS, CLARA. "Dramatic Play." Elementary Education, 26
       (April 1949), 201.
       Discusses the perimeters of dramatic play.

1675   FATHERSON, ELIZABETH. "Analysis of Methods and Practices in
       Dramatic Activities of Children." Master's thesis,
       University of Iowa, 1940.
       Explores all aspects of dramatic play in school, home,
       church, and social organizations.

1676   FERRIS, ANITA BROCKWAY. Following the Dramatic Instinct: An
       Elementary Handbook on the Use of Dramatics in Missionary
       and Religious Education. New York: Missionary Education
       Movement of the United States and Canada, 1922.

1677   FINLAY-JOHNSON, HARRIET. The Dramatic Method of Teaching.
       Boston: Ginn and Company, 1912.
       Advocates the use of informal drama to create an
       atmosphere of awareness in the kindergarten and elementary
       school child.

1678   FIRTH, ROXIE ANDREWS. "Creating School Assembly Programs."
       Instructor, 52 (May 1943), 13.

1679   FLAGELAND, ELEANORE. "An Evaluation of Creative Dramatics
       in Terms of Current Educational Objectives." Master's
       thesis, University of Denver, 1948.
       Slanted toward elementary education.

1680   FOSTER, JOSEPHINE C. AND KEITH E. HEADLEY. Education in the
       Kindergarten. 2nd ed. New York: American Book Company,
       1948.
       Emphasizes mental growth and self-awareness as out-
       growths of informal drama; advises the use of simple
       stories.

CREATIVE DRAMATICS

1681   FREAR, CAROLINE. "Imitation." Pedagogical Seminary, 4
        (April 1897), 382-86.
            A very early exploration of spontaneous dramatics and
        its adjunct disciplines.

1682   GARRISON, CHARLOTTE; EMMA D. SHEEHY; ALICE DAGLIESH. The
        Horace Mann Kindergarten for Five-Year-Old Children.
        New York: Bureau of Publications, Columbia University
        Teachers College, 1937.
            The curriculum of the Horace Mann School at Columbia
        University, which evolved over a fifty year period,
        included regular work in Creative Dramatics; methods are
        discussed.

1683   GILBERT, EDNA E. "Materials Suitable for Dramatization in
        the Intermediate Grades." Master's thesis, Northwestern
        University, 1930.
            Concerned with literature for informal drama.

1684   GRATZ, MARGARETTA. "The Auditorium and the Child." Platoon
        School, 12 (December 1938), 13-18.
            Advocates using the auditorium period for informal
        dramatics on all curricular subjects.

1685   GREEN, ETHEL M. Creative Activities in Second Grade: Building
        a Theatre. Milwaukee: Milwaukee State Normal School, n. d.
            Bulletin discusses creative steps involved in making
        a semi-formal play.

1686   GROUP OF TEACHERS OF THE SHADY HILL SCHOOL. "Acting Things
        Out." Progressive Education, 5 (January-February-March
        1928), 28-31.
            Discusses a variety of dramatic activities and their
        application to the entire school year: warm-ups, informal
        drama, and ultimately, one formal play.

1687   HALL, BETTY K. "A Consideration of Three Creative Dramatic
        Productions by Grade School Children Motiviated by Like
        Stimuli." Master's thesis, Ohio University, 1938.
            Analyzes the social, emotional and dramatic benefits
        of informal drama for fourth, fifth and sixth grade
        students.

1688   HALL, G. STANLEY. Educational Problems. 2 vols. New York:
        D. Appleton and Company, 1911.
            Slanted toward informal dramatics for elementary
        school children; discusses mime, dance, rhythmic movement
        and creative dramatics.

IN EDUCATION AND THE SCHOOLS, GENERAL: PRE-1950

1689   HARDY, MYRTLE. "The Place of Speech Arts in Auditorium
       Activities of the Platoon School." Master's thesis,
       University of Southern California, 1932.
           Gives the history of the Platoon School, founded by
       William Wirt, and shows the application of dramatic
       activities to it.

1690   HARTER, MILDRED. "Auditorium Round Table." Platoon School,
       3 (March-April-May 1929), 28-33.
           Report concerned the discussion of dramatics at the
       Fourth National Platoon School Conference.

1691   _____. "Auditorium Round Table." Platoon School, 3 (June-
       July-August 1929), 67-70.
           For annotation, see above.

1692   HILDRETH, GERTRUDE. Child Growth through Education: Effective
       Teaching in the Modern School. New York: Ronald Press
       Company, 1948.
           Author feels that dramatic play is vitally necessary
       to the future of progressive education.

1693   HIRSHBERG, BERNARD. "Classroom 'Movies' I." Instructor,
       52 (June 1943), 13, 60.
           Describes how the author used mime and creative
       dramatics to re-create a movie-like presentation.

1694   _____. "Classroom 'Movies' II." Instructor, 52 (September
       1943), 23, 67.
           For annotation, see above.

1695   _____. "Classroom 'Movies' III." Instructor, 52 (October
       1943), 26.
           For annotation, see above.

1696   HOLMES, EDMOND GORE ALEXANDER. What Is and What Might Be: A
       Study of Education in General and Elementary Education in
       Particular. New York: E. P. Dutton and Company, 1912.
           Author describes a utopian school of the future;
       creative dramatics figure heavily in his predictions.

1697   HOLMES, MARGARET C. "Play Activities in the First Grade."
       Childhood Education, 2 (December 1925), 174-76.
           Emphasis is on rhythm, movement and their application
       to creative dramatics.

CREATIVE DRAMATICS

1698   HOLSTEIN, PAULINE N. "Creative Expression." Instructor, 53
(September 1944), 27-28, 56, 65.
Explores some steps in the creative process of young
children: idea, written expression, then dramatic
expression.

1699   HORN, JOHN LOUIS AND THOMAS WHITE CHAPMAN. The Education of
Children in the Primary Grades. New York: Farrar and
Rinehart, 1935.
Gives some attention to informal dramatization from
literary sources and storytelling.

1700   HOROWITZ, TILLIE. "The Play-Acting Period." Elementary
English, 26 (January 1949), 32-34.
Defines the steps necessary to have successful
spontaneous dramatic play.

1701   _____. "What Shall We Play?" Grade Teacher, 64 (May 1947),
44, 88-89.
Included is a list of thirty-nine stories suitable for
informal dramatics; evaluations and suggestions are given.

1702   HUNTER, MAUDE W. "Creative Dramatics." Instructor, 54
(February 1945), 26-27.
Emphasizes the need for critical evaluation, by
children, of each creative dramatics session; based on
the author's observation of six first-grade classes.

1703   JANDELL, EULA MARIE. "Creative Dramatics in the Primary
Curriculum." Master's thesis, University of Utah, 1934.
An outline for creative dramatics work in grades one
through three, for an academic year, is given.

1704   JERSILD, ARTHUR T. AND RUTH J. TASCH. Children's Interests
and What They Suggest for Education. New York: Bureau
of Publications, Columbia University Teachers College,
1949.
Gives some attention to the spontaneous dramatic
activities of primary school children.

1705   JOHNSON, GEORGE ELLSWORTH. Education by Plays and Games.
Boston: Ginn and Company, 1907.
Concerned with the physical development of young
children; devotes some time to dramatic and imaginative
play activities.

188

Children's Theatre and Creative Dramatics

1706   JOHNSON, HARRIET M. "Dramatic Play in the Nursery School." Progressive Education, 8 (January 1931), 16-19.

1707   JOHNSON, MARY T. "Creative Dramatics." Instructor, 54 (June 1945), 11.
Discusses a primary school creative dramatization of Peter Pan.

1708   JUNIGER, OLGA. "We Played That in School." Instructor, 42 (October 1933), 21.
Summarizes techniques for teaching kindergarten and first grade students about safety and how to react to emergencies.

1709   KETLER, FRANK C. "Dramatics in the Elementary School." School Executive, 56 (June 1937), 396-97.
Explores many facets of informal drama and cites general sources for creative enactment.

1710   KNOX, ROSE B. "New Schools for Old." Progressive Education, 4 (April-May-June 1927), 95-99.
Discusses dance, mime, puppetry, choral drama, architecture and their relationship to creative activities.

1711   LAMBERT, CLARA. "Identification through Play." Childhood Education, 25 (May 1949), 402-05.
Advocates that the child dramatize events that are contemporary to his immediate situation: a quasi-form of role playing.

1712   LANE, ROBERT HILL. The Teacher in the Modern Elementary School. Boston: Houghton Mifflin Company, 1941.
Part of the teacher's methodology, according to the author, should include work in informal drama related to the language arts.

1713   LEE, JOSEPH. Play in Education. New York: National Recreation Association, 1942.
Concerned with the dramatic play and recreation of very young children and elementary school children; the emphasis is on the educational merits of directed play.

1714   LENSKI, LOIS. "Helping Children to Create." Childhood Education, 26 (November 1949), 101-05.
Places the burden of creative stimulation, at its inception, on the instructor.

CREATIVE DRAMATICS

1715   LEWIS, MARY H. <u>An Adventure with Children</u>. New York: Macmillan, 1928.
The author describes her twelve years of work in
elementary education; many creative dramatics methods are
discussed.

1716   MALVEY, CLARA M. "Dramatizing the Toy Store." <u>Instructor</u>,
43 (December 1933), 31, 66-67.

1717   MERRILL, JOHN. "Dramatics a Mode of Study." <u>Progressive
Education</u>, 8 (January 1931), 58-70.
An extended discussion of the techniques of dramatic
play and their natural use in the education of children.

1718   _____. AND MARTHA FLETCHER. <u>Play-Making and Plays: The
Dramatic Impulse and Its Educative Use in the Elementary
and Secondary Schools</u>. New York: Macmillan Company, 1930.
Combines a discussion of formal and informal drama in
the schools.

1719   MESSINGER, MARGARET BARCLAY. "Creative Dramatics and Its
Relationship to Progressive Education." Master's thesis,
University of Wisconsin, 1940.
Primarily a history of creative dramatics and its
techniques, and their general applicability to progressive
education; the author finds that the two are very conso-
nant with each other.

1720   MEUDEN, EMMA. "Dramatics in Progressive School." <u>Playground</u>,
23 (April 1929), 17-18.

1721   MOTE, JERRINE. "Teaching Dramatization in Preparing Class
Plays." <u>Grade Teacher</u>, 65 (May 1948), 20, 85.
Makes a specific distinction between formal and
informal drama.

1722   MOWRY, SUSAN W. "Dramatization in the Primary Grades."
<u>Elementary English Review</u>, 2 (February 1925), 50-53.
Advocates reading good plays and good literature in
general to produce good creative drama.

1723   NAUMBERG, MARGARET. <u>The Child and the World: Dialogues in
Modern Education</u>. New York: Harcourt, Brace and Company,
1928.
Discusses the merits of creative dramatics in
progressive schools.

CHILDREN'S THEATRE AND CREATIVE DRAMATICS

IN EDUCATION AND THE SCHOOLS, GENERAL: PRE-1950

1724 ____. "Playmaking in a Modern School." Survey, 60
      (September 1923), 550-53, 560.
      Reprinted from The Child and the World; makes a
      distinction between formal and informal drama, and
      recommends the latter.

1725 NEAL, HELEN W. "Toddler Dramatics Make Play Delightful and
      Routines Fun." Parents' Magazine, 15 (May 1940), 32-33,
      78-79.

1726 NICHOLS, CECILE. "Outline of a Syllabus for Teaching 'Crea-
      tive Dramatic Play' to Prospective Kindergarten Teachers."
      Master's thesis, Whittier College, 1949.

1727 OVERTON, GRACE SLOAN. Drama in Education: Theory and Tech-
      nique. New York: Century Company, 1926.
      Surveys all facets of dramatic activity in general
      and religious education.

1728 PARKER, SAMUEL CHESTER. Types of Elementary Teaching and
      Learning Including Practical Technique and Scientific
      Evidence. New York: Ginn and Company, 1923.
      Discusses puppetry, formal and informal drama and
      their value in teaching the liberal and social arts.

1729 ____. AND ALICE TEMPLE. Unified Kindergarten and First-
      Grade Teaching. Boston: Ginn and Company, 1925.
      Some discussion of formal and informal dramatic
      techniques for teachers.

1730 PEABODY, MAY E. "Study Course of the Pre-School Child."
      Parent's Magazine, 15 (May 1940), 106-08.
      Evaluates an article by Helen Neal [see above] in the
      same issue.

1731 POOLE, IRENE. "Suggested Methods for Dramatics." Quarterly
      Journal of Speech, 19 (April 1933), 304-05.

1732 PRATT, CAROLINE. "Growing Up and Dramatics." Progressive
      Education, 8 (January 1931), 7-10.

1733 ____. I Learn from Children. New York: Simon and Schuster,
      1948.
      Devotes some space to reminiscence about informal
      drama in the classroom.

CREATIVE DRAMATICS

1734   PRESSLER, FRANCES. "Developing Dramatics in the Public
       School." Progressive Education, 8 (January 1931), 43-46.

1735   _____. "Including Child Interest in Plan for a Curriculum -
       II." Instructor, 48 (October 1939), 16-17, 76-77.

1736   PUTNAM, GUSTAVA. "A Study of a Selected Number of Stories
       Suitable for Dramatization in the Third Grade." Master's
       thesis, North Texas State Teacher's College, 1948.

1737   RASMUSSEN, CARRIE. "Creative Dramatization in the Auditori-
       um." Quarterly Journal of Speech, 20 (April 1934), 279-
       82.

1738   RICE, REBECCA. "Minute Dramatizations for Primary and Middle
       Grades." Instructor, 50 (October 1941), 44.

1739   ROBERTS, MARGARET MANNING. "When 'The Play's the Thing'."
       Child Education, 12 (June 1936), 394-98.
           Gives criteria for evaluating dramatic play at
       different age levels; some discussion of puppetry is
       given, but the emphasis is on creative dramatics.

1740   ROGERS, E. W. "The Show-Off in Educational Dramatics."
       Quarterly Journal of Speech, 28 (April 1941), 210-12.

1741   ROSENBLUM, FLORENCE M. "The Children Write a Play."
       Recreation, 39 (February 1946), 594-95, 610-11.
           Work in a settlement house is described; through
       informal drama, children create and perform a non-
       written play.

1742   RUGG, HAROLD AND ANN SHUMAKER. The Child-Centered School:
       An Appraisal of the New Education. Yonkers-on-Hudson:
       World Book Company, 1928.
           Gives a partial discussion of the merits of informal
       dramatization in the elementary school.

1743   RYAN, CALVIN T. "You Can Dramatize It." School Activities,
       14 (February 1943), 219-20.
           Gives a strict interpretation of creative dramatics in
       the classroom, discourages performance, and shows its
       value in teaching history.

1744   SAAL, MARY ELIZABETH. "Creative Dramatics in the Elementary
       School." Western Speech, 4 (March 1940), 15-19.
           Suggests methods of using creative dramatics with good
       literature; analyzes the procedure of selecting literature
       for dramatization.

Children's Theatre and Creative Dramatics

IN EDUCATION AND THE SCHOOLS, GENERAL PRE-1950

1745 SHAW, DEBBIE. "The Great First-Grade Circus." Instructor,
      45 (June 1936), 24, 73.
          A study of animals produces a creative dramatics
      exercise.

1746 SIMPSON, BERYL M. "An Experiment in Creative Dramatics."
      School Activities, 11 (January 1940), 191-92.
          Analyzes the steps involved in formal and informal
      dramatics in education.

1747 SMUCK, NANCY TAFT. "Creative Dramatics for Children."
      Western Speech, 10 (May 1946), 3-6.
          Mentions The Play Centers in Seattle and describes the
      author's methods of producing a formal play using creative
      dramatics techniques.

1748 SPOONER, JULIA A. "The Auditorium and the Home Room."
      Platoon School, 4 (March-April-May 1930), 22 25.
          Suggests that all aspects of the curriculum should be
      saturated with creative dramatics, and it is the respon-
      sibility of the teacher to see that this happens.

1749 STAFF OF THE ELEMENTARY DIVISION OF THE LINCOLN SCHOOL OF
      TEACHERS COLLEGE, COLUMBIA UNIVERSITY. Curriculum Making
      in an Elementary School. Boston: Ginn and Company, 1927.
          Discusses an experiment using dramatic play at
      Lincoln Elementary School.

1750 STEELE, ELLEN. "The Growth of Dramatic Forms in the School
      Life." Progressive Education, 8 (January 1931), 20-25.

1751 STORMS, NELLIE M. "Dramatic Play Growing Out of a Community
      Project." Childhood Education, 1 (April 1925), 372-76.

1752 STRODE, BARBARA. "A Study of Dramatics in the First, Second,
      and Third Groups of the Smith College Day School."
      Master's thesis, Smith College, 1940.

1753 THORNDIKE, EDWARD L. Education: A First Book. New York:
      Macmillan Company, 1912.
          Briefly analyzes the educational merits of creative
      dramatics and informal drama.

1754 VIOLA, WILLIAM NELSON. Creative Dramatics for Secondary
      Education. Boston: Expression Company, 1932.
          Many methods discussed are applicable to elementary
      education; includes a bibliography of related sources.

CREATIVE DRAMATICS

1755   WALKER, MORILLAE. "The Drama Yesterday and Today." Elementary English Review, 4 (January 1927), 15-18.
Gives some attention to mime and spontaneous dramatics.

1756   WARD, WINIFRED. "Creative Dramatics as a Background for High
School Drama." The High School Thespian, (May-June 1936),
4, 17.
Emphasizes the value of creative dramatics in elementary school to prepare the student for formal drama in
high school.

1757   _____. Creative Dramatics for the Upper Grades and Junior
High School. New York: D. Appleton and Company, 1930.
Evaluates formal and informal dramatic techniques for
grades six through nine, lists appropriate formal plays
and literature for dramatization, and includes suitable
reference sources.

1758   _____. "Creative Dramatics in the Elementary School."
Quarterly Journal of Speech, 28 (December 1942), 445-49.
Advocates that the child interact personally with
literature and ideas rather than passively view them
through formalized plays.

1759   _____. "Frills or Fundamentals." Players Magazine, 5
(November-December 1928), 2.
Justifies educator's indifference to dramatic activities because, historically, they have been of an
exhibitional nature; suggests that creative dramatics
should change this.

1760   _____. "Techniques in Dramatization." Chicago School
Journal, March-April, 1948, pp. 108-13.
Concerned with creative dramatics techniques in the
elementary school.

1761   WASHBURN, RUTH W. "Study Course on the School-Age Child."
Parents' Magazine, 22 (March 1947), 185-86.
Suggests additional materials for creative dramatics,
derived from an article by Earl W. Blank in the same
issue; See 1506.

1762   WATKINS, EVELYN. "Beauty Through Dramatization." Childhood
Education, 25 (March 1949), 313-15.
Discusses first graders' informal dramatization of
Bambi.

CHILDREN'S THEATRE AND CREATIVE DRAMATICS

IN EDUCATION AND THE SCHOOLS, GENERAL: PRE-1950

1763   WEISS, EDNA S. "Dramatization in the Rural School." Instruc-
       tor, 58 (September 1949), 10-11.
          Advises using informal and impromptu dramatics for all
       subjects in the rural school.

1764   WHITTENBURG, CLARENCE. "Playing Safe - An Experience Unit
       for Grades One and Two." Instructor, 56 (May 1947),
       16-17, 72, 81.
          Children learn about safety by acting out potential
       hazards.

1765   WILSON, CLARA O. "Play Activities in the Kindergarten and
       Primary Grades: Spontaneous Dramatic Play in Early
       Childhood." Childhood Education, 2 (December 1925),
       166-68.

1766   WOOD, WALTER. Children's Play and Its Place in Education:
       With an Appendix on the Montessori Method. New York:
       Duffield and Company, 1913.

1767   WOOLRIDGE, OPAL. "Creative Play Activities." Grade Teacher,
       61 (January 1944), 28.
          Covers puppetry and informal dramatic activities,
       among other related subjects.

       See also the following entries. 151, 190, 228, 230, 234,
       240-41, 261, 265, 274, 295-96, 302, 305, 332, 339, 340-41,
       344, 346, 348-49, 357-58, 365, 369, 371, 409-10, 417, 618,
       885, 1436, 1496-97, 1507, 1517, 1526-27, 2009, 2013, 2229.

IN EDUCATION AND THE SCHOOLS, GENERAL: 1950-1973

1768   ADAMS, FAY. Educating America's Children. 2nd ed. New
       York: The Ronald Press, 1954.
          Makes a definitional distinction between free play and
       directed and undirected dramatic play; applies them to
       the educational methods of elementary schools.

1769   ALINGTON, ARGENTINE F. Drama and Education. Chester Springs,
       Pennsylvania: Dufour Editions, 1961.
          A British approach to creative drama through the
       vehicles of mime, literature and improvisation; a brief
       discussion of teacher training in colleges is included.

CREATIVE DRAMATICS

1770   APPLEGATE, MAUREE. "And the Children Followed...." Child-
        hood Education, 33 (January 1957), 197-202.
            Concerned with the excitement and "joy" creative
        dramatics produces in elementary education.

1771   _____. Everybody's Business - Our Children. New York:
        Row, Peterson and Company, 1952.
            A parents and teachers guide to creative activities for
        young children.

1772   BARNFIELD, GABRIEL. Creative Drama in Schools. New York:
        Hart Publishing Company, 1970.
            Explores the role of spontaneity in creative drama
        and its ancillary disciplines: characterization, dance,
        improvisation, mime, music and rhythm.

1773   BAYNE, JOSEPHINE. "A Unit and a Program on 'Peter and the
        Wolf'." Instructor, 72 (December 1962), 19, 80.

1774   BECK, ROBERT H.; WALTER W. COOK; NOLAN C. KEARNEY. Curriculum
        in the Modern Elementary School. 2nd ed. Englewood
        Cliffs, New Jersey: Prentice-Hall, 1960.
            Links creative dramatics, puppetry, mime and story
        dramatization with crafts and the fine arts.

1775   BERTRAM, JEAN DeSALES. "Creative Dramatics in the School."
        Elementary English, 35 (December 1958), 515-18.
            Evaluates educators' knowledge of creative drama, and
        concludes that it is not extensive.

1776   BIGBY, CHARLES WESLEY. "A Survey of the Use of Dramatics as
        a Teaching Medium in the Public Schools of the Dallas
        Area." Master's thesis, Southern Methodist University,
        1955.
            Finds that the application of creative dramatics to
        elementary school work is quite feasible; results are less
        productive in junior high.

1777   BIRDSALL, RUTH. "Book Week Is a Good Time to Use Creative
        Dramatics." Instructor, 64 (November 1954), 81.

1778   _____. "Creative Dramatics." Instructor, 62 (September
        1952), 46-47.
            Comments on the changed attitude of education toward
        creative dramatics.

Children's Theatre and Creative Dramatics

1779 _____. "Creative Dramatics." Instructor, 62 (October 1952), 45, 74, 83.
Concerned with formal and informal dramatic activities related to Hallowe'en.

1780 _____. "Creative Dramatics." Instructor, 62 (November 1952), 77, 83, 106.
Explains how to use creative dramatics with special holidays in November.

1781 _____. "Creative Dramatics." Instructor, 62 (January 1953), 65, 84.
Includes commentary on creative drama activities that lead to informal productions with volunteer crew work.

1782 _____. "Creative Dramatics." Instructor, 62 (March 1953), 58, 88, 100.
Gives suggestions for creative work during International Drama Month.

1783 BLANCHARD, DAGNY HANSON. "Creative Dramatic Activities in the Elementary Classroom. Parts I and II." Ph.D. dissertation, New York University, 1958.
Part I discusses the applicability of creative dramatics to education; Part II is a systematic guide for applying theory.

1784 BLOOM, KATHRYN. "The Arts in Education." Children's Theatre Review, 19 (May 1970), 10-13.
Concerned with a cross-arts, mixed-media program being funded by John D. Rockefeller III, and lists projects already in progress.

1785 BROWN, IDA STEWART. "How We Act in Groups." Childhood Education, 27 (December 1950), 156-60.
Discusses informal dramatic activities.

1786 BROWN, VIRGINIA T. "Monkeys - Fictional and Human: An Adventure in Creative Dramatics." Instructor, 69 (October 1959), 65, 75.
Initial work with a fifth grade class in creative dramatics is discussed.

1787 BURGER, ISABEL B. "Creative Dramatics: An Educational Tool." Instructor, 73 (September 1963), 133-36.
An expansion of an article in Players Magazine, October 1962 [see below].

CREATIVE DRAMATICS

1788   BURGER, ISABEL B. "Creative Dramatics - An Educational Tool."
        Players Magazine, 39 (October 1962), 9-10.
            Advocates creative dramatics in the educational
        situation when teachers are concerned with informal
        dramatic situations, and discusses the benefits of
        dramatics in the middle grades.

1790   BURROWS, ALVINA TROUT. Teaching Children in the Middle
        Grades. Boston: D. C. Heath and Company, 1952.
            Gives some attention to the teacher's role in informal
        dramatic situations, and discusses the benefits of
        dramatics in the middle grades.

1791   BUSBEE, VIVIAN. "Dramatic Interpretation in the Elementary
        School." Elementary Education, 34 (October 1957),
        394-96, 424.
            Shows the way that children's natural abilities to
        dramatize can be channeled into informal productions.

1792   CARPENTER, N. E. "The Influence of Acting in a Play on
        Adjustment." Teachers College Journal, 38 (January 1967),
        178-81.

1793   CIRELLI, JUANITA. "The Third Grade Writes a Play." Grade
        Teacher, 78 (September 1960), 66-67, 114, 146.
            A program about American Indians, involving four
        third grade classes, is described.

1794   "A Class Full of Creators." Life, 40 (March 5, 1956), 105-06.
            Illustrates a creative dramatics class at Greenburgh,
        New York.

1795   COHEN, EDWARD A. "Helen Keller." Instructor, 66 (April
        1957), 41, 63, 65-66.
            Discusses a fourth grade class' creative dramatics
        project on Helen Keller.

1796   CORNWALL, VIRGINIA. "Magic Road to Class Dramatics."
        Instructor, 79 (March 1970), 65-66.
            The author discusses two plays written by third
        graders.

1797   COURTNEY, RICHARD. Teaching Drama. London: Cassell and
        Company, 1965.
            A two-part discussion concerned with (1) the dramatic
        method; and (2) specific techniques such as improvisation,
        movement, mime and playmaking.

Children's Theatre and Creative Dramatics

IN EDUCATION AND THE SCHOOLS, GENERAL: 1950-1973

1798 CRADDOCK, MYRTLE. "Creative Dramatics for 9's, 10's, 11's."
Childhood Education, 29 (January 1953), 230-34.
Commentary on the author's experience in creative
dramatics in the middle school.

1799 Creative Dramatics Handbook. Philadelphia: Office of Early
Childhood Programs, 1971.
This elementary school handbook for initiated practitioners of creative dramatics is concerned with the
philosophy and practicum of programs related to child
drama in the schools. A bibliography of material to be
used in creative dramatics is included.

1800 CROSBY, MURIEL. "Creative Dramatics as a Developmental
Process." Elementary English, 33 (January 1956), 13-18.
Discusses the role of creative dramatics in producing
self-awareness and self-understanding.

1801 CULLUM, ALBERT. Push Back the Desks. New York: Citation
Press, 1967.
Treats the author's twenty years of teaching the
fifth grade.

1802 DAVIS, GEORGE L. "A Dramatics Activity Manual for Use in the
Primary, Intermediate, and Junior High School." Master's
thesis, University of Denver, 1951.
Discusses many drama-related activities, as well as
creative dramatics.

1803 DICKINSON, MARY ELIZABETH. "Some Suggested Methods, Materials and Activities for a Handbook of Creative Dramatics."
Master's thesis, Kent State University, 1958.

1804 Drama Curriculum: Levels C-D Grades Three and Four, Teacher's
Guides. Eugene, Oregon: University of Oregon, 1971.
Supplementary materials include texts of The Hammer of
Thor, The Squire's Bride, The Indian Cinderella, Rumpel-
stiltskin, The Fool of the World and the Flying Ship,
Two Neighbors, The Magic Drum, Deucalion and the Flood,
and The Contest.

1805 Drama Curriculum - V and VI: Grades Five and Six, Teacher's
Guide. Eugene, Oregon: University of Oregon Press, 1971.
These curricular guides cover a broad range of formal
and informal dramatic techniques. Supplementary materials
include texts of The Magic Drum, The Squire's Bride, The
Fool of the World and the Flying Ship, The Cat Who
Walked by Himself, and The Story of Keesh.

CREATIVE DRAMATICS

1806   "Drama in Education," English in Education, I:3 (Autumn 1967).
       (Special Issue for the National Association for the
       Teaching of English.)
          The entire issue focuses on drama in British
       education and materials for creative dramatics.

1807   Drama in the Classroom: Papers Related to the Anglo-American
          Seminar on the Teaching of English. Champaign, Illinois:
       National Council of Teachers of English, 1968.
          Although this monograph is devoted to practices in
       secondary education, there is an appendix which discusses
       approaches for primary school dramatics.

1808   DUKE, CHARLES R. "Creative Dramatics: A Natural for the
       Multiple Electives Program." Virginia English Bulletin.
       21 (Winter 1971), 6-10.

1809   DURLAND, FRANCES CALDWELL. Creative Dramatics for Children:
       A Practical Manual for Teachers and Leaders. Yellow
       Springs, Ohio: Antioch Press, 1952.
          A handbook for the uninitiated.

1810   ECHEVERRIA, P. "Following the Drinking Gourd: A Program in
       Creative Dramatics." Independent School Bulletin, 30
       (October 1970), 61-63.

1811   ELLISOR, MILDRED. "Classroom Opportunities to Express
       Feelings." Childhood Education, 45 (March 1969), 373-78.
          Shows the effect of artistic, dramatic and literary
       creation on self-image and the ability to continue to
       create.

1812   EVANS, HELEN KITCHELL. "Let's Give a Play!" Grade Teacher,
       71 (March 1954), 48, 109.
          Concerned with the mental growth and maturation of
       the child through the vehicle of creative and improvisa-
       tional dramatics.

1813   FARIDAY, MARY JANICE. "Creative Dramatics: An Exciting
       Newcomer in the Elementary Curriculum." Minnesota
       Journal of Education, 48 (January 1968), 20-21.
          Gives a brief definition of the aims of creative
       dramatics.

1814   FESSENDEN, SETH A.; ROY IVAN JOHNSON; P. MERVILLE LARSON.
       The Teacher Speaks. New York: Prentice-Hall, 1954.
          Includes a discussion of how creative dramatics aid
       speech improvement.

Children's Theatre and Creative Dramatics

1815   FIRTH, ROXIE ANDREWS. "What We Did in First Grade."
       Instructor, 66 (May 1957), 61, 71.
           Shows the benefits of creative and improvisational
       dramatics over formal drama in the early years of
       schooling.

1816   FLETCHER, JUANITA. "Theatre Teaching in the Elementary
       School." Educational Theatre Journal, 19 (Special Issue,
       June 1967), 288-90.
           Although the emphasis of this article is on Creative
       Dramatics and its various dimensions, a definitional
       distinction is made between Creative Drama and actual
       play production.

1817   FRANK, MARY AND LAWRENCE K. FRANK. How to Help Your Child in
       School. New York: Viking Press, 1950.
           Creative dramatics is discussed under the category of
       educational objectives.

1818   GANS, ROMA; CELIA BURNS STENDLER; MILLIE ALMY. Teaching
       Young Children in Nursery School, Kindergarten, and the
       Primary Grades. Yonkers-on-Hudson, New York: World Book
       Company, 1952.
           Includes discussions of informal drama as it relates
       to speech improvement, problem-solving, the language
       arts, and mental stability.

1819   GILLIES, EMILY. Creative Dramatics for All Children.
       Patricia M. Markum and Monroe De Cohen, eds. Washington,
       D.C.: American Council on Education, 1973.

1820   HADDEN, JANE. "Developing Creativity Through Dramatization."
       Central States Speech Journal, 7 (Spring 1956), 28-32.

1821   HAMLIN, HARRIET D. "A Descriptive Study of First Grade
       Children's Behavior in Informal Dramatizations."
       Master's thesis, Boston University, 1959.

1822   HAMM, HARLEN L. "A Study of Creative Dramatics in the
       Kindergarten, First, Second, and Third Grades of the
       Bowling Green Public Elementary Schools." Master's
       thesis, Bowling Green State University, 1965.

1823   HARTSHORN, EDWINA AND JOHN C. BRANTLEY. "The Effects of
       Dramatic Play on Classroom Problem-Solving Ability."
       Journal of Educational Research, 66 (February 1973),
       243-6.

CREATIVE DRAMATICS

(HARTSHORN, EDWINA)
Second and third graders in the experimental group
received higher grades on a post-test that the control
group also took, with negligible results.

1824   HEATHCOTE, DOROTHY. "How Does Drama Serve Thinking, Talking,
and Writing?" Elementary English, 47 (December 1970),
1077-81.
The author limits the definition of educational drama
to role-playing, coping, and general creative work.

1825   HEFFERNAN, HELEN. "Dramatic Play in Kindergarten." Grade
Teacher, 75 (February 1958), 14, 76, 78.
Gives techniques for using creative dramatic play in
early childhood education.

1826   _____. Ed. Guiding the Young Child. Boston: D. C. Heath
and Company, 1951.
Combines a series of studies prepared for the
Committee of the California School Supervisors Association, based on work in the elementary school.

1827   HILL, EMILY. "The Child's the Thing." National Education
Association Journal, 46 (January 1957), 36-37.
Illustrates seven steps for enacting creative
dramatics.

1828   HOLDEN, MARGARET. "We Invited Townspeople to Help Us
Dramatize." Instructor, 65 (February 1956), 39.
Describes a sixth grade project associated with the
March of Dimes.

1829   HOROWITZ, TILLIE. "Dramatizing the Story." American Childhood, 35 (February 1950), 17-18.
Discusses the author's work in adapting folk tales to
creative dramatics exercises in the elementary school.

1830   HUNT, JOHN H. "Dramatic Experiences: Fads or Frills?"
New York State Education, 49 (April 1962), 36-37.
Author discounts educators' and parents' disapproval
of dramatics, especially informal dramatics, in education.

1831   INGERSOLL, RICHARD L. AND JUDITH B. KASE. The Effects of
Creative Dramatics on Learning and Retention of Class-
room Material. Washington, D.C.: Office of Education,
Department of Health, Education, and Welfare, 1970.

Children's Theatre and Creative Dramatics

IN EDUCATION AND THE SCHOOLS, GENERAL: 1950-1973

(INGERSOLL, RICHARD L.)
A study conducted at the University of New Hampshire with eight classes of fifth and sixth graders concludes that girls' retention is affected favorably, boys' unfavorably.

1832   JARZEN, CYNTHIA L. "Magic Compass: An Adventure in Creative Dramatics." Instructor, 75 (June 1966), 56-57.
A brief description of a play created and performed by forty-four fourth graders - based on Mary Poppins and world geography.

1833   KASE, JUDITH B. "Theatre Resources for Youth in New Hampshire." Educational Theatre Journal, 21 (May 1969), 205-13.
Discusses TRY (Theatre Resources for Youth) a project of PACE (Projects to Advance Creativity in Education) and its impact on New Hampshire children and the state's educational network.

1834   KIRKPATRICK, MARGARET. "The Baits Must Be Many." Childhood Education, 31 (November 1954), 119-122.
Discusses the way teachers must be creative if they expect creativity from their students.

1835   KISER, EVELYN J. "Concerning Mr. Todd and His Doughnuts." Instructor, 63 (March 1954), 63, 90.
Describes an informal performance of a third grade class.

1836   KNAPP, KATHERINE. "Guiding Creative Experiences in the Primary Grades." Social Education, 15 (January 1951), 74-75.

1837   KOLBE, NADINE A. "'Witches' Can Be Fun." Elementary English, 34 (October 1957), 373-74.
Shows how dramatization of witches eliminated a fear of them at Hallowe'en.

1838   KOMMEL, EVE. "Speech in the Upper Elementary Curriculum." Master's thesis, University of Michigan, 1955.
Covers both formal and informal dramatic activities.

1839   KOZARA, MARILYN JOANNE. "Let Children Pretend!" Grade Teacher, 80 (October 1962), 63, 143.
Advocates the extensive use of creative dramatics in the elementary school curriculum.

CREATIVE DRAMATICS

1840   KRAUS, RICHARD. Play Activities for Boys and Girls (Six
        Through Twelve): A Guide for Teachers, Parents, and
        Recreational Leaders. New York: McGraw-Hill Book
        Company, 1957.

1841   KRUSE, MARY. "Terminology and Definitions of Terms Dealing
        with Dramatics in the Elementary and Secondary Schools."
        Master's thesis, Queen's College, 1954.

1842   LEE, J. MURRY AND DORRIS MAY LEE. The Child and His Curricu-
        lum. 3rd ed. New York: Appleton-Century-Crofts, 1960.
            Included in a chapter on creative experiences is a
        discussion of creative and improvisational dramatization.

1843   LETTON, MILDRED C. "How Do Children Communicate?" Childhood
        Education, 32 (October 1955), 64-66.

1844   LEVIN, ESTHER. "They Lived Happily Ever After." Instructor,
        65 (September 1955), 66, 142, 146.
            Describes a first grade project in dramatizing
        "Cinderella."

1845   LINDMAN, MARGARET. "Just Imagine." Instructor, 67 (June
        1958), 45, 56, 91.
            Concerned with a summer school project for eight-year-
        olds in creative dramatic activities.

1846   LIPTON, HELEN. "A Fourth Grade Creates a Hallowe'en Program."
        Instructor, 75 (October 1965), 107.

1847   LOGAN, LILLIAN M. Teaching the Young Child: Methods of Pre-
        school and Primary Education. Boston: Houghton Mifflin
        Company, 1960.
            Includes a discussion of dramatic play, story enact-
        ment, and creative dramatics.

1848   LOWNDES, POLLY ROBBINS. "Creative Assemblies." Players
        Magazine, 30 (October 1953), 10-11.

1849   _____. Creative Assemblies. Minneapolis: T. S. Denison and
        Company, 1961.
            The emphasis is on creative expression rather than
        formalized drama.

1850   MacINSKAS, SARA P. "Movement Exploration in the Elementary
        School." Grade Teacher, 81 (December 1963), 101.

CHILDREN'S THEATRE AND CREATIVE DRAMATICS

1851   MARTIN, WILLIAM AND GORDON VALLINS. Exploration Drama:
        Teacher's Book and Four Student Texts. London: Evans
        Brothers, 1968.
        A thematic approach to drama experiments with fifth
        through eighth graders; texts for plays are based on the
        themes of legend, carnival, horizon, routines, and others.

1852   McCASLIN, NELLIE. "'A Bell Is to Ring': A Creative Dramatics
        Experience." Instructor, 75 (September 1965), 83, 155.
        Concerned with characterization and plot in creative
        dramatics exercises.

1853   _____. Creative Dramatics in the Classroom. 2nd ed. New
        York: McKay, David Company, 1974.
        Shows the uninitiated creative dramatics leader how to
        get started; includes a discussion of pantomime,
        characterization, and story playing.

1854   McCOY, GAY. "Dramatics Play in Primary Grades." Instructor,
        59 (March 1950), 13.
        Analyzes the creative and dramatic instincts of
        young children.

1855   McCRACKEN, JANET. "Ingredients of Success in Creative Group
        Action." Education, 79 (October 1958), 105-08.

1856   McCREA, LILLIAN. Stories to Play in the Infant School.
        London: Oxford University Press, 1956.
        Anthologizes and discusses numerous works from
        children's literature which are suitable for informal
        drama in the classroom.

1857   McINTYRE, BARBARA M. "Creative Dramatics." Education, 79
        (April 1959), 459-98.
        Excellent article on the choice of materials for
        creative dramatics, their relation to the child partici-
        pant, and how to achieve quality work.

1858   McKENNA, MARIAN. "Dramatic Play in the Middle Grades." Grade
        Teacher, 73 (January 1956), 56, 77.
        Discusses the lack of attention given to creative
        dramatics in the middle grades; shows ways to eliminate
        apathy in the classroom.

1859   McSPADDEN, ANNE. "So You're Going to Put on a Program!"
        Childhood Education, 31 (November 1954), 115-18.
        Concerned with the use of creative dramatics and
        informal dramatizations for special events.

CREATIVE DRAMATICS

1860 MIKOLOSKI, VANDA. "Dramatics in the Classroom." Grade
      Teacher, 75 (November 1959), 59, 122, 124.
         Describes a fifth grade project based on the life of
      Helen Keller.

1861 MILLICENT, SISTER M. "Creative Dramatics in the Classroom."
      Elementary Education, 40 (April 1963), 382-85, 389.
         Emphasizes the value of creative dramatics for the
      elementary school child.

1862 MORTENSEN, LOUISE HOVDE. "Creative Drama Combined with
      Formal Drama." Elementary English, 30 (December 1953),
      513-14.

1863 _____. "The Good Voice, The Bad Voice, and The Actor."
      Elementary English, 31 (February 1954), 98.
         Discusses a creative dramatics workshop at Drake
      University.

1864 NASH, GRACE. "Creating a Play." Instructor, 69 (September
      1959), 66.
         Advises a democratic approach to performing a creative
      dramatics-type play.

1865 NETTLES, DEBBIE G. "Combining Creative Activities." Instruc-
      tor, 63 (October 1953), 61, 72.
         Discusses mixed-media projects in the first grade.

1866 _____. "Christopher Robin and His Friends Come Alive."
      Instructor, 65 (May 1956), 52.
         Describes a creative dramatics activity based on
      Winnie the Pooh.

1867 NICHOLS, HILDRED AND LOIS WILLIAMS. Learning about Role-
      Playing for Children and Teachers. Washington, D.C.:
      Association for Childhood Education International, 1960.
         An how-to bulletin which demonstrates role-playing
      techniques more for their creative product than their
      therapeutic benefits.

1868 O'DAY, JEANNETTE. "The Wizard's a Whiz." Instructor, 65
      (January 1956), 71, 81, 85.
         Describes a first grade dramatization of Frank Baum's
      The Wizard of Oz.

CHILDREN'S THEATRE AND CREATIVE DRAMATICS

1869 PARKER, BEATRICE FORD. "Dramatic Play for Primary Grades."
Instructor, 60 (June 1951), 26, 64.

1870 PARKER, FAYE. "What to Do in 10 Periods of Creative Dramatics." _Instructor_, 74 (January 1965), 96-97.

1871 PETERSON, DOROTHY. "Creative Living in the Kindergarten."
Education, 80 (October 1959), 109-12.
Finds that creative dramatics is one of the most
popular creative activities in early childhood education.

1872 PETTY, WALTER AND TONI ANDERSON. "A Dramatization of a
Familiar Story." _Instructor_, 67 (September 1957), 47, 75.
Discusses personality development and social growth
in first grade through the vehicle of creative dramatics.

1873 PICOZZI, RAYMOND L. "Creative Dramatics: Experience in
Wonder." _NCEA Bulletin_, 64 (August 1967), 142-44.

1874 _____. "The Construction and Evaluation of a Series of
Exercises in Creative Dramatics." Ph.D. dissertation,
Boston University, School of Education, 1961.

1875 PIERINI, FRANCIS. _Creative Dramatics: A Guide for Educators_.
New York: Seabury Press, 1971.

1876 PIERSON, HOWARD. "Pupils, Teachers, and Creative Dramatics."
Elementary English, 32 (February 1955), 82-89.
Discusses creative dramatics and related dramatic
techniques, and their place in early education.

1877 PIQUETTE, JULIA C. "Creative Dramatics for Pre-Adolescence."
New York State Education, 43 (May 1956), 553-54.
Analyzes the use of creative dramatics and formal
drama in early education and questions the fact that
they are not used more extensively with adolescent
children.

1878 POLSKY, MILTON. "Who? What? Where?" _Grade Teacher_, 88
(February 1971), 74.
The author discusses how the grade teacher gets
ready to use creative dramatics.

1879 POMERANZ, REGINA ESTHER. "A Creative Drama Club." _English
Journal_, 41 (June 1952), 303-06.

CREATIVE DRAMATICS

1880   RANSON, JOAN NELL. "An Adventure in Group Planning."
        Instructor, 62 (April 1953), 53, 79, 85.
            Describes an informal performance by fourth graders
        on the subject of Mexico; the work was initiated through
        creative dramatics.

1881   RAVICH, LEONARD E. "Discover the Playwrights in Your
        Classroom." Dramatics, 43 (April 1972), 10-12.
            A blow by blow description of how improvisational
        theatre works when it works.

1882   RAVIS, HOWARD S. "Creative Drama: The 'Acting Up' You Love to
        See." Grade Teacher, 90 (September 1972), 48-53.
            Children in Long Island, New York, find that creative
        dramatics has become a necessary part of their curriculum.

1883   REYNOLDS, SALLY O'CONNOR. "Creative Dramatics in the School-
        room." Master's thesis, Wayne State University, 1952.

1884   ROBERTS, ALICE. "Eddie Found a Good Story." Instructor, 65
        (December 1955), 68, 89.
            Discusses a spontaneous creative dramatics exercise in
        kindergarten.

1885   ROPER, MARIE LEONORA. "Children's Theatre in the Rhett
        Elementary School, Charleston, South Carolina." Master's
        thesis, University of Michigan, 1952.
            Considers both formal and informal drama in elementary
        education.

1886   RUSSELL, AMY T. "Let's Make Believe!" Grade Teacher, 74
        (September 1956), 32, 71, 76.
            Emphasis is on the teacher's role in creating informal
        dramatization.

1887   SAWYER, RICHARD. "Whirling and Swirling." Childhood Educa-
        tion, 40 (September 1964), 298-300.
            The author discusses a cross-arts project with third
        graders involving creative dramatics.

1888   SCANLON, EILEEN. "A Creative Dramatics Manual for Use by the
        Second Grade Teacher." Master's thesis, Newark State
        College, 1958.

1889   SEALEY, L. G. W. AND   IAN GIBBON. Communication and
        Learning in the Primary School. New York: Schocken
        Books, 1972.

Children's Theatre and Creative Dramatics

IN EDUCATION AND THE SCHOOLS, GENERAL: 1950-1973

(SEALEY, L. G. W.)
Predicating their work on the assumption that "learn-ing arises from experience which is absolutely bound up with communication," the authors give their attention to movement, dramatic play, and music in the infant school.

1890   SEELING, MARTHA. "Creative Experience for Young Children." Education, 75 (February 1955), 355-60.
Gives lists of necessary creative experiences in elementary schools and includes materials for dramatic work.

1891   Self-Directed Dramatization Project, Joliet, Illinois. Elementary Program in Compensatory Education 2. Palo Alto, California: American Institute for Research in Behavioral Sciences, 1969.
This brief pamphlet discusses the effect of creative dramatics on self-concept and reading achievement of second through fifth graders. It covers two projects (1) with children grades two through seven, and (2) with predominately disadvantaged black children grades one through four. The conclusions suggest that reading ability and self-concept were most improved with the younger children.

1892   SHARPHAM, JOHN R. "Creative Drama in an Arts Education Program: Core I at Illinois State University." Paper presented at the Annual Meeting of the American Theatre Association, New York, August 1973. Available on ERIC fiche # ED 081 052.
Gives a discussion of Illinois' teacher preparation in the arts via creative dramatics, and the value of this approach.

1893   SHAW, ANN MARIE. "The Development of a Taxonomy of Education-al Objectives in Creative Dramatics in the United States Based on Selected Writings in the Field." Ph.D. disser-tation, Columbia University, 1968.

1894   _____. "A Taxonomical Study of the Nature and Behavioral Objectives of Creative Dramatics." Educational Theatre Journal, 22 (December 1970), 361-72.

1895   SHEEHY, EMMA DICKSON. The Fives and Sixes Go to School. New York: Henry Holt and Company, 1954.
A portion of this book is concerned with the teacher's part in organizing and leading creative dramatics activities.

CREATIVE DRAMATICS

1896 SHIELDS, VIOLA MANVILLE. "A Plan for Integrating Creative
       Dramatics into the Secondary Program." Master's thesis,
       University of Virginia, 1954.
         Has implications for, and applicability to, the
       elementary school situation.

1897 SILVER, RENEE AND ANNE AVERY. "Classroom Experiments 2:
       Experiences in Creative Dramatics." English Quarterly, 5
       (February 1972), 110-14.
         An Opportunities for Youth Creative Arts Project which
       emphasizes the value of creative dramatic play for
       primary children is discussed.

1898 SINKS, THOMAS A. "A Creative Play." National Elementary
       Principal Yearbook, 34 (September 1955), 131-34.
         Describes an informal dramatization originated through
       creative dramatics.

1899 "Six Curriculums that Turn Kids On." Nation's Schools, 90
       (September 1972), 49-54.
         Gives some attention to the value of creative dramatics
       in the development of educational tools and student
       motivation.

1900 SLADE, PETER. Child Drama and Its Value in Education.
       Bromley, Kent: Stacey Publication for Educational Drama
       Association, 1967.
         The pamphlet contains a speech "Given at the first
       drama conference of the Department of Education and
       Sciences for Wales, Bangor University, April 1965" as
       well as a series of questions and answers.

1901 SNYDER, HELEN EMILY. "A Kindergarten Circus." Instructor,
       40 (June 1951), 14, 69.
         Describes an informal, out-of-doors performance that
       originated through creative drama techniques.

1902 STAINS, KATHERINE BERLE. "Creative Expression." Instructor,
       41 (November 1951), 31, 73, 81.
         Discusses daily creative activities in a kindergarten.

1903 STARKS, ESTHER B. "Dramatic Play." Childhood Education, 37
       (December 1960), 163-67.
         The article is concerned primarily with a definition
       of creative dramatics and the teacher's role in leading
       it.

CHILDREN'S THEATRE AND CREATIVE DRAMATICS

1904 STONE, BERENICE HUFSTUTLER. "Creative Dramatics in the Primary Grades." Master's thesis, Southwestern University, 1957.

1905 TAYLOR, A. L. "A Sitting-Thing." CITE [Center for Information on the Teaching of English] Newsletter, 2 (January 7, 1969), 25-27.
Describes an acting, writing, role-playing experience with reluctant learners, and how the project worked.

1906 TOLES, MYRIAM. "The Classroom Play...MEANS or END?" Instructor, 65 (September 1955), 43, 89, 102-03.
The author feels that the classroom play should be a means to allow the child his natural spontaneity, rather than an end in formalized drama.

1907 TORRANCE, E. PAUL. Encouraging Creativity in the Classroom. Dubuque, Iowa: William C. Brown Company, 1970.
Gives a discussion of creative dramatics and how it encourages the child to develop his mental and social capacities.

1908 _____. Rewarding Creative Behavior: Experiments in Classroom Creativity. Englewood Cliffs, New Jersey: Prentice-Hall, 1965.
A brief discussion of creative dramatics is given in terms of its value in language arts programs.

1909 TUCH, CLAIRE. "Make-Believe with a Purpose." Instructor, 76 (May 1967), 39.
Concerned with a viable classroom atmosphere for creative dramatics.

1910 VAN RIPER, CHARLES AND KATHERINE G. BUTLER. Speech in the Elementary Classroom. New York: Harper and Brothers, 1955.
Discusses creative dramatics and informal dramatization, and their effect on speech improvement.

1911 VENT, HERBERT J. AND DONALD W. COX. "Creative Dramatics in the Elementary Grades." Educational Administration and Supervision, 42 (December 1956), 461-65.
Advises using creative dramatics to enliven classroom activities.

CREATIVE DRAMATICS

1912 WAGNER, GAY. "What Schools Are Doing: Creative Dramatics."
      Education, 80 (January 1960), 317.
          Concerned with drama-related activities and how they
      motivate the student to learn.

1913 WARD, WINIFRED. "Dramatics - A Creative Force." School
      Executive, 69 (August 1950), 54-55.
          Miss Ward cites work in the Evanston, Illinois, School
      System, and shows how creative dramatics aids in learning.

1914 _____. "Let's Pretend." Junior League Magazine, 60
      (February 1953), 6.

1915 _____. Playmaking with Children from Kindergarten Through
      Junior High School. 2nd ed., 1957; rpt. New York:
      Appleton-Century-Crofts, 1969.
          A companion work to Stories to Dramatize, by the
      same author.

1916 _____. "The Teacher's Role in Creative Dramatics." Instruc-
      tor, 64 (February 1955), 35.
          Discusses creative dramatics methodology through the
      vehicle of "The Emperor's New Clothes."

1917 WEINIGER, OTTO. "Unstructured Play as a Vehicle for Learn-
      ing." International Journal of Early Childhood, 4:2
      (1972), 63-69.
          Briefly touches the value of dramatic play in cogni-
      tive learning for pre-school children, and emphasizes
      its worth for culturally-deprived children.

1918 WILLIAMS, KATHERINE TAYLOR. "Young Children Dramatize a
      Christmas Carol." Elementary English, 27 (December 1950),
      511, 526.

1919 WILLIAMS, LAURENE ESTHER. "A Study of Creative Dramatics As
      an Enrichment of a Fourth Grade Curriculum in Language
      Arts." Master's thesis, University of Washington, 1953.

1920 WILT, MIRIAM E. Creativity in the Elementary School. New
      York: Appleton-Century-Crofts, 1959.
          A portion of this book is devoted to a discussion of
      creative dramatics and ancillary subjects.

1921 WINTON, REBECCA A. AND BERNICE FLEISS. "You're Asking Us: I
      Need Some Zesty New Ideas for Role-Playing and Creative
      Dramatics." Instructor, 75 (June-July, 1966), 31.

CHILDREN'S THEATRE AND CREATIVE DRAMATICS

IN EDUCATION AND THE SCHOOLS, GENERAL: 1950-1973

(WINTON, REBECCA A.)
Gives some very brief suggestions for developing creative dramatics materials.

1922 WISE, NANCY SUSAN. "A Study of Certain Creative Dramatics Techniques as Applied in the Second Grade Classroom of the North Texas State University Laboratory School." Master's thesis, North Texas State University, 1964.

1923 WOODS, MARGARET S. "Creative Dramatics." National Education Association Journal, 58 (May 1959), 52-53.
Discusses the teacher's role in creative dramatics.

1924 _____. "Learning Through Creative Dramatics." Educational Leadership, 18 (October 1960), 19-23.
The author is concerned with teacher training in creative dramatics, and its impact on the teacher and the taught.

1925 _____. "A Survey of Effective Classroom Practices in Creative Dramatics." Master's thesis, University of Washington, 1955.
Covers creative dramatics techniques as they apply to elementary and secondary education.

1926 _____. "The Teaching of Creative Dramatics." Grade Teacher, 78 (November 1960), 54, 130-31.
Gives suggestions for initiating creative dramatic activities.

1927 _____. Thinking, Feeling, Experiencing: Toward Realization of Full Potential. Washington, D.C.: National Education Association, 1962.
Emphasizes the role of creative dramatics in elementary education, and gives methods for making it work.

1928 YOUNG, MABEL E. "The Play's the Thing." Childhood Education, 31 (September 1954), 30-33.
An outgrowth of the Make It With and For Children Committee of the Association of Childhood Education International; the author discusses puppetry and other creative drama activities, and the way they relate to elementary education.

CREATIVE DRAMATICS

See also the following entries. 43, 109, 126, 146, 162, 173,
189, 191, 242, 248-49, 254, 259, 264, 267, 279, 284, 287, 298-99,
303, 308-09, 311, 313, 337-38, 342, 347, 355-56, 361, 364, 373,
375, 383, 517, 525, 747, 1467, 1532, 1540-42, 1544, 1551,
1557-58, 1565-66, 1574, 1587, 1594, 1597, 1599, 1600, 1602,
1608-09, 1631-32, 1638, 1640, 1768, 1806, 1965, 1979, 1997,
2154, 2216, 2235, 2254.

LITERATURE AND LANGUAGE ARTS

1929   ALLEN, ARTHUR T. "Literature for Children: An Engagement for
          Life." Horn Book, 43 (December 1967), 732-37.
          The author feels that the child's involvement with
          literature should be a totally absorbing one in which
          listening, participating (creative dramatics, pantomime
          and play-acting), and then literary creation are the main
          ingredients.

1930   ALLEN, ELIZABETH GODWIN. "An Investigation of Change in
          Reading Achievement, Self-Concept, and Creativity of
          Disadvantaged Elementary School Children Experiencing
          Three Methods of Training." Ph.D. dissertation,
          University of Southern Mississippi, 1968.
          Investigations showed that only those children who
          participated in creative dramatics learned as many
          reading and creative skills as those children who
          remained in the formal classroom.

1931   ALLEN, JOAN GORE. "Creative Dramatics and Language Arts
          Skills." Elementary English, 46 (April 1969), 436-37.
          Shows a logical inter-relationship between the two
          disciplines; see Gwen Osten, "Structure in Creativity,"
          in the same issue for a companion article.

1932   ALLSTROM, ELIZABETH C. Let's Play a Story. New York:
          Friendship Press, 1957.
          Discusses a wide variety of drama-related activities,
          including story telling, puppetry, choral speaking, panto-
          mime, rhythm and role-playing.

1933   AMMERMAN, KATHLEEN G. "Can Children Interpret Literature?"
          Elementary English Review, 21 (October 1944), 207-10,
          223.
          Discusses a number of creative drama activities which
          allow a child to freely interpret and understand litera-
          ture.

LITERATURE AND LANGUAGE ARTS

1934   APPLEGATE, MAUREE. Easy In English: An Imaginative Approach
         to the Teaching of the Language Arts. Evanston, Illinois:
         Harper and Row, 1960.
               Gives a large variety of suggestions for teaching the
         language arts in the elementary school.

1935   ASHLEY, ROSALIND MINOR. Successful Techniques for Teaching
         Elementary Language Arts. West Nyack, New York: Parker
         Publishing Company, 1970.
               A considerable portion of this book is devoted to
         creative dramatics and imaginative play.

1936   ATKINSON, D. "New Approach: Drama in the Classroom." English
         Journal, 60 (October 1971), 947-51, 956.
               Discusses the ground rules for working with improvisa-
         tion in the English classroom.

1937   BAKER, ZELMA W. The Language Arts, the Child, and the
         Teacher. San Francisco: Fearon Publishers, 1955.
               A text book for future elementary school teachers;
         many examples of dramatic techniques are given.

1938   BALCH, MARSTON. "Start Them Young." Children's Theatre
         Review, 17 (May 1968), 11, 18.
               Emphasizes the importance of starting work in creative
         activities early in the child's school career.

1939   BANKS, ANGELA RITA. "The Integration of Speech Improvement
         Activities into a Public School Kindergarten." Master's
         thesis, University of Pittsburgh, 1951.

1940   BANNERMAN, ANDREW. "Approach to Shakespeare." Use of
         English, 20 (Spring 1969), 239-41.
               A British mixed-media approach to The Tempest
         involving tapes, interviews, improvisation and music.

1941   BARNARD, RAYMOND H. "Speech in the Elementary School."
         Childhood Education, 11 (March 1935), 271-74.
               Discusses some aspects of informal drama and how they
         aid good speech.

1942   BARNES, DOUGLAS. Drama in the English Classroom: Papers
         Relating to the Anglo-American Seminar on the Teaching
         of English at Dartmouth College, New Hampshire, 1966.
         Champaign, Illinois: National Council of Teachers of
         English, 1968.

CREATIVE DRAMATICS

(BARNES, DOUGLAS)
A Dartmouth Seminar Project compiled at the University of Leeds; among other things, it is concerned with drama as it relates to British teaching, primary education, democracy and general education.

1943 _____. Ed. Drama in English Teaching, Study Group Paper No. 2. New York: Modern Language Association, 1966.
Includes reports on drama "as threat", drama and composition, drama in primary and secondary education, and a view of the contemporary scene.

1944 BARUCH, DOROTHY W. "An Experiment with Language Expression in the Nursery School." Childhood Education, 8 (November 1931), 139-45.
The experiment includes work with informal dramatics, story telling, and rhythmic activities.

1945 BIRDSALL, RUTH. "Creative Dramatics: Motivates Reading." Instructor, 64 (January 1955), 75.

1946 BLAISDELL, THOMAS C. Ways to Teach English. Garden City, New Jersey: Doubleday, Doran and Company, 1930.
Gives a partial discussion of informal drama and literature.

1947 BLANK, EARL WILLIAM. "The Effectiveness of Creative Dramatics in Developing Voice, Vocabulary and Personality in the Primary Grades." Ph.D. dissertation, University of Denver, 1953.
Research finds that creative dramatics is productive in increasing the language arts skills of second graders; a bibliography follows.

1948 BORDAN, SYLVIA DIANE. Plays as Teaching Tools in the Elementary School. West Nyack, New York: Parker Publishing Company, 1970.
The author discusses playwriting with slow, average and superior students.

1949 BRACK, KENNETH H. "Creative Dramatics: Why? How? When?" Elementary English, 36 (December 1959), 565-67.
Emphasis is on spontaneous combustion in the classroom, with all curricular activities, in both a structured and non-structured fashion.

LITERATURE AND LANGUAGE ARTS

1950   BUCKEY, NADINE G. "We Start with a Story." Instructor, 63
        (November 1953), 69, 85.
            A discussion of how to begin creative dramatics
        activities; an example based on "The Princess Who Could
        Not Cry" is given.

1951   CATHER, KATHERINE DUNLAP. Educating by Story-Telling.
        Yonkers, New York: World Book Company, 1920.
            Shows the inter-relationship between story telling and
        spontaneous dramatic activity.

1952   C-D Grades 3 and 4: Teacher's Guide. Eugene: University of
        Oregon, 1971.
            Although these curricular guides are directed toward
        the teaching of composition, the major medium for
        initiating the subject is dramatic play.

1953   CHAMBERS, DEWEY W. "Children's Literature and the Allied
        Arts." Elementary English, 48 (October 1971), 622-27.
            A brief portion of this article (pp. 625-26) discusses
        children's literature and creative dramatics.

1954   _____. Literature for Children: Storytelling and Creative
        Drama. Dubuque, Iowa: William C. Brown and Company,
        1970.
            Included is a curriculum guide for work in creative
        dramatics.

1955   CHANDLER, RUTH F. "We Dramatized the Newberry Medals Books."
        Instructor, 67 (November 1957), 86-88.

1956   CHUBB, PERCIVAL. The Teaching of English in the Elementary
        and the Secondary School. Rev. ed. New York: Macmillan
        Company, 1929.
            Considers the use of informal dramatics in the school
        curriculum from kindergarten through high school.

1957   Classroom Practices in Teaching English, 1968-69: A Sixth
        Report of the NCTE Committee on Promising Practices.
        Champaign, Illinois: National Council of Teachers of
        English, 1968.
            This work, through a series of articles, discusses
        innovative programs that have high potential for teaching
        the language arts; included is a section on language
        development through creative dramatics.

CREATIVE DRAMATICS

1958   COHEN, LORRAINE. "Macbeth in the Fifth Grade." Grade
        Teacher, 87 (November 1969), 108, 110, 112, 114, 116, 118,
        120, 122.
            A re-counting of how fifth graders developed the
        Longfellow Theatre and Stock Company, sold shares,
        financed their creative dramatics production of Macbeth,
        and performed it.

1959   COMER, VIRGINIA LEE. Language Arts for Today's Children.
        New York: Appleton-Century-Crofts, 1954.
            Discusses several dramatic activities and their
        relationship to the language arts in the elementary
        school.

1960   COMMISSION ON THE ENGLISH CURRICULUM OF THE NATIONAL COUNCIL
        OF TEACHERS OF ENGLISH. The English Language Arts. New
        York: Appleton-Century-Crofts, 1952.
            Shows the application of creative dramatics to
        elementary and secondary education.

1961   COMMITTEE FOR THE ADVANCEMENT OF SPEECH EDUCATION IN ELEMEN-
        TARY SCHOOLS. "Speech in the Schools." Quarterly Journal
        of Speech, 19 (April 1933), 297-309.
            Defines the special role of creative dramatics in
        speech education.

1962   Composition: Grade Five. Teacher's Guide. Eugene: University
        of Oregon, 1971.
            The subject of composition is approached via imagina-
        tive and dramatic play.

1963   Composition: Grade Six. Teacher's Guide. Eugene: University
        of Oregon, 1971.
            For annotation, see above.

1964   COREY, EVELYN BROWN. "Speech Education Through Creative
        Channels." Quarterly Journal of Speech, 25 (December
        1939), 621-23.
            Gives suggestions for using dramatic activities with
        kindergarten and elementary school children.

1965   CORNWALL, PAUL. Creative Playmaking in the Primary School.
        London: Chatto and Windus, 1970.
            Concerned with the relationship between drama and
        writing, as well as other communicative and humanistic
        disciplines in the primary grades; detailed examples
        are given.

LITERATURE AND LANGUAGE ARTS

1966   COX, GLENDA SUE. "A Study of the Effectiveness of Teaching
        Language Through Creative Dramatics." Master's thesis,
        Texas Technological College, 1961.
            Results show that creative dramatics can help to
        teach the language arts.

1967   CRAWFORD, CAROLINE. "The Teaching of Dramatic Arts in the
        Kindergarten and Elementary School." Teacher's College
        Record, 16 (September 1915), 60-77.
            Advocates that teachers teach children how to synthesize
        facts in their creative dramatic activities, rather than
        just learn them.

1968   "Creative Dramatics Spurs Verbal Development: Rhode Island."
        Nation's Schools, 90 (September 1972), 51-52.
            A report on a Rhode Island program called IMPROVISE,
        manned by five teachers who tour the state teaching
        creative dramatics. One fifteen week experiment with
        fourth graders showed that their vocabulary growth rate
        doubled over a control group's.

1969   CROSBY, MURIEL. "Language as a Means of Expression."
        Educational Forum, 3 (May 1939), 430-37.
            Discusses creative dramatics and rhythmic activities
        with second graders in a language arts program.

1970   _____. "Values of Creative Dramatics." Recreation, 49
        (November 1956), 427-29.

1971   CRUST, ANITA WALTRIP. "Creative Dramatics." Grade Teacher,
        72 (January 1955), 28-29.
            Defines the term and shows it applicability to the
        classroom.

1972   DALLMAN, MARTHA. Teaching the Language Arts in the Elementary
        School. Dubuque, Iowa: W. C. Brown and Company, 1966.
            Includes some discussion of creative dramatics, puppet-
        ty and spontaneous drama.

1973   DAWSON, MILDRED AND FRIEDA HAYES DINGEE. Children Learn
        the Language Arts. Minneapolis: Burgess Publishing
        Company, 1959.
            Replaces Directing Learning in the Language Arts
        by the same author.

CREATIVE DRAMATICS

1974   DAWSON, MILDRED AND GEORGIANA C. NEWMAN. Language Teaching in Kindergarten and the Early Primary Grades. New York: Harcourt, Brace and World, 1966.
        Replaces Language Teaching in Grades 1 and 2 by Mildred A. Dawson.

1975   _____.; MARION ZOLLINGER; ARDWELL ELWELL. Guiding Language Learning. 2nd ed. New York: Harcourt, Brace and World, 1963.
        A revision of Teaching Language in the Grades.

1976   DELANCEY, FLOY W. "Playmaking and Children's Literature." Instructor, 63 (November 1963), 84.
        In the article, playmaking is synonymous with creative dramatics; the author shows its value in a language arts situation.

1977   De ROO, EDWARD. "Teaching Procedures for Writing a Play." Speech Teacher, 19 (November 1970), 257-61.
        Concerned with various creative methods which elicit informal and formal drama.

1978   DOBBS, ELLA VICTORIA. "Literature Through Dramatic and Graphic Art." Elementary English Review, 5 (February 1928), 52-54.

1979   DUNN, MARIE TERESE. "The Importance of the Speech Arts Program Within a Settlement House." Master's thesis, Emerson College, 1958.
        Work at the Elizabeth Peabody Settlement House, in Boston, from 1896 through 1957 is discussed; both formal and informal drama are covered.

1980   EDMONDS, EDITH. "Dramatic Play from Books." Elementary English, 30 (March 1953), 159-62.
        Lists fifty-three books as sources for creative drama materials.

1981   EMERSON, CORA. "A Fifth Grade's Adventure in Dramatics." Elementary English Review, 11 (November 1934), 247-49.
        Work with creative and improvisational drama in the language arts is discussed.

1982   "Emotional Balance Through the Language Program." National Education Association Journal, 41 (October 1952), 404-06.
        One section of the article is devoted to dramatic expression, through creative dramatics.

LITERATURE AND LANGUAGE ARTS

1983   ERWIN, RACHEL. "Rise! Lady Hilda Floradale!" Progressive
       Education, 8 (January 1931), 26-31.
           A third grade class presents a creative dramatization
       of a Medieval miracle play.

1984   FALBER, BALYA. "Speech Improvement Program for the Primary
       Grades of Levittown Public Schools." Master's thesis,
       Queen's College, 1966.
           Discusses a creative dramatics program for primary
       school children in Levittown, Long Island.

1985   FAULK, PEARL H. "Speech Education in the Elementary School:
       Neither Accidental or Incidental." National Education
       Association Journal, 56 (March 1967), 34.
           One of the techniques open to the classroom speech
       teacher, interested in creative responses, is informal
       drama.

1986   FERRY, ELIZABETH DUDLEY. "Our Own Plays: An Experiment in
       Creative Writing." Elementary English, 28 (March 1951),
       133-35.
           A creative dramatics exercise yields a script and an
       assembly program.

1987   FESSENDEN, SETH A. Ed. Speech for the Creative Teacher.
       Dubuque, Iowa: William C. Brown Company, 1968.
           Includes sections on creative dramatics and puppetry
       and discusses their uses in good speech and speech
       improvement.

1988   FITZGERALD, BURDETTE S. Let's Act the Story: A Leader's
       Guide for Dramatic Fun with Children's Literature.
       San Francisco: Fearon Publishers, 1957.
           Gives the methodology of initiating creative dramatics
       activities through good children's literature.

1989   FORDHAM, BELA. "A Study of Oral Language Objective and
       Content." Master's thesis, George Peabody College for
       Teachers, 1936.
           Gives some attention to the values of creative
       dramatics in the intermediate grade language program;
       shows the advantages of spontaneous work over methodical
       drill work.

1990   FREED, CATHERINE M. "A Study of the Status of General Speech
       Education in the Public Elementary Schools of the United
       States, 1961." Master's thesis, University of Kansas,
       1961.

CREATIVE DRAMATICS

(FREED, CATHERINE M.)
Elementary schools in 319 cities are surveyed; concludes that creative dramatics is one of the most effective techniques for teaching language arts.

1991   FURNER, BEATRICE A. "Creative Writing Through Creative Dramatics." Elementary English, 50 (March 1973), 405-08, 416.
The author gives some methodology for teaching writing using creative drama warm-ups.

1992   GLICKER, FRANK. J. "Shakespeare Made a Hit with My Sixth Grade." Instructor, 68 (March 1959), 64, 66.
Discusses a creative dramatics activity based on the Comedy of Errors.

1993   GRAUBARD, PAUL S. "Adapting Literature to Drama." Childhood Education, 38 (March 1962), 322-24.
Discusses an adaptation of The Gift of the Magi.

1994   GREENE, HARRY A. AND WALTER A. PETTY. Developing Language Skills in the Elementary Schools. 3rd ed. Boston: Allyn and Bacon, 1967.
Many aspects of informal drama, including creative dramatics and puppetry, are discussed in relation to a language arts program.

1995   HAARSTICK, WILMINE L. "A Projected Course of Study in Speech for Grades Three to Eight, Inclusive, of the Winner (South Dakota) Public Schools." Master's thesis, University of South Dakota, 1942.
The work suggests a heavy reliance on informal dramatic techniques in the elementary school speech program.

1996   HAHN, ELISE. "Speech Improvement in the Classroom." Master's thesis, Wayne State University, 1942.
Makes a distinction between speech correction and speech improvement and shows how creative dramatics benefits the latter.

1997   _____. AND WALDO PHELPS. "A Speech Course for Elementary School Teachers." Western Speech, 16 (March 1952), 93-101.
Advocates a strong background in creative dramatics for elementary school teachers in speech arts programs.

CHILDREN'S THEATRE AND CREATIVE DRAMATICS

1998   HAHN, RUTH HARRIET. "Primaries Dramatize Favorite Stories."
        Instructor, 72 (March 1963), 59, 125.

1999   HATCHETT, ETHEL. AND DONALD H. HUGHES. Teaching Language
        Arts in the Elementary Schools: A Functional-Creative
        Approach. New York: The Ronald Press, 1956.
            Many aspects of informal drama are included in this
        discussion of a language arts program.

2000   HATFIELD, WALTER WILBUR. An Experience Curriculum in English:
        A Report of the Curriculum Commission of the National
        Council of Teachers of English. New York: C. Appleton
        and Century Company, 1935.
            Creative dramatics in many disciplines of the elemen-
        tary school curriculum is discussed.

2001   HAYES, ELOISE. "Drama, Big News in English." Elementary
        English, 47 (January 1970), 13 16.
            Author discusses how creative drama is becoming the
        center of the English program in elementary education
        because of the vitality and insight it brings to
        language arts.

2002   HENRY, MABLE WRIGHT. Ed. Creative Experiences in Oral
        Language. Champaign, Illinois: National Council of
        Teachers of English, 1967.
            Parts IV and V contain eight essays on creative
        dramatics and formal theatre for children; a valuable
        source book for a wide cross-section of children and
        drama-related subjects.

2003   HERMAN, DELDEE M. AND SHARON TARLIFFE. Eds. Speech Activities
        in the Elementary School. Michigan Speech Association
        Curriculum Guide I. Skokie, Illinois: National Textbook
        Company, 1972.
            This pamphlet updates the 1968 Michigan Speech Associa-
        tion curriculum guide for elementary school children. It
        deals with nonverbal communication, story telling, informal
        dramatics and the teacher's role in child communication.

2004   _____. AND SHARON TARLIFFE. Eds. Speech and Drama in the
        Intermediate School. Michigan Speech Association Guide
        II. Skokie, Illinois: National Textbook Company, 1972.
            Similar in concept to Curriculum Guide I, this
        pamphlet treats six primary subjects: interpersonal
        communication, group communication, formal speaking,
        story telling, reading aloud and creative dramatics.

CREATIVE DRAMATICS

2005   HOETKER, JAMES. Dramatics and the Teaching of Literature.
       Champaign, Illinois: National Council of Teachers of
       English, 1969.
              A monograph concerned with the influence of drama on
       the teaching of literature. Techniques such as creative
       dramatics, oral expression and role-playing are discussed.

2006   HUCKLEBERRY, ALAN W. AND EDWARD S. STROTHER. Speech Education
       for the Elementary Teacher. Boston: Allyn and Bacon,
       1966.
              Discusses formal and informal drama in the elementary
       school language arts program.

2007   Improvisation and the Teaching of Literature: The Proceedings
       of a Symposium. St. Ann, Missouri: Central Midwestern
       Regional Lab, 1969.
              The monograph analyzes improvisational sessions and
       the value of improvisation in self-expression, self-
       confidence and sensitivity. Comments on the conclusions
       are given by Geoffry Summerfield and Robert F. Hogan.

2008   JACOBS, LELAND B. "Enjoy Literature at School." Education,
       78 (January 1958), 259-62.
              Informal drama is suggested as one method for enjoying
       literature.

2009   JAMES, KATHRINA BROWN. "A Handbook of Speech Training for
       the Elementary Teacher." Master's thesis, University of
       Alabama, 1941.
              Some materials for creative dramatics are included in
       the thesis.

2010   JENNINGS, ALICE. "Incidental Dramatics." Elementary English
       Review, 2 (November 1925), 330-31.
              The term "incidental dramatics" includes both formal
       and informal drama in the elementary curriculum.

2011   JOHNSON, GLADYS. "Dramatizing 'Rip Van Winkle'." Instructor,
       56 (March 1947), 32, 75.

2012   JONES, CAROLYN. "The Status of Speech Improvement in Elemen-
       tary Classrooms of the Public Schools of the United
       States." Master's thesis, Louisiana State University,
       1958.
              Among other things, the thesis discusses the status of
       creative dramatics programs in speech improvement.

CHILDREN'S THEATRE AND CREATIVE DRAMATICS

2013   JONES, EMILY. "Children Should Learn to Talk." Instructor,
        56 (September 1947), 22, 85, 91.
            Gives a brief discussion of children and story acting.

2014   KING, CAROLYN JOYCE. "The Development of a Suggestive Speech
        and Drama Program for the Negro Elementary Schools of
        Tennessee." Master's thesis, Tennessee Agricultural and
        Industrial State University, 1952.

2015   KING, CAROLINE VIRGINIA. "Guides to the Teaching of Speech
        in Florida Elementary Schools." Master's thesis,
        University of Florida, 1952.

2016   KIRKTON, CAROLE M. "Classroom Dramatics: Developing Oral
        Language Skills. NCTE/ERIC Report." Elementary English,
        48 (February 1971), 254-61.
            The article justifies the use of creative dramatics
        in the elementary classroom and surveys some of the major,
        recent works related to creative dramatics and the
        language arts.

2017   KRAMER, MAGDALENE. "Everybody Talks, But How?" National
        Education Association Journal, 45 (December 1956), 561-63.
            Discusses formal and informal drama in the classroom.

2018   LILLYWHITE, IRIS. "An Analysis of Techniques for the Improve-
        ment of Speech as Incorporated in the General Curriculum
        of One Fifth Grade Class of the Nettie L. Waite School
        in Norwalk, California, During the Year of 1948-49."
        Master's thesis, Whittier College, 1950.

2019   LUSTY, BEVERLY L. "Speech Contents in Language Arts Text-
        books." Speech Teacher, 16 (November 1967), 289-94.
            Summarizes the work of three Northwestern University
        doctoral dissertations; some mention of creative dramatics
        is given.

2020   MABIE, ETHEL. "Free Speech for Children." Childhood Educa-
        tion, 12 (January 1936), 152-57.
            Emphasis is on free expression through improvisation
        and informal drama.

2021   MacCLINTOCK, PORTER LANDER. Literature in the Elementary
        School. Chicago: University of Chicago Press, 1908.
            Analyzes the creative process in children in relation-
        ship to literature and informal dramatics.

CREATIVE DRAMATICS

2022   MACKINTOSH, HELEN K. "How Fundamental Are the Language Arts?"
        Childhood Education, 35 (December 1958), 157-61.
            Stresses the value of creative dramatics in a
        language arts program.

2023   MALATESTA, ANNE. "An Unexpected Outgrowth of Creative
        Dramatization." Instructor, 63 (May 1954), 57.
            Discusses a sixth grade creative dramatics approach to
        Alice in Wonderland, and its effect on the students'
        creative ability to express.

2024   MARGRETTA, SISTER. O.S.B. "Foreign Language Dramatizations."
        Catholic School Journal, 64 (February 1964), 64-65.
            Sixth graders' work in German is discussed.

2025   MARSHMAN, ROGER. "Aspects of Junior School Drama - A
        Discursion." Opinion: The Journal of the South Australian
        English Teachers' Association, 11 (May 1967), 31-34.
            Gives a discussion of creative dramatics and dance as
        tools for literature understanding and appreciation in
        elementary education.

2026   MARTIN, CAROLYN LOUISE. "Creative Dramatics Techniques in
        the Elementary School Speech Improvement Program."
        Master's thesis, University of Virginia, 1959.

2027   MARTIN, MARY R. "Acting Out a Story - Primary Grades."
        Instructor, 55 (March 1946), 15, 32.

2028   McLEOD, FRANCIS. "Play-Acting with Our Reading." Volta
        Review, 54 (February 1952), 60, 84.
            Discusses a variety of informal dramatics techniques
        in a special reading program.

2029   MEADER, EMMA GRANT. "Speech Teaching in the Elementary
        Schools of England and the United States." Quarterly
        Journal of Speech, 16 (February 1930), 156-62.

2030   MEKEEL, SUSAN J. "Idea Bag: Characterization - Love It or
        Leave It." Media and Methods: Explorations in Education,
        6 (April 1970), 60.
            The author describes a dramatic activity wherein
        students pick a character from literature and dramatize
        the role for the class.

2031   MELODY, PATRICIA L. "Children's Interests in Story Content
        for Children's Theatre." Master's thesis, University of
        Kansas, 1967.

LITERATURE AND LANGUAGE ARTS

2032 MENAUGH, H. BERESFORD. "Creative Dramatics." Guiding Children's Literature, Pose Lamb. Ed. Dubuque, Iowa: William C. Brown Company, 1967. Pp. 63-91.
An extensive discussion of the application of creative dramatics to elementary education.

2033 MERRILL, JOHN. "Creative Effort - Dramatizing Mother Goose Rhymes." Francis W. Parker Studies in Education, 8 (1925), 82-95.

2034 MEYER, ROSE D. "Third Graders Act Out Their Reading." Grade Teacher, 83 (May 1956), 54, 90.

2035 MILLER, EDITH F. "Dramatization and the Language Arts Program." Elementary English, 29 (January 1952), 14-19.
Emphasis is on creative dramatization in the primary grades, and its value to the student.

2036 MILLER, ELIZABETH CHRISTINE. "Dramatic Play." Instructor, 53 (October 1944), 32, 62.
Discusses a creative dramatics exercise based on "The Town Musicians."

2037 _____. "Let's Play 'Sleeping Beauty'." Instructor, 56 (April 1947), 49, 80-81.

2038 MILLSAP, LUCILLE. "The Ubiquitous Book Report." Reading Teacher, 24 (November 1970), 99-105.
Emphasizes the correlation of writing with other creative activities, such as creative dramatics.

2039 MOFFET, JAMES. Drama - What Is Happening: The Use of Dramatic Activities in the Teaching of English. Champaign, Illinois: National Council of Teachers of English, 1967.
This monograph deals with the process of dramatic interaction in the study of literature; some attention is given to playwriting.

2040 MOORE, WALTER J. "A Thousand Topics for Composition: Revised Elementary Level." Illinois English Bulletin, 58 (February 1971), 1-32.
Category three deals with dramatization, playwriting, characterization and related subjects.

2041 MULLER, HERBERT J. The Uses of English: Guidelines for the Teaching of English from the Anglo-American Conference at Dartmouth College. New York: Holt, Rinehart and Winston, 1967.

CREATIVE DRAMATICS

(MULLER, HERBERT J.)
Report shows that there was more informal dramatic involvement in British education than American.

2042 MUNKRES, ALBERTA. <u>Helping Children in Oral Communication</u>. New York: Bureau of Publications, Columbia University Teachers College, 1959.
Discusses the advantages of using informal drama in a language arts program.

2043 MUSSOFF, LEONORE. "Not By Mind Alone: A Workshop Approach to the English Classroom." <u>English Journal</u>, 62 (March 1973), 446-47.
The author feels that improvisational drama in the classroom enhances a student's ability to express, and gratifies his needs for recognition and reinforcement.

2044 NICHOLSON, DAVID. "It'll Change Your Life." <u>Independent School Bulletin</u>, 32 (December 1972), 30-32.
Advocates that creative approaches to, and activities in, dramatics give the student self-awareness and an understanding of life and literature.

2045 OBERLE, MARCELLA. "A Contemporary View of Elementary Education." <u>Speech Teacher</u>, 19 (December 1960), 267-70.
Gives the rationale for having speech education and language arts programs in the elementary curriculum.

2046 OGILVIE, MARDEL. "Creative Speech Experiences in the Elementary Schools." <u>Speech Teacher</u>, 7 (January 1958), 6-10.
Discusses the uses of story telling, which broaden into creative dramatics.

2047 _____. <u>Speech in the Elementary School</u>. New York: McGraw-Hill, 1954.
Gives some attention to creative dramatics and puppetry; discourages teachers from working with formal dramatics in the elementary school.

2048 O'LEARY, HELEN AND ROBERT F. MURPHY. "Creative Book Reporting." <u>Instructor</u>, 75 (September 1965), 60.
Gives thirty-five creative ways to do book reports.

2049 OSBAND, HELEN. "Making Stories Live for Children." <u>Quarterly Journal of Speech</u>, 20 (April 1935), 252-55.
Surveys a course in story telling at Alabama College for Women.

228

LITERATURE AND LANGUAGE ARTS

2050   OSTEN, GWEN. "Structure in Creativity." Elementary English,
        46 (April 1969), 438-53.
            A companion piece to "Creative Dramatics and Language
        Arts" by Joan Gore Allen, in the same issue. Discusses
        creative development and motivation through various
        activities.

2051   PAINE, M. J. AND A. J. PARSONS. "Acting the Reader."
        English Language Teaching, 25 (October 1970), 27-32.
            The authors show how to motivate students to dramatize
        reading material and thus enrich their motivation and the
        classroom situation.

2052   PARENT, NORMA. "Speech Techniques and Children's Literature."
        Elementary English, 27 (November 1950), 45-53.

2053   PARRET, MARGARET. "The Program in Spoken English." Elemen-
        tary English, 24 (April 1947), 225-29.
            Describes the various ingredients of a good speech
        program in elementary education.

2054   PARRY, CHRISTOPHER. English Through Drama: A Way of Teaching.
        New York: Cambridge University Press, 1972.
            Results of the author's work with eleven through
        thirteen year olds in the Peese School, Cambridge, Eng-
        land, are given. Parry sees dramatic expression and
        literature as inseparable, and advocates "creative
        discipline" but with none of the pejorative connotations
        the term might imply.

2055   PEABODY, PAMELA. "English: Relevance of School Dramatics."
        Independent School Bulletin, 28 (May 1969), 70-71, 73.
            A report from the National Association of Independent
        Schools, February 1969.

2056   PEARSON, FRANCES. "'The Play's the Thing' for Speech
        Training." Elementary English Review, 16 (December 1939),
        291-93, 296.

2057   _____. "Speech Training through Children's Plays." Quarter-
        ly Journal of Speech, 22 (October 1936), 660-68.
            Puppetry is linked with good speech in the elementary
        school.

2058   PEINS, MARYANN. "Speech Techniques for the Classroom."
        Elementary English, 27 (November 1950), 446-49.
        Emphasizes the value of creative dramatics in speech
        training.

CREATIVE DRAMATICS

2059   PERRY, HILDA IDA. "An Exploratory Study of Methods for
        Speech Improvement in Lower Elementary Grades." Master's
        thesis, Michigan State University, 1956.

2060   PIERSON, HOWARD. "Pupils, Teachers and Creative Dramatics."
        Creative Ways in Teaching the Language Arts: A Portfolio
        of Elementary Classroom Procedures. Alvina Trout Burrows.
        Ed. Champaign, Illinois: National Council of Teachers of
        English, 1957. Pp. 5-8.

2061   PIQUETTE, JULIA C. "Needed: Adequate Speech Training for
        Elementary Education Majors." Speech Teacher, 19
        (October 1960), 275-77.

2062   POOLE, IRENE. "Introducing the Speech Program." Quarterly
        Journal of Speech, 20 (February 1934), 85-96.
            Shows how to initiate a speech program, through
        creative dramatics, in the elementary grades.

2063   _____. "Speech Achievement in the Elementary School."
        Quarterly Journal of Speech, 17 (November 1931), 478-92.
            Gives attention to both formal and informal dramatics
        in the elementary school, but recommends the use of the
        latter.

2064   POPOVICH, JAMES. "Creative Dramatics." National Education
        Association Journal, 49 (November 1960), 29-30.
            Gives a definition of the term and shows its applica-
        tion.

2065   PORTER, E. JANE. "Reflections of Life Through Books."
        Elementary English, 50 (February 1973), 189-95.
            Concerned with sensitivity training, reading games
        and creative dramatics, as well as their effect on
        learning through books.

2066   POSSIEN, WILMA M. They All Need to Talk: Oral Communication
        in the Language Arts Program. New York: Appleton-
        Century-Crofts, 1969.
            Gives some attention to creative dramatics and creative
        play in the classroom.

2067   POTTER, LOIS SHEFTE. "A Plan for Individualized Speech
        Activities in the Elementary School." Speech Teacher, 15
        (September 1966), 200-06.
            Explains the value of creative dramatics in speech
        improvement.

LITERATURE AND LANGUAGE ARTS

2068   PRONOVOST, WILBERT AND LOUISE KINGMAN. The Teacher of Speak-
        ing and Listening in the Elementary School. New York:
        Longmans, Green and Company, 1959.
        A teacher training manual that includes a discussion
        of both formal and informal dramatics.

2069   PRUIS, JOHN J. "General Speech Training in the Elementary
        School." Quarterly Journal of Speech, 36 (December 1950),
        524-27.
        Advocates spontaneity in beginning speech exercises.

2070   _____. "A Study of Concepts Concerning General Speech Train-
        ing in the Elementary School." Ph.D. dissertation,
        Northwestern University, 1951.

2071   PURVIS, ALAN C. Ed. How Porcupines Make Love: Notes on a
        Response-Centered Curriculum. Lexington, Massachusetts:
        Xerox Education Group, 1972.
        This English curricular approach is concerned with
        acclimating the student to his response to himself and
        others. Chapter V discusses "Ways of using classroom
        drama to enhance literature."

2072   QUINTUS, BERNICE MAE. "Stories Suitable for Dramatization on
        the Seven-to-Eight-Year Old Level." Master's thesis,
        University of Washington, 1950.
        Lists and analyzes sixty-seven stories.

2073   RANGER, PAUL. Experiments in Drama. London: University of
        London Press, 1970.
        Primary school experiments with words, sounds and
        poetry are applied to traditional elementary school
        projects.

2074   RASMUSSEN, CARRIE. Speech Methods in the Elementary School.
        Rev. ed. New York: The Ronald Press, 1960.
        A teacher-training manual for learning to apply
        creative techniques to elementary speech curricula.

2075   RAUBICHECK, LETITIA. How to Teach Good Speech in Elementary
        Schools. New York: Noble and Noble Publishers, 1937.
        Surveys many aspects of informal dramatics and their
        application to a speech program.

2076   REASONER, CHARLES F. "Enjoying Literature Visually." Using
        Literature with Young Children. Leland B. Jacobs. Ed.
        New York: Bureau of Publications, Columbia University
        Teachers College, 1965. Pp. 41-47.

CREATIVE DRAMATICS

2077   REID, VIRGINIA M. "Language Opportunities." Childhood
        Education, 38 (January 1962), 212-14.
            Discusses the application of creative dramatics and
        story telling to the language arts program.

2078   RISSO, SHIRLEY HIGHLAND. "Creative Dramatics Sugar Coats
        Learning." School and Community, 59 (November 1972), 32,
        74.
            Despite the pejorative title, the author advocates
        creative drama usage in reading classes.

2079   ROBERTS, OLYVE J. "Dramatization of Memory Poems for Grades
        III and IV." Primary Education-Popular Educator, 45
        (March 1928), 532.

2080   ROGERS, CHRISTINE. "Kindergarten Theatre." Instructor, 80
        (November 1970), 30.
            A description of a kindergarten improvisation of
        "The Three Bears."

2081   SCHUELL, HILDRED. "An Approach to Speech in the Elementary
        Curriculum." Quarterly Journal of Speech, 27 (April
        1941), 262-66.
            Discusses the function of many informal dramatics
        procedures in the elementary school.

2082   SEEDS, CORINNE. "The Language Arts and the Elementary School
        Activities." Progressive Education, 10 (April 1933),
        204-09.
            Gives some attention to creative dramatics and
        dramatic play.

2083   SHANE, HAROLD G; MARY E. REDDIN; MARGARET C. GILLESPIE.
        Beginning Language Arts Instruction with Children.
        Columbus, Ohio: Charles E. Merrill Books, 1961.
            Describes work with puppets as well as creative
        dramatics activities; includes an extensive bibliography.

2084   SHARP, ELIZABETH. "Relieving the Monotony in Primary
        Recitations." Instructor, 42 (September 1933), 31, 66.
            Advocates the use of rhythmic activities and informal
        drama.

2085   SMITH, JAMES A. Creative Teaching of the Language Arts.
        Boston: Allyn and Bacon, 1967.

LITERATURE AND LANGUAGE ARTS

2086   SMITH, RODNEY P., JR. Creativity in the English Program.
        Champaign, Illinois: National Council of Teachers of
        English, 1970.

2087   STEWIG, JOHN WARREN. "Creative Drama and Language Growth."
        Elementary School Journal, 72 (January 1972), 176-88.
            An elementary primer of creative dramatics concepts
        for the language arts teacher.

2088   STRICKLAND, RUTH G. The Language Arts in the Elementary
        School. 3rd ed. Lexington, Massachusetts: D. C. Heath
        and Company, 1969.
            Gives some attention to dramatic play and its effect
        on a language arts program.

2089   THOMPSON, BARBARA K. "Improving the Young Child's Speech."
        National Education Association Journal. 48 (December
        1959), 13-14.
            Elaborates on the value of informal dramatic
        activities in speech improvement.

2090   TIDYMAN, WILLARD F.; CHARLENE W. SMITH; MARQUERITE BUTTERFIELD.
        Teaching the Language Arts. 3rd ed. New York: McGraw-
        Hill, 1969.
            Chapter I contains references to a multitude of
        informal drama techniques for kindergarten and elementary
        school children.

2091   TIEDT, IRIS M. AND SIDNEY W. TIEDT. Contemporary English in
        the Elementary School. Englewood Cliffs, New Jersey:
        Prentice-Hall, 1967.
            Shows the link between speech and literature; there
        is some discussion of creative dramatics and puppetry.

2092   TRAUGER, WILMER K. Language Arts in Elementary Schools.
        New York: McGraw-Hill Company, 1963.
            Discusses many aspects of informal dramatics and
        their use in the language arts program.

2093   TOMMER, CAROLINE J. AND TERESA A. REGAN. Directing Language
        Power in the Elementary School Child Through Story,
        Dramatization, and Poetry. New York: Macmillan Company,
        1933.

2094   TROXELL, ELEANOR. Language and Literature in the Kindergarten
        and Primary Grades. New York: Charles Scribner's Sons,
        1927.

CREATIVE DRAMATICS

2095   TUCKER, JOANNE KLINEMAN. "The Use of Creative Dramatics as an Aid in Developing Reading Readiness with Kindergarten Children." Ph.D. dissertation, University of Wisconsin, 1971.
        Results of the study were directed towards (1) developing a curriculum of creative drama in the kindergarten; (2) analyzing the role of the "classroom teacher and the specialist in leading creative dramatics activities"; and (3) the effect of creative dramatics on specific learning ability in a reading readiness program.

2096   WAGNER, GUY; MAX HOSIER; MILDRED BLACKMAN. Language Games: Strengthening Language Skills with Instructional Games. Darien, Connecticut: Teachers Publishing Corporation, 1963.

2097   WARD, WINIFRED. "Creative Dramatics." The Role of Speech in the Elementary School. A Bulletin of the Department of Elementary School Principals. Washington, D.C.: National Education Association, 1947. Pp. 75-79.

2098   _____. "Creative Dramatics as a Medium for Teaching Literature." Elementary English Review, 10 (February 1933), 40-44.

2099   WATSON, MARY STONE. "A Survey of the Teaching of Speech in the First Six Grades in the Maryland Puplic Schools." Master's thesis, University of Maryland, 1965.

2100   WELSCH, J. DALE. "A Speech Program in a Small School System." Quarterly Journal of Speech, 20 (November 1934), 557-64.
        Applies the concepts of story telling to all elementary grades.

2101   WERNER, LORNA SHOGREN. Speech in the Elementary School. Evanston, Illinois: Row, Peterson and Company, 1947.
        Advocates the use of a variety of improvisational techniques including rhythmic activities, pantomime, and dramatic play.

2102   ZIEGLER, ELSIE MAE. "A Study of the Effects of Creative Dramatics on the Progress in Use of the Library, Reading Interests, Reading Achievement, Self-Concept, Creativity, and Empathy of Fourth and Fifth Grade Children." Ph.D. dissertation, Temple University, 1970.
        Results suggest there is negligible effect.

Children's Theatre and Creative Dramatics

LITERATURE AND LANGUAGE ARTS

See also the following entries. 146, 157, 257, 259, 265, 278, 289-90, 319, 333-34, 360, 367, 1438, 1540, 1557, 1608, 1705, 1728, 1769, 1786, 1824, 1856, 1887, 1907, 1980, 2155, 2171-72, 2179, 2195.

SCIENCES AND SOCIAL SCIENCES

2103 ABBOTT, CHRISTABEL. "Dramatic Training in the Normal Schools of New York State." Education, 32 (October 1911), 99-104.
      Advocates the use of informal dramatic exercises to teach character building and development. Emphasis is on teacher training.

2104 ADAMS, RUTH. "How We Play Store." Instructor, 58 (October 1949), 11.
      Concerned with teaching mathematics to second grade students through the vehicle of creative dramatics and simple plot creation.

2105 ADLAND, DAVID. "Drama as a Social Activity." Opinion: The Journal of South Australian English Teachers, 12 (August 1968), 7-18.
      Demonstrates a wide spectrum of formal and informal dramatic activities and the effect they have on a child's emotional growth.

2106 ANDREWS, HAZEL M. "Vocational and Moral Guidance through Dramatics." Education, 41 (September 1921), 130.

2107 ARTH, ALDRED A. AND J. HOWARD JOHNSTON. "Dramatization and Gaming for Optimum Environmental Survival." Elementary English, 50 (April 1973), 539-43.
      Stresses teaching environmental awareness through informal drama.

2108 BALLOU, BARBARA. "The Fifth Grade Makes Up a Play." Grade Teacher, 73 (May 1956), 55, 88.
      Describes an American History project dealing with westward expansion, and the development of a performed play through creative dramatics.

2109 BIRDSALL, RUTH. "Learning to Know Latin Americans by Acting Out Stories About Them." Instructor, 65 (April 1956), 43, 87-88.
      A brief bibliography of related materials is included with this creative dramatics introduction to Latin Americans.

CREATIVE DRAMATICS

2110   BLACK, ELIZABETH. "Informal Dramatics as a Socializing
        Force." Instructor, 54 (Spetember 1945), 38.
            Emphasizes self awareness, analysis and criticism
        through informal drama. Costumes, scenery and conscious
        rehearsal are discouraged.

2111   BRATTON, DOROTHY ANN. "Dramatization in the Social Studies."
        Social Education, 4 (April 1940), 250-57.
            Suggests that informal dramatics is a natural approach
        to learning about social studies because of the pleasure
        involved in dramatic activities. Side benefits include
        improved language skills and esthetic appreciation.

2112   BRITTIN, ARTHUR. "Role Playing." Speech and Drama, 23
        (Spring 1974), 2-8.
            A British approach to dramatics, sociology and the
        methodology of role playing.

2113   CAFFIERE, BLANCHE H. "Science Through Creative Dramatics."
        Grade Teacher, 78 (April 1961), 50, 127.
            Process includes creative dramatics, dance, rhythmic
        activities and pantomime to teach elementary science.

2114   CLAPP, ELSIE RIPLEY; ELISABETH SHEFFIELD; GEORGE BEECHER.
        "Plays in a Country School." Progressive Education, 8
        (January 1931), 35-38.
            Explores creative dramatic activities in three rural
        school classrooms. Reprinted in Creative Expression,
        Gertrude Hartman and Ann Shumaker, eds.as "Plays in a
        Kentucky School."

2115   CLARK, ELIZABETH. "The Seed That Grew." Instructor, 70
        (March 1961), 60-61.
            A third grade science project on plants, through
        creative dramatics, grows into a formalized assembly
        program with costumes, music, dance and narration.

2116   COFFIN, REBECCA J. "'Let's Play.'" Progressive Education,
        8 (January 1931), 46-53.
            The study of one aspect of ancient Egypt leads to
        dramatization of the material. Reprinted in Creative
        Expression, Gertrude Hartman and Ann Shumaker, eds.

2117   COGGIN, LEONARD P. "Creative Drama: Bringing History up to
        Date." Instructor, 65 (September 1955), 43.
            Deals specifically with a creative dramatics scene
        between Queen Elizabeth and Sir Walter Raleigh; other
        suggestions for enlivening history are given.

SCIENCES AND SOCIAL SCIENCES

2118   CORY, FRANCIS McGUIRE, JR. "The Utilization of Creative
        Dramatics with Social Studies Units in the Sixth Grade,
        Everett, Washington." Master's thesis, University of
        Washington, 1954.
            Argues that all forms of informal dramatics are
        valuable for teaching and enriching social studies.

2119   CURTIS, NELL C. "We Could Have a Market." Progressive
        Education, 10 (February 1933), 89-91.
            Describes the author's work with third and fourth
        graders in a private school in Southern California; gives
        specific suggestions for dramatizing scenes about markets
        in other countries.

2120   DALLMANN, MARTHA. "The Role of Dramatics in the Social
        Studies." Grade Teacher, 78 (April 1961), 64-65, 143-47.
            Discusses the role of puppetry, formal and informal
        drama in teaching social studies; several examples are
        given.

2121   DENECKE, LENA. "'My Country is the World' - A Fifth Grade
        Project." Elementary English, 24 (November 1947), 435-53.
            An extended explanation of an inter-racial project in
        local history and geography; an original play with music
        was developed.

2122   DIENES, Z. P. Mathematics through the Senses: Games, Dance
        and Art. New York: Fernhill House Ltd., 1973.
            An informal approach to informal dramatics.

2123   DOLLIVER, LONA. "Making a Visit to Congo Land." Instructor,
        43 (September 1934), 21, 64.
            Study plans for a creative dramatics project in
        geography are given; the exercise ultimately lead to a
        formal production with sets and costumes.

2124   ESTERLY, ELIZABETH NORCROSS. "Can Children Understand Social
        Justice?" Progressive Education, 11 (November 1934),
        407-10.
            Work with eleven-year-old history students is described;
        creative dramatics yields a formal play.

2125   FITZGERALD, VIRGINIA. "Creative Dramatics: An Aid to
        Character Education." Grade Teacher, 64 (January 1947),
        17, 80-81.
            Briefly describes the beginning steps of creative
        dramatics and stresses the value of character and

CREATIVE DRAMATICS

(FITZGERALD, VIRGINIA)
imagination building; following the Reynard principle,
the author discourages heros who are also villains.

2126   FLAGG, ANN. "Helping Children Understand the Negro's
Contribution to American Society." Children's Theatre
Review, 16 (May 1967), 13-15.
Concerned with the improvement of self-image among
Black children who participated in a program of creative
dramatics based on the history of the American Negro.

2127   FUSSHIPPEL, MARTHA. "History is Dramatic." Instructor, 77
(February 1968), 124-126.
Discusses creative dramatic play and a production of a
playlet based on the Boston Tea Party.

2128   GORDON, VIRGINIA. "'Ham' and Arithmetic." Instructor, 67
(January 1958), 32.
A fourth grade creative dramatic project based on
problems in arithmetic ultimately leads to an auditorium
assembly program.

2129   GREELEY, ERMA E. "A Third Grade Studies Indian Life."
National Education Association Journal, 26 (April 1937),
121.
Using the example of dramatized scens from "Hiawatha,"
the author discusses the value of dramatic activity to
tie numerous different subjects together for study.

2130   HAHN, H. H. "How History May be Made Real to Children in the
Grades." Education, 58 (September 1937), 26-34.
Nine techniques to make history become real to students
are given; the author stresses the use of informal
dramatics at all times.

2131   HALL, CECILE B. "Dramatization of History: Suggestions for
Motivating the Recitation Period." Grade Teacher, 49
(September 1931), 40-41, 71.
Urges teachers to allow students to take the role of
prominent historical figures to learn about them and to
avoid the boredom of memorizing facts.

2132   HALLOCK, GRACE TABOR. Dramatizing Child Health: A New Book
of Health Plays, with Chapters on the Writing, the
Producing, and the Educational Value of Dramatics. New
York: American Child Health Association, 1925.

SCIENCES AND SOCIAL SCIENCES

(HALLOCK, GRACE TABOR)
The manual stresses the value of formal and informal
dramatics and their related arts for health instruction;
several plays are given plus a bibliography of additional
plays.

2133 HARLAN, BETTY LaVERNE. "The Value of the Theatre as an
Integrating Experience." Master's thesis, Baylor
University, 1954.

2134 HORN, ERNEST. Methods of Instruction in the Social Studies:
American Historical Association Report of the Commission
on the Social Studies, Part XV. New York: Charles
Scribner's Sons, 1937.
A critical evaluation of techniques used in elementary
education; the author advocates the use of both formal
and informal dramatics in teaching social studies, but
feels that most teachers are not qualified to lead
dramatic activities in the classroom.

2135 HOROWITZ, TILLIE. "Possibilities in Dramatic Play."
Instructor, 62 (February 1953), 31.
Advises teachers to use students' innate enthusiasm
for dramatics to teach American History.

2136 HOUSTON, CELESTINE; DOROTHY KROH; AUDREY JOYCE. "Hawaii."
Instructor, 68 (April 1959), 34-35.
Each author describes her method of studying Hawaii
through creative dramatics in the elementary classroom;
brief bibliographies are included.

2137 HOYT, HELE E. "Creating a Program on Water Conservation."
Instructor, 54 (February 1945), 28, 53.
An improvisational assembly program on water conserva-
tion is described.

2138 HUBBARD, ELEANOR E. "History Through Drama." Education, 55
(June 1935), 609-13.
Advocates totally spontaneous dramatic play to re-create
great moments in history; examples are given.

2139 _____. The Teaching of History through Dramatic Presentation.
Chicago: Benjamin H. Sanborn and Company, 1935.
A radical departure from the work above; author
advocates the use of structured drama to teach history,
although suggestions for informal dramatics are given.
The author feels that only "subnormal and supernormal"
children function well in a totally spontaneous situation.

CREATIVE DRAMATICS

2140   LOCKWOOD, MARGARET M. AND HELEN J. TOWSON. "The Creation of
       a Dramatic Unit." National Education Association Journal,
       26 (February 1937), 47.
            A creative dramatics playlet "Sokar and the Crocodile"
       which grew out of a study of Egypt is discussed.

2141   LUDEMAN, W. W. "The Lewis and Clark Expedition." Instructor,
       46 (March 1937), 24, 77.
            Among other things, the author advocates the use of
       creative dramatics in the study of history, and focuses on
       a Lewis and Clark project in his classroom.

2142   MARGOLIS, ANNETTE KRASSNER. "Education, Dramatics and
       Character." Speech Magazine, 5 (December 1940), 178-81.
            Suggests that literature with high moral value is the
       best for creative activities in the schools.

2143   MARIS, IRENA. "Promoting Courtesy through Acting and Art."
       Instructor, 65 (September 1955), 43.
            Shows the effectiveness of creative dramatics to teach
       politeness and courtesy; dramatic activities are most
       effective when followed by a discussion of what has been
       learned.

2144   MICHAELIS, JOHN U. Social Studies for Children in a Democracy.
       New York: Prentice-Hall, Inc., 1955.
            The author feels that creative dramatics, rhythmic
       activities and improvisation greatly enhance the study of
       social studies in elementary school situations; techniques
       and approaches are discussed.

2145   MILLER, EDITH F. "Dramatizing the Social Studies." Instruc-
       tor, 55 (January 1946), 29, 60, 62.
            Stresses the use of creative dramatics to enliven
       social studies in elementary education; several different
       approaches are discussed.

2146   MITCHELL, JULIA D. "Making an Historical Play." Chicago
       Schools Journal, 14 (January 1932), 224-27.
            Work with third and fourth graders in dramatizing the
       invention of the skin boat is described; emphasis is on
       improvisation, but pre-structuring is necessary.

2147   PETERSON, AILEEN. "Easter Far and Near, Then and Now."
       Instructor, 62 (March 1953), 32-65.
            Dramatizing different stories about Easter with fourth
       through eighth graders is discussed; the author feels
       that the final product should be appropriate to classroom
       or assembly production.

SCIENCES AND SOCIAL SCIENCES

2148 _____. "The Great Corn Feast." Instructor, 65 (November
    1955), 73, 86.
        Discusses an informal play that resulted from the
    study of American Indians; the author shows several ways
    of formalizing the play.

2149 PINE, TILLIE S. "We Dramatize the United Nations." Child-
    hood Education, 23 (May 1947), 435-36.
        Work with inter-racial fourth graders in New York
    City and how they dramatized the founding of the United
    Nations in San Francisco is discussed.

2150 PRESTON, RALPH C. Teaching Social Studies in the Elementary
    School. 3rd ed. New York: Holt, Rinehart and Winston,
    Inc., 1968.
        Using formal and informal dramatics is one of the
    methods for enhancing a student's involvement in social
    studies and his understanding of himself and others in a
    social situation.

2151 RUSSELL, MARY M. Drama as a Factor in Social Education. New
    York: George H. Doran Company, 1924.
        Shows how formal and informal dramatics can be used in
    the classroom; several examples are given.

2152 RYAN, MARGARET A. "The Play's the Thing." Instructor, 45
    (June 1936), 26, 76.
        A creative dramatics project based on the history of
    the Fulton Steamboat ultimately leads to a pageant
    production for an assembly.

2153 SANFORD, JEAN. "Our Garden Assembly." Instructor, 53 (June
    1944), 16, 57.
        The planting and cultivating of Victory gardens is
    acted out creatively.

2154 SCHWARTZ, CAROLE. "A Suggested Creative Dramatic Workshop
    Based on the Social Study Curriculum Utilized in the New
    York Syosset School System." Master's thesis, University
    of Denver, 1959.
        Plans for a twenty hour training program in creative
    dramatics for elementary school teachers are given;
    methods and materials are included.

2155 SCOTT, COLIN ALEXANDER. Social Education. Boston: Ginn and
    Company, 1908.

CREATIVE DRAMATICS

(SCOTT, COLIN ALEXANDER)
Based on Dewey's philosophy of education, the work advocates openness in the classroom; special emphasis on informal drama in language arts and social studies programs.

2156 SEEDS, CORINNE. "Dramatic Play as a Means to Democratic Social Living." Childhood Education, 19 (January 1943), 128-22.
Stresses the role of dramatic play in the maturation process.

2157 _____. "Playing Ukrainian Farmer." Progressive Education, 22 (May 1945), 30-31.
A fourth grade creative dramatics exercise based on a social studies unit on Russia grows into a formal play entitled "A Day on the Hammer and Sickle Collective."

2158 SIMOS, JACK. Social Growth through Play Production. New York: Association Press, 1957.
A potpourri book with sections on creative drama, formal drama, performing for disturbed children, play production, social growth and drama, and the technical aspects of children's plays for and by children.

2159 SPARLING, JOSEPH J. "Dramatic Play in Science." Instructor, 75 (February 1966), 28.
Simple science projects related to biology, mathematics and physics lend themselves to dramatic play.

2160 STEVENS, BERTHA. "Earth Sciences and Children." Progressive Education, 7 (November 1930), 326-33.
Creative dramatics, rhythmic activities and poetry are used to teach seven-year-old children about the earth sciences; some methods are included.

2161 TOWNSEND, W. B. "Modern Methods of Teaching the Social Sciences." Instructor, 43 (April 1934), 14, 31.
Advocates a multi-disciplinary approach to social studies, including dramatic activities.

2162 TUTTLE, H. S. "Drama for Democratic Citizenship." Journal of the National Education Association, 33 (January 1944), 18.

SCIENCES AND SOCIAL SCIENCES

2163   VOORHEES, MARGARETTA A. "Social Studies in the Beaver
        County Day School." Progressive Education, 2 (October-
        November-December 1925), 241-46.
            Describes a project with primary and intermediate
        school children in social studies using creative
        dramatics and improvisation to play the roles of histori-
        cal characters.

2164   WALKER, ALBERTA. "Dramatization and Current Events."
        Elementary School Journal, 16 (November 1915), 125-31.
            An historical piece that shows the author's shift
        from formal play creation in the classroom to informal
        dramatics, and the benefits gained.

2165   WALKER, EDITH V. AND MARTHA A. BENNETT. "Using Dramatic
        Experiences to Instill Democratic Ideals." National
        Elementary Principal, 22 (July 1943), 403-09.

2166   WARD, WINIFRED. "Wave of the Future." Motive, 5 (February
        1945), 19-20.
            Describes a semester-long project with sixth graders
        studying Chinese history; the final product is a performed
        play and the author gives her methodology and approach as
        well as philosophy.

2167   WOODS, MARGARET S. "Creative Dramatics: An Exciting New Way
        to Teach Safety." Safety Education, 43 (May 1964),
        14-17.
            Gives examples of ways children can use creative
        dramatics to learn safety rules, and ultimately think
        creatively about safety.

2168   ZINO, BETTY. "Pirate Songs and Play Acting Aid in Study of
        'Early Exploration' Period." New York State Education,
        47 (February 1960), 22-23.
            Stories about pirates are dramatized using dance and
        music along with creative dramatics.

2169   ZINMASTER, WANNA M.   "Contributions of Creative Dramatics to
        Teachings Social Studies." Speech Teacher, 14 (November
        1965), 305-13.
            Concerned with the sense of reality that creative
        dramatics lends to social studies; work with third
        graders in the classroom is discussed.

CREATIVE DRAMATICS

2170   ZINMASTER, WANNA M. "Exploring the Art of Creative Dramatics
        in the Teaching of Social Studies." Ed.D. dissertation,
        Columbia Teachers College, 1962.
            An in-depth analysis of the role of creative dramatics
        in the social studies program; a bibliography is included.

        See also the following entries. 265, 332, 341, 348, 366,
        560, 804, 1286, 1431, 1500, 1684, 1710-11, 1728, 1791, 1793,
        1887, 1907.

SPECIAL EDUCATION

2171   ARCHER, KAY MORGAN. Drama for the Disadvantaged: Boston-
        Northampton Language Arts Program, ESEA, 1965. Washing-
        ton, D.C.: Office of Education, Department of Health,
        Education and Welfare, 1968.
            Report describes a Title I summer program for academi-
        cally handicapped students, using creative dramatics.

2172   AXLINE, VIRGINIA MAE. "Play Therapy - A Way of Understanding
        and Helping 'Reading Problems'." Childhood Education,
        26 (December 1949), 156-61.
            Gives a definitional distinction between play therapy
        and the therapy of play, and discusses methods to aid
        backward readers.

2173   BARRY, DOROTHY O. "Creative Dramatics: Its Relation to Speech
        Correction." Master's thesis, University of Wisconsin,
        1951.
            Creative dramatics, puppetry and play therapy are
        offered as methods to correct speech problems when
        individual instruction on a one-to-one basis is not
        available to the handicapped child; techniques are
        discussed.

2174   BRAGG, BERNARD. "The Human Potential of Human Potential: Art
        and the Deaf." American Annals of the Deaf, 117 (October
        1972), 508-11.
            Mr. Bragg, a member of the National Theatre of the
        Deaf, strongly advocates the use of the creative arts in
        the education of the deaf.

2175   BROWN, HELEN MOORE. "The Account of an Experiment Showing
        the Effects of a Year's Work in Creative Dramatics on a
        Group of Problem Children." Master's thesis, Northwestern
        University, 1936.

SPECIAL EDUCATION

(BROWN, HELEN MOORE)
Work with maladjusted children is discussed, but results are inconclusive.

2176 BURNS, BRENDA S. "The Use of Play Techniques in the Treatment of Children." Child Welfare, 49 (January 1970), 37-41.
Describes play techniques (some of which are communicative) and their application to the treatment of emotionally disturbed children.

2177 CARLSON, KAY. "Singing Roles for Pinocchio." Dramatics, 44 (November 1972), 24-26.
Developing talents of the deaf through the Junior National Association of the Deaf at the South Dakota School for the Deaf is discussed.

2178 CARLSON, RUTH KEARNEY. "Raising Self-Concepts of Disadvantaged Children through Puppetry." Elementary English, 47 (March 1970), 349-55.
Treats the procedures for elevating student motivation and self-appreciation, emphasizing the advantages of puppets as alter ego factors.

2179 COOPER, DAVID. "Relevancy and Involvement: Literature for the Disadvantaged." English Record, 19 (October 1968), 47-51.
Advocates flexibility of approach (through creative dramatics) and relevancy and contemporariness in materials for disadvantaged youths studying literature.

2180 CRYSTAL, JOSIE. "Role-Playing in a Troubled Class." Elementary School Journal, 69 (January 1969), 169-79.
Concerned with involving Black and disadvantaged children in problem-solving through role-playing in the classroom.

2181 DIETRICH, J. R. "Dramatics That Are Out of Sight: Illinois Braille and Sight Saving School." School Activities, 40 (April 1969), 12-13.
Work at a Jackson, Illinois School for the Blind is discussed.

2182 EBSEN, NANCY. "Performing for Handicapped Children." Children's Theatre Review, 16 (February 1967), 9-10.
Examines the work of the Children's Theatre Guild of Newport Harbor for mentally retarded children; some attention to the methods for choosing suitable plays.

245

CREATIVE DRAMATICS

2183   EICHMANN, GRACE SHULL. "Drama in Juvenile Delinquency Pre-
       vention." Recreation, 37 (January 1944), 563-64, 586.
           Discusses the eighth season of the Children's Theatre
       of Visalia, California.

2184   ENGLAND, A. W. "Caliban, Beatie Bryant and 1H." English in
       Education, 4 (Spring 1970), 42-6, 48.
           Shows the moral development of remedial students
       through improvisation and role playing.

2185   ERVIN, JEAN C. "Speech Improvement in the Elementary School."
       Speech Teacher, 7 (September 1958), 185-90.
           Makes a distinction between speech correction and
       speech improvement - the latter being a technique that a
       layman can use, especially in conjunction with creative
       activities.

2186   FLIEGLER, LOUIS A. "Play-Acting with the Mentally Retarded
       Children'." Journal of Exceptional Children, 19
       (November 1952), 56-60.
           The author finds that creative dramatic play is
       especially beneficial in developing reading readiness,
       improving language and stimulating speech and listening
       awareness with mentally retarded children.

2187   GAFFNEY, JOHN P., JR. "Creative Dramatics for Hard-of-
       Hearing Children." Volta Review, 54 (October 1952),
       321-26.
           Advocates the use of creative dramatics with hard-of-
       hearing students because of the free atmosphere under
       which it is conducted.

2188   GIANELLONI, SISTER MARY EDWARD, O. P. "A Survey of the
       Professional Attitudes, Objectives and Basic Approaches
       to Speech Improvement in the Elementary Schools with
       Suggested Courses of Study in Speech for the Parochial
       Schools in New Orleans." Master's thesis, Louisiana
       State University, 1948.
           A portion of the thesis is devoted to creative
       dramatics activities.

2189   GILMORE, IRIS PAVEY. "The Use of Informal Dramatic Projects
       in Developing Social Adjustment on the Elementary Level."
       Master's thesis, University of Denver, 1944.
           Testing indicates that informal dramatics are benefi-
       cial in developing personality as well as a broader
       understanding of inter-related arts.

SPECIAL EDUCATION

2190 GITTER, L. L. "Creative Dramatics as a Teaching Tool."
The Journal for Special Educators of the Mentally
Retarded, 8 (Winter 1972), 128-34.
Explores the potential of creative dramatics in work
with the mentally retarded student.

2191 GOODE, JESSIE MAE. "A Description of the Expressive Language
of Five Psychotic Children Before and After a Program of
Speech Therapy." Master's thesis, University of Pittsburgh, 1957.

2192 GRAMS, JEAN D. "Dynamics of Psycho-Drama in the Teaching
Situation." Sociatry, March 1948, pp. 393-400.
Gives a definition of terms and application of
procedures related to psycho-drama.

2193 HAHN, ELISE. "Role-Playing, Creative Dramatics, and Play
Therapy in Speech Correction." Speech Teacher, 4
(November 1955), 232-39.
Defines these three forms of creative expression and
shows their relevance to creativity development; some
mention of puppetry is included.

2194 HAYES, ELOISE. "Creative Drama at Kalihi-Uka." Today's
Education, 57 (September 1968), 30-32.
Discusses creative dramatics with elementary school
children who have language problems.

2195 HENDRICKSON, RICHARD H. AND FRANCES S. GALLEGOS. Using
Creative Dramatics to Improve the English Language Skills
of Mexican-American Students. Washington, D.C.: Office
of Education, Department of Health, Education and Welfare,
1972.
Study involved children in grades two through seven;
conclusions suggest positive results and a general
applicability of the program to the classroom situation.

2196 HOLBROOK, DAVID. English for the Rejected: Training Literacy
in the Lower Streams of the Secondary School. New York:
Cambridge University Press, 1964.
An appendix to this book includes a discussion of
dramatic work with backward children and is applicable to
pre-secondary school children.

2197 JACKSON, LYDIA AND KATHLEEN M. TODD. Child Treatment and the
Therapy of Play. 2nd ed. New York: The Ronald Press,
1950.

CREATIVE DRAMATICS

(JACKSON, LYDIA)
Discusses the therapy of play (as opposed to the non-generic "play therapy") and its benefit to the child who has some form of neurosis. The subject is well delineated and the authors hope to convince the reader that this is a "highly specialized branch of child treatment and one not to be embarked upon by the untrained, however enthusiastic...."

2198 JODER, ANNA BEST. "Children's Theatres and Juvenile Delinquency." Players Magazine, 5 (May 1943), 8, 16.
Advocates using Children's Theatres to fight the rising crime rate during the war.

2199 KENNY, VIRGINIA. "A Better Way to Teach Deaf Children." Harper's Magazine, 42 (March 1962), 61-68.
States that deaf children are the best pantomimists in the world, and that teachers and parents should allow their deaf children to use their talent.

2200 KENT, MARGARET SCOTT. Suggestions for Teaching Rhythm to the Deaf. Frederick, Maryland: Maryland School Press, 1934.
Includes a bibliography of related sources.

2201 KOENIG, FRANCES G. "Implications in the Use of Puppetry with Handicapped Children." Journal of Exceptional Children, 17 (January 1951), 111-12, 117.
Because of physical limitations, the author feels that handicapped children can not respond well to creative dramatics; however, she advocates the use of puppets as an adequate substitute.

2202 KRISE, MORLEY. "Creative Dramatics and Group Psychotherapy." Journal of Child Psychiatry, 2 (January 1952), 3, 337-42.

2203 LEMAN, G. "Creative Dramatics for the Deaf and Hard of Hearing Pupils." Volta Review, 69 (November 1967), 610-13.

2204 LESHER, MIRIAM. "The Use of Dramatics as an Aid in Rehabilitation in Psychological Speech Disorders." Master's thesis, Penn State University, 1950.
Tests the ability of creative dramatics techniques to elevate speech disorders of a psychological nature; results are not totally conclusive.

SPECIAL EDUCATION

2205   LUDWIG, CHARLOTTE. "The Effect of Creative Dramatics Upon
        the Articulation Skills of Kindergarten Children."
        Master's thesis, University of Pittsburgh, 1955.
            Test shows that creative dramatics has some beneficial
        effect on speech improvement.

2206   MARCHAND, LOUIS V., JR. "A Study of Adolescent Psychology
        and Its Relation to Dramatic Arts." Master's thesis,
        University of Denver, 1950.
            Concerned with the role of the director of dramatic
        activities in the school situation; conclusions are
        concerned with improving the role and the calibre of the
        occupation.

2207   McGILL, AUDREY JANET. "The Effectiveness of the Use of
        Puppets in Oral Language Development of Culturally
        Disadvantaged First-Grade Children." Ph.D. dissertation,
        North Texas State University, 1970.
            The general conclusion of this four month study is
        that "The puppets were best used for entertainment or
        play and were a hindrance during goal-directed activities"
        especially when students were highly motivated to communi-
        cate interpersonally.

2208   McINTYRE, BARBARA M. "The Effect of a Program of Creative
        Activities upon the Consonant Articulation Skills of
        Adolescent and Pre-Adolescent Children with Speech
        Disorders." Ph.D. dissertation, University of Pitts-
        burgh, 1957.

2209   _____. Informal Dramatics: A Language Arts Activity for the
        Special Pupil. Pittsburgh: Stanwix House, 1963.
            A three part book which (1) discusses creative
        dramatics and the average child, (2) treats creative
        activities for mentally retarded children, and (3) gives
        a list of source materials applicable to the subjects.

2210   _____. AND BETTY JANE McWILLIAMS. "Creative Dramatics in
        Speech Correction." Journal of Speech and Hearing Dis-
        orders, 24 (August 1959), 275-79.
            Work at the Speech Clinic at the University of Pitts-
        burgh from 1952 to 1959 is described.

2211   MORKOVIN, BORIS V. "Thought Patterns of Deaf Children: What
        Does This Imply for the Classroom Teacher?" Volta Review,
        66 (September 1964), 491-94.
            Implications are applicable to the creative dramatics
        leader.

CREATIVE DRAMATICS

2212   MOSKOWITZ, ESTELLE. "Dramatics as an Educational Approach to
       the Mentally Handicapped." The Quarterly Journal of
       Speech, 28 (April 1942), 215-18.

2213   MUNNS, W. E. "Theatre for Upward Bound." The Teacher's
       College Journal, 38 (January 1967), 158-60.
            Suggestions for a theatre-oriented program related to
       Upward Bound are given.

2214   MYERS, DONALD GEORGE. "A Comparison of the Effects of Group
       Puppet Therapy and Group Activity with Mentally Retarded
       Children." Ph.D. dissertation, Lehigh University, 1970.
            Study envolved forty-eight students at Penn State's
       Demonstration School who ranged in age from seven to
       fifteen. It concludes that puppet therapy significantly
       improves mentally retarded student's ability to adjust
       and adapt, although there was no vidence of an effect on
       intelligence. See McGill, Audrey Janet above for
       comparison.

2215   NASH, WILLIAM ROSCOE. "Facilitating the Creative Functioning
       of Disadvantaged Young Black Children." Ph.D. disserta-
       tion, University of Georgia, 1971.
            The author theorizes that young black children perform
       better during creativity testing when they have experi-
       enced a period of creative warm-up before the test. One
       device used is creative dramatics.

2216   NICHOLS, HILDRED. "Role-Playing in Primary Grades." Group
       Psychotherapy, 7 (December 1954), 238-41.

2217   OLSON, JACK R. AND CARROLL HOVLAND. "The Montana State
       University Theatre of Silence." American Annals of the
       Deaf, 117 (December 1972), 620-25.
            Describes a summer touring theatre company composed of
       deaf as well as normal hearing actors and its benefits to
       the exceptional child.

2218   PIERINI, PATRICIA MARIES. "Application of Creative Dramatics
       to Speech Therapy." Master's thesis, Penn State Univer-
       sity, 1956.

2219   PROKES, SISTER DOROTHY, F.S.P.A. "Exploring the Relationship
       between Participation in Creative Dramatics and Develop-
       ment of the Imagination Capacities of Gifted Junior High
       School Students." Ph.D. dissertation, New York University,
       1971.
            Deals with "the nature and characteristics of gifted-

SPECIAL EDUCATION

(PROKES, SISTER DOROTHY, F.S.P.A.)
ness, as well as the issues and problems concerning it;
and the nature, educational implications, and values of
creative dramatics were considered."

2220 The Reticent Child in the Classroom: Oral Communication
      Concepts and Activities. A Manual for Teachers.
      Hayward, California: Almeda County School Department,
      1969.
          Of relevance are models for eight lesson plans and a
      bibliography on creative dramatics related to the reti-
      cent child.

2221 RICH, J. DENNIS. "The National Theatre of the Deaf." Players
      Magazine, 47 (February-March 1972), 115-19.
          Part of the article is devoted to a discussion of the
      Little Theatre of the Deaf, its purposes and products.

2222 ROBINSON, LILLIAN. "Role Play with Retarded Adolescent
      Girls: Teaching and Therapy." Mental Retardation, 8
      (April 1970), 36-37.
          Briefly shows the effects of dramatic play with
      mentally handicapped girls.

2223 ROYCE, ELIZABETH S. "The Play Is the Thing: Dramatics Can
      Do a Lot for Special Class Pupils." New York State
      Education, 54 (January 1967), 41-43.
          Work with retarded children in elementary education
      is discussed.

2224 SAVAGE, MRS. GEORGE. "Children's Theatre: Theatre for Spastics."
      Players Magazine, 26 (November 1949), 38.
          Discusses the materials and program of the Seattle
      Junior Programs.

2225 _____. "Recreation for Spastics." Players Magazine, 25
      (November 1948), 38-39.
          Emphasis is on participation rather than placid
      observation.

2226 SCHATTNER, REGINA. Creative Dramatics for Handicapped
      Children. New York: John Day Company, 1967.
          Describes creative dramatics work with physically
      handicapped children; nine playlets with a narrator and
      music are included.

CREATIVE DRAMATICS

2227   SCHISGALL, JANE. "The Creative Use of Multimedia (Or the
        Shape of Strings to Come)." Teaching Exceptional Child-
        ren, 5 (Summer 1973), 162-69.
            Lists eight multimedia approaches to creative dramatics
        and their use with emotionally and academically disturbed
        children.

2228   SHAPIRO, MARVIN I. The Development of Communication Skills
        Project. Final Report. Pittsburgh: Pittsburgh Child
        Guidance Center, 1965.
            Discusses a clinically-controlled project with five
        and six year old inarticulate children using a non-
        clinical teacher of creative dramatics. The resulting
        level of articulation and emotional response of the
        children showed that the project was profitable.

2229   SHELLHAMMER, LOIS B. "Solving Personal Problems through
        Sociodrama." English Journal, 38 (November 1949), 503-05.

2230   WHITE-BASKIN, JAQUELYN. "Slow Learning Children: Self-
        Expression and School Subjects." Instructor, 62
        (January 1953), 60.
            Advocates using creative dramatics to motivate slow
        learners in reading, science, social science and music.

2231   WILSON, DOROTHY B. "Creative Dramatics for Speech Therapy."
        Instructor, 79 (December 1969), 76.
            Shows how creative dramatics eliminates tensions and
        provides for spontaneous expression in speech therapy.

2232   YOAKAM, DORIS G. "Speech Games for Children." The Quarterly
        Journal of Speech, 30 (February 1944), 85-87.
            Concerned with correcting speech impediments.

        See also the following entries. 113, 127, 201, 319, 323, 399,
        400, 472, 607, 686, 1070, 1438, 1531, 1578, 1608, 1776, 1891,
        1905, 1915, 1917, 1982, 2015, 2028, 2158.

RELIGIOUS EDUCATION

2233   ATKINS, ALMA NEWELL. Drama Goes to Church. St. Louis:
        Bethany Press, 1931.
            Discusses both formal and informal drama and their
        benefits to religious education; however emphasis is on
        spontaneous creation. Materials and methods are given.

RELIGIOUS EDUCATION

2234   BROWN, JEANETTE PERKINS. <u>Storytelling in Religious Education</u>.
         Boston: The Pilgrim Press, 1951.
         Analyzes techniques of story-telling for children
         nursery age through fourteen, and their place in
         religious education; a source book related to beginning
         work in creative dramatics.

2235   CITRON, SAMUEL J. <u>Dramatics for Creative Teaching</u>. New York:
         United Synagogue Book Service, 1961.
         Procedures and methods for using creative dramatics,
         pantomime, sociodrama and storytelling in a Jewish school
         curriculum are given.

2236   _____. "Socio-Drama in Teaching Bible or Hunrash." <u>New York</u>
         <u>Jewish Education Committee Bulletin</u>, 13 (March 1954),
         n. p.
         Informal dramatic techniques are stressed.

2237   EDLAND, ELIZABETH. <u>Children's Dramatizations</u>. Boston: The
         Pilgrim Press, 1926.
         Explores methods and techniques of formal and informal
         drama in religious situations.

2238   EGGLESTON, MARGARET W. <u>The Use of the Story in Religious</u>
         <u>Education</u>. Garden City, New York: Doubelday, Doran and
         Company, 1920.
         Some attention to informal dramatics, as an outgrowth
         of storytelling, and as an adjunct to religious education,
         is given.

2239   EHRENSPERGER, HAROLD A. <u>Conscience on Stage</u>. New York:
         Abingdon-Cokesbury Press, 1947.
         Advocates the use of spontaneous drama to stimulate
         religious living and education; creative dramatics and
         storytelling are stressed. A bibliography of related
         works is included.

2240   _____. <u>Religious Drama: Ends and Means</u>. New York: Abingdon
         Press, 1962.
         A wide spectrum of dramatic activities are covered;
         a large annotated bibliography of related materials is
         included.

2241   EMMANUEL, SISTER MARY, S.M. "Drama as a Means of Religious
         Education." <u>Catholic School Journal</u>, 54 (April 1954),
         64A, 66A, 68A.

CREATIVE DRAMATICS

(EMMANUEL, SISTER MARY, S.M.)
Stresses the use of creative dramatics to teach Bible-related stories; author feels that the teacher's role should be one of non-interference, and creativity should not be hampered by props, scenery or costumes.

2242   FIELD, ELLIOT. "Drama in the Church: A Religious Drama Workshop." Players Magazine, 26 (May 1950), 188.
Techniques developed in a one week summer workshop related to religious education are given.

2243   KESSLER, HARRY L. Creative Dramatics for Young Judean Clubs. New York: New York Leaders' Council Series, 1944.

2244   LAMB, DOROTHEA MARY KREUGER. "The Drama in Religious Education." Master's thesis, University of Denver, 1938.
The author's research related to formal and informal drama in religious education is given plus a brief history of religious drama; recommendations for materials and methods are offered.

2245   LOBINGIER, ELIZABETH ERWIN MILLER. The Dramatization of Bible Stories: An Experiment in the Religious Education of Children. Chicago: University of Chicago Press, 1918.
Stresses the leader's role in creative dramatics related to Bible stories; proposes that the leader stay aloof from activities unless requested to give suggestions. Some methodology is given.

2246   _____. Stories of Shepherd Life: A Second-Grade Course of Study Suitable for Primary Departments of Church Schools, Week-Day Schools of Religion, and Church Sunday Schools. Chicago: University of Chicago Press, 1924.

2247   LOOMIS, AMY. "Drama in the Church: Summer Workshop." Players Magazine, 28 (March 1952), 141.
Announces the Fourth Annual Religious Drama Workshop and its program of study.

2248   MEREDITH, WILLIAM V. Pageantry and Dramatics in Religious Education. New York: Abingdon Press, 1921.
Stresses informal dramatics and its value for character building and moral education.

2249   MORRISON, ELEANOR SHELTON AND VIRGIL E. FOSTER. Creative Teaching in the Church. Englewood Cliffs, New Jersey: Prentice-Hall, Inc., 1963.

RELIGIOUS EDUCATION

(MORRISON, ELEANOR SHELTON)
Discusses creative dramatics, improvisation and puppetry and their value in stimulating pre-school and elementary school aged children in a religious atmosphere.

2250 MURPHY, F. DELFINE. "Drama in the Church Community: A Training Program in Religious Education." Ph.D. dissertation, University of Denver, 1949.
Surveys the use of dance, puppetry and creative dramatics in religious education for leaders with little or no previous experience.

2251 NIEBUHR, HULDA. Ventures in Dramatics for Boys and Girls of the Church School. New York: Charles Scribner's Sons, 1935.
Primarily a collection of plays written and produced by nine to fourteen year olds; the introduction summarizes the goals of informal and formal dramatics in religious education.

2252 RAINE, JAMES WATT. Bible Dramatics. New York: Century Company, 1927.
Discusses informal dramatics for primary children and formal approaches for older children.

2253 RICHARDSON, NORMAN E. The Church at Play: A Manual for Directors of Social and Recreational Life. New York: Abingdon Press, 1922.
Surveys informal dramatics methods for adults and children; includes a bibliography and source materials.

2254 SHAFTEL, GEORGE AND FANNIE R. SHAFTEL. Role Playing the Problem Story. New York: Commission on Educational Organizations, National Conference of Christians and Jews, 1952.
Concerned with various approaches to human relations and moral education in the religious classroom, and in cross-ethnic situations.

2255 SIKS, GERALDINE B. "Children Learn through Dramatic Activity." International Journal of Religious Education, 37 (February 1961), 16-17, 45-46.
Suggests that creative dramatics is a good method for teaching religious education, but advises the leader to be selective in choosing materials to dramatize. Procedures for working with elementary school children are given.

CREATIVE DRAMATICS

2256   SMITHER, ETHEL L. The Use of the Bible with Children: A Text-
        book in the Standard Course in Leadership Training,
        Approved by the Curriculum Committee of the Board of
        Education of the Methodist Episcopal Church. New York:
        Abingdon-Cokesbury Press, 1937.
            Shows the methods of using dramatic play with kinder-
        garten aged children, informal dramatics with primary
        children, and quasi-formal drama with junior high school
        aged children.

2257   TAYLOR, MARGARET FISK. Time of Wonder. Philadelphia:
        Christian Education Press, 1961.
            Suggestions for creative dramatics and rhythmic
        movement exercises related to religious education are
        given.

2258   _____. A Time to Dance: Symbolic Movement in Worship.
        Philadelphia: United Church Press, 1967.
            Gives procedures for developing a creatively-oriented
        dance choir for children and adults.

2259   WALLARAB, BARBARA JEAN. "Creative Dramatics in Religious
        Education." Master's thesis, Michigan State University,
        1960.
            Emphasis is on story dramatization and creative
        movement for kindergarten through junior high school aged
        children; procedures are given.

2260   WARD, WINIFRED. "It's Fun to Dramatize." The Baptist Leader,
        June 1953, pp. 30-31.
            Shows leaders and potential leaders how to use creative
        dramatics to enhance Bible studies.

2261   _____. "It's Fun to Dramatize." Child Guidance in Christian
        Living, June 1953, pp. 3-4.
            See above for annotation.

2262   _____. "It's Fun to Dramatize." Children's Religion, June
        1953, pp. 7-8.
            See above for annotation.

2263   _____. "Meaning Coming Through with Power: The Values of
        Creative Drama in the Church School." Motive, April 1958,
        pp. 30-31.
            Gives a definition of creative dramatics, and stresses
        its value in teaching moral and religious awareness.

RELIGIOUS EDUCATION

2264 _____. "Play the Story." Child Guidance in Christian Living,
June 1947, pp. 241-43.
Shows how children learn character development through
informal dramatizations; a short bibliography is given.

2265 WARGO, DAN AND DOROTHY WARGO. Dramatics in the Christian
School. St. Louis: Concordia Publishing House, 1966.
A two part book concerned with (1) creative dramatics,
socio-drama and puppetry in the church school, and (2)
religious-oriented play production for child audiences.
Seven plays with production notes are included.

2266 WILCOX, HELEN L. Bible Study through Educational Dramatics.
New York: Abingdon Press, 1924.
Emphasis is on creative dramatics techniques.

2267 WINTHER, ALICE MEYERS. "Littlest Ones Play-Act What Stories
Mean." Christian Science Monitor, 83 (June 1956), 13.
Describes creative activities with kindergarten aged
children.

2268 WOOD, WILLIAM CARLETON. The Dramatic Method in Religious
Education. New York: Abingdon Press, 1931.

2269 WYKELL, ESTHER. Creative Dramatics in the Jewish School: A
Manual for Teachers with Suggested Materials. Chicago:
Board of Jewish Education, 1962.
Discusses the advantages of using creative dramatics
in the religious school; a ten page outline of methods is
included.

See also the following entries. 127, 148, 281, 611, 747,
1612, 1627, 1675-76, 1727, 1915.

Author Index

Bemet, Merlin Edwin, Jr., 1318
Benary, Blanche, 254
Bendick, Jeanne, 1319
Benet, Rosemary, 1018
Bennett, Martha A., 2165
Benson, Myra, 660
Berk, Barbara, 1319
Berman, Sadye A., 1649
Bertram, Jean De Sales, 1188, 1775
Best, Mrs. A. Starr, 553
Bethea, Sara Kathryn [Kay], 255-56
Bice, Margaret Garrett, 1650
Bienstock, Sylvia F., 296
Bigby, Charles Wesley, 1776
Birdsall, Ruth, 661, 1535, 1777-82,
  1945, 2109
Birner, William B., 1189
Biroc, John, 1536
Black, Donald, 554
Black, Elizabeth, 2110
Blackie, Pamela, 1537
Blackman, Mildred, 2096
Blaisdell, Thomas C., 1946
Blanchard, Dagny Hanson, 1783
Blanchard, Dorothy, 550
Bland, Jane C., 1538
Blank, Earl W., 1506, 1947
Block, Dorothy, 5
Bloom, Kathryn, 1784
Bloyom, Marian, 1019
Blumberg, Fredric, 1190
Boas, Guy, 1651
Bobbett, Celeste S., 1020
Bock, Frank George, 1320
Bodwin, Shirley, 1539
Bogen, Melvin, 118
Bolte, Denslow E., 376
Bolten, Mary, 846
Bonar, Hugh S., 119
Bordan, Sylvia D., 1948
Borgers, Edward W., 120
Bork, Kurt, 436
Borten, Helen, 257
Bourne, John, 121
Bowen, Frances Cary, 663, 664
Boyer, Martha May, 6
Boynton, Portia Cecelia, 1191
Brack, Kenneth H., 1949
Braden, George, 557
Bradley, David, 1540
Brady, Bea, 1541

Bragg, Bernard, 2174
Brain, Geraldine M., 651. [See
  Geraldine B. Siks].
Brainwaite, Mary R., 1193
Bramwell, Ruby Phillips, 1194
Brantley, John C., 1823
Bratton, Dorothy Ann, 2111
Braucher, Howard S., 377
Braucher, Mrs. Howard S., 122-123
Braun, Marilyn Helene, 1195
Brazier, Harriet, 847
Brenes, Eleanor H., 1542
Briggs, Elizabeth D., 7
Brinkerhoff, Mary, 1022
British Children's Theatre
  Association, 8
Brittin, Arthur, 2112
Broadbent, R. J., 258
Broadman, Muriel, 665
Brocker, Sharon Loretta, 1023
Brockett, Joseph, 1321
Brockett, Oscar G., 9
Brown, Corinne, 1507, 1652
Brown, Eva, 1653
Brown, Grace Anderson, 259
Brown, Helen, 2175
Brown, Ida Stewart, 1785
Brown, Jeanette Perkins, 2234
Brown, Virginia T., 1786
Bruford, Rose, 260
Brush, Martha S., 124, 666, 1322
Bryan, Betty Brooks, 1196
Buckhanan, Roberta M., 1024
Buckey, Nadine G., 1950
Buckley, Rose, 261
Bullough, Bess, 912
Bulow-Hanson, Tage, 438
Burger, Isabel B., 439, 849,
  1508-1511, 1543, 1654, 1787-
  88
Burkart, Ann Kammerling, 10, 54
Burke, Barbara Willock, 1197
Burnett, Beatrice, 1323, 1789
Burnett, Hazel Manzor, 782
Burns, Brenda S., 2176
Burrows, Alvina Trout, 1790
Busbee, Vivian, 1791
Bush, Sadie, 850
Butler, Donna L., 106, 1198
Butler, Karolyn Kay, 557
Butler, Katherine G., 1910

Author Index

Melnitz, William W., 66
Melody, Patricia L., 2031
Menaugh, H. Beresford, 2032
Mendelson, Marilyn, 67
Meredith, William V., 2248
Merew, Erva Loomis, 1103
Merrill, John, 1717-1718, 2033
Meserve, Ruth I., 503
Meserve, Walter, J., 503
Messinger, Margaret Barclay, 1719
Metz, Susan, 1104
Meuden, Emma, 1720
Meyer, Jeanette R., 1105
Meyer, Rose D., 2034
Michaelis, John U., 68, 2144
Michaeloof, Goni, 69
Mikoloski, Vanda, 1860
Miller, Anne Folker, 1106, 2035
Miller, Edith F., 2145
Miller, Elizabeth Christine, 2036-2037
Miller, Irwin Bennett, 504
Miller, James Hull, 1375
Miller, Vera V., 1591
Millicent, Sister M., 1861
Millikin, Maxine Winston, 1257
Millsap, Lucille, 2038
Milne, A. A., 174
Mishoe, Emma Lee, 1107
Mitchell, Albert O., 938, 1376
Mitchell, Elmer D., 415, 424
Mitchell, Julia D., 2146
Mlakar, Dusan, 505
Moffet, James, 2039
Mohn, Margaret E., 1108
Montgomery, Anne E., 1258
Moore, Steve, 748
Moore, Walter J., 2040
More, Grace Van Dyke, 1462
Moreno, J. L., 175
Morgan, Esther, 311
Morkovin, Boris V., 2211
Morris, Mrs. George Spencer, 936
Morris, Lizabeth A., 176
Morrison, Adrienne, 620
Morrison, Eleanor Shelton, 2249
Morrison, J. S., 1377
Morrow, Sara Sprott, 749
Morse, William Northrop, 940
Mortensen, Louise Hovde, 1592, 1862-63

Morton, Beatrice Kerr, 177
Morton, Evelyn Alice, 1378
Morton, Miriam, 506
Moses, Irene E. Phillips, 312
Moses, J. Garfield, 941
Moses, Montrose, 178-182
Moskowitz, Estelle, 2212
Moss, Allyn, 1593
Mote, Jerrine, 1721
Motter, Thomas H. Vail, 508
Mowry, Susan W., 1722
Muller, Herbert J., 2041
Munkres, Alberta, 2042
Munns, W. E., 2213
Murphy, F. Delfine, 2250
Murphy, Sister Mary Honora, O. P., 183
Murphy, Robert F., 2048
Murray, Ruth Lovell, 313, 1463
Musselman, Virginia, 416, 1594
Mussoff, Leonore, 2043
Mycue, Marguerite, 1260
Myers, Donald George, 2214
Myers, Susanna, 315

Nadel, Norman S., 184
Nancrede, Edith De, 943
Nash, Moris, 912
Nash, Grace, 1864
Nash, William Roscoe, 2215
Naumberg, Margaret, 1723-1724
Neal, Helen W., 1725
Nebeker, Jolene, 1261
Neidermeyer, Fred C., 1464
Nettles, Debbie G., 1865-66
Neumeyer, Esther S., 417
Neumeyer, Martin H., 417
Newman, Georgiana C., 1974
Newmeyer, Sara, 944
Newton, Peter, 1379
Newton, Robert G., 316
Nichols, Byron, 1112
Nichols, Cecile, 1726
Nichols, Hildred, 1867, 2216
Nichols, Lewis, 945
Nichols, Martha, 1112
Nicholson, Anne, 1113
Nicholson, David, 2044
Nicholson, Mary Agnes, 1262
Nickell, Marion F., 946
Niebur, Hulda, 2251

AUTHOR INDEX

Nightswander, Mary, 1114
Noble, Helen S., 622
North, Marion, 318
Norton, Sandra K., 1595

Oberle, Marcella, 750, 1116, 1596, 2045
Oberreich, Bob, 1117
O'Day, Jeanette, 1868
Oden, Virgil H., 1263
Odom, Helen B., 418
Ogden, Jean Carter, 948, 1380
Ogden, Jess, 1380
Ogilvie, Mardel, 70, 2046-2047
Oglebay, Kate, 71, 185, 590
O'Leary, Helen, 2048
Olin, Donald Todd, 1264
Oliver, George H., 949
Oliver, Linda, 1464
Olson, Jack R., 2217
Olwell, Georgiana P., 319
Ommanney, Katherine Anne, 1465
Ommanney, Pierce C., 1465
Osband, Helen, 2049
Osborn, D. Keith, 320
Osborne, Rosalie Hoff, 1466, 1597
Osten, Gwen, 2050
Ottemiller, John Henry, 72
Overton, Grace Sloan, 1727
Owen, Gene Nielson, 1118-1119, 1266
Owen, Hal, 1266, 1267
Owens, Florence, 261

Paine, M. J., 2051
Palfrey, Thomas R., 73
Palmer, Luella A., 186
Palmer, Winthrop, 951
Pantenberg, Sister Rosaleen, O. P., 1268
Parent, Norma, 2052
Parker, Beatrice Ford, 1869
Parker, Faye, 1870
Parker, Samuel Chester, 1728, 1729
Parret, Margaret, 2053
Parry, Christopher, 2054
Parsons, A. J., 2051
Partridge, Pauline, 952
Patten, Cora Mel, 72-78, 187, 623-624, 953-954
Patten, Hazel R., 1372
Paulmier, Hilah, 79
Pawley, Thomas D., 91

Peabody, Pamela, 2055
Peabody, May E., 1730
Pearson, Frances, 2056, 2057
Peck, Seymour, 1123
Peins, Maryann, 2058
Peixiotta, Sidney S., 420
Pengel, Georgia, 1269
Perry, Hilda Ida, 2059
Peterson, Aileen, 2147, 2148
Peterson, Dorothy, 1871
Pethybridge, David C., 752
Pettet, Edwin Burr, 753
Petty, Walter A., 1872, 1994
Phelps, Waldo, 1997
Philbrick, Norman, 754-756
Philippe, Herbert, 1381
Phillips, Leila D., 719, 757
Pickard, P. M., 1598
Picozzi, Ramond L., 1873
Pierce, Lucy France. 955, 956
Pierini, M. Francis, 1875
Pierini, Patricia Maries, 2218
Pierson, Howard, 1876, 2060
Pine, Tillie S., 2149
Piquette Julia C., 1599, 1877, 2061
Pirtle, Ann B., 1600
Pitcher, Evelyn G., 1601
Place, Richard, 803
Plescia, Gillian L., 1467
Pollack, Peter, 1382
Pollette, John, 1124
Polsky, Milton, 321-323, 1125, 1270, 1602-1607, 1878
Pomeranz, Regina Esther, 1879
Poole, Irene, 80, 1731, 2062. [See Irene Poole Davis].
Popovich, James E., 81, 758, 759, 1608, 2064
Porvat, Orna, 510
Porter, E. Jane, 2065
Possemeirs, Jean, 83
Possien, Wilma M., 2066
Potter, Lois Shefte, 2067
Potts, Norman B., 1126
Powell, Anne, 958
Powell-Arnold, Jessie, 959
Pratt, Caroline, 1732-33
Preece, Marian, 422
Prelinger, Ernst, 1601
Pressler, Frances, 1734-35

270

Author Index